REA's Test Prep Books Are The Best!
(a sample of the hundreds of letters REA receives each year)

" I studied this guide exclusively and passed the [CLEP Introductory Sociology] test with 12 points to spare. "
Student, Dallas, TX

" This book was right on target with what was on the [CLEP Introductory Sociology] test. I highly advise studying it before you take the exam. "
Student, Washington, DC

" Your book was such a better value and was so much more complete than anything your competition has produced—and I have them all! "
Teacher, Virginia Beach, VA

" Compared to the other books that my fellow students had, your book was the most useful in helping me get a great score. "
Student, North Hollywood, CA

" Your book was responsible for my success on the exam, which helped me get into the college of my choice... I will look for REA the next time I need help. "
Student, Chesterfield, MO

" Just a short note to say thanks for the great support your book gave me in helping me pass the test... I'm on my way to a B.S. degree because of you! "
Student, Orlando, FL

(more on next page)

(continued from front page)

" I just wanted to thank you for helping me get a great score
on the AP U.S. History exam... Thank you for making great test preps! "
Student, Los Angeles, CA

" Your *Fundamentals of Engineering Exam* book was the absolute best
preparation I could have had for the exam, and it is one of the major
reasons I did so well and passed the FE on my first try. "
Student, Sweetwater, TN

" I used your book to prepare for the test and found that the advice and the
sample tests were highly relevant... Without using any other material, I earned
very high scores and will be going to the graduate school of my choice. "
Student, New Orleans, LA

" What I found in your book was a wealth of information sufficient to shore up
my basic skills in math and verbal... The section on analytical ability was
excellent. The practice tests were challenging and the answer explanations most
helpful. It certainly is the *Best Test Prep for the GRE!* "
Student, Pullman, WA

" I really appreciate the help from your excellent book. Please keep up
the great work. "
Student, Albuquerque, NM

" I am writing to thank you for your test preparation... your book helped me
immeasurably and I have nothing but praise for your *GRE* preparation."
Student, Benton Harbor, MI

(more on front page)

THE BEST TEST PREPARATION FOR THE

CLEP

Principles of Management

 With REA's TESTware® on CD-ROM

John R. Ogilvie, Ph.D.
Associate Professor of Management
Barney School of Business
University of Hartford
West Hartford, CT

 Research & Education Association
Visit our website at
www.rea.com

Research & Education Association

61 Ethel Road West
Piscataway, New Jersey 08854
E-mail: info@rea.com

The Best Test Preparation for the
CLEP PRINCIPLES OF MANAGEMENT EXAM
With TEST*ware*® on CD-ROM

Published 2008

Printed in the United States of America

Library of Congress Control Number 2005938205

ISBN 13: 978-0-7386-0125-0
ISBN 10: 0-7386-0125-X

D08-0101

About the Author

Dr. John Ogilvie, Associate Professor of Management and Department Chair, received his Ph.D. in Industrial/Organizational Psychology from Michigan State University and has taught courses in Human Resource Management, Organizational Behavior, and Bargaining and Negotiations at the University of Hartford since 1988. His current research explores topics related to organizational commitment, emotional intelligence, and HR roles. He has also co-authored a CD-ROM simulation and student workbook on Strategic Assessment of Human Resource Management.

About Research & Education Association

Founded in 1959, Research & Education Association (REA) is dedicated to publishing the finest and most effective educational materials—including software, study guides, and test preps—for students in middle school, high school, college, graduate school, and beyond.

REA's test preparation series includes books and software for all academic levels in almost all disciplines. REA publishes test preps for students who have not yet entered high school, as well as high school students preparing to enter college. Students from countries around the world seeking to attend college in the United States will find the assistance they need in REA's publications. For college students seeking advanced degrees, REA publishes test preps for many major graduate school admission examinations in a wide variety of disciplines, including engineering, law, and medicine. Students at every level, in every field, with every ambition can find what they are looking for among REA's publications.

REA's series presents tests that accurately depict the official exams in both degree of difficulty and types of questions. REA's practice tests are always based upon the most recently administered exams, and include every type of question that can be expected on the actual exams.

REA's publications and educational materials are highly regarded and continually receive an unprecedented amount of praise from professionals, instructors, librarians, parents, and students. Our authors are as diverse as the subject matter represented in the books we publish. They are well known in their respective disciplines and serve on the faculties of prestigious colleges and universities throughout the United States and Canada.

We invite you to visit us at *www.rea.com* to find out how "REA is making the world smarter."

Acknowledgments

In addition to our author, we would like to thank Larry B. Kling, Vice President, Editorial, for his overall guidance, which brought this publication to completion; Pam Weston, Vice President, Publishing, for setting the quality standards for production integrity and managing the publication to completion; John Paul Cording, Vice President, Technology, for the design, development, and testing of REA's TEST*ware*® software; Diane Goldschmidt, Associate Editor, for editorial project management; Christine Reilley, Senior Editor, for preflight editorial review; and Amy Jamison and Heena Patel, software project managers, for their tireless software testing efforts. Susan T. Cooper of Sam Houston State University technically reviewed the manuscript, and our cover was designed by Christine Saul, REA Senior Graphic Designer.

We also gratefully acknowledge the team at Publication Services for page composition, copyediting, and proofreading; and REA's Jeremy Rech, Graphic Designer, for pre-production file mapping.

CONTENTS

Independent Study Schedule:
CLEP Principles of Management x

Passing the CLEP Principles of Management Exam xi

    About this Book and TEST*ware*® xiii
    About the Exam xiii
    How to Use this Book xv
    Format and Content of the CLEP xv
    About Our Course Review xvi
    Scoring Your Practice Tests... xvi
    Practice-Test Raw Score Conversion Table xvii
    Studying for the CLEP xviii
    Test-Taking Tips... xviii
    The Day of the Exam xix

Installing REA's TEST*ware*® xx

Chapter 1: The World of Management 1

Chapter 2: Development of Management Thought 15

Chapter 3: The Environments of Business 33

Chapter 4: Managerial and Group Decision-Making 49

Chapter 5: Ethics and Social Responsibility 67

Chapter 6: Planning 85

Chapter 7: Organizing 101

Chapter 8: Human Resource Management..................**123**

Chapter 9: Budgeting and Control..................**143**

Chapter 10: Operations and Information Management **157**

Chapter 11: Motivation in the Workplace **175**

Chapter 12: Making Teams Work **195**

Chapter 13: Leadership **209**

Chapter 14: Conflict, Change, and Communication **225**

Practice Test 1 ....**245**
  Test 1..247
  Answer Key..277
  Detailed Explanations of Answers........................278

Practice Test 2 ....**305**
  Test 2..307
  Answer Key..338
  Detailed Explanations of Answers........................339

Answer Sheets **365**

Index **367**

To my valiant wife, Gerri, who taught me perseverance
and managing with grace and dignity.

CLEP PRINCIPLES OF MANAGEMENT
Independent Study Schedule

The following study schedule allows for thorough preparation for the CLEP Principles of Management. Although it is designed for four weeks, it can be reduced to a two-week course by collapsing each two-week period into one. Be sure to set aside enough time—at least two hours each day—to study. But no matter which study schedule works best for you, the more time you spend studying, the more prepared and relaxed you will feel on the day of the exam.

Week	Activity
1	Read and study the Introduction section of this book, which will introduce you to the CLEP Principles of Management exam. Then take Practice Test 1 on CD-ROM to determine your strengths and weaknesses. Assess your results by using our raw score conversion table. You can then determine the areas in which you need to strengthen your skills.
2 & 3	Carefully read and study the Principles of Management Review included in Chapters 1 through 14 of this book.
4	Take Practice Test 2 on CD-ROM and carefully review the explanations for all incorrect answers. If there are any types of questions or particular subjects that seem difficult to you, review those subjects by studying again the appropriate sections of the Principles of Management Review.

Note: If you care to, and time allows, retake Practice Tests 1 and 2. This will help strengthen the areas in which your performance may still be lagging and build your overall confidence.

Passing the
CLEP Principles of
Management Exam

PASSING THE CLEP PRINCIPLES OF MANAGEMENT EXAM

ABOUT THIS BOOK & TEST*ware*®

This book provides you with complete preparation for the CLEP Principles of Management exam. Inside you will find a concise review of the subject matter, as well as tips and strategies for test-taking. We also give you two practice tests, which are based on the official CLEP Principles of Management exam. Our practice tests contain every type of question that you can expect to encounter on the actual exam. Following each practice test you will find an answer key with detailed explanations designed to help you more completely understand the test material.

The practice exams in this book and software package are included in two formats: in printed format in this book, and in TEST*ware*® format on the enclosed CD. **We strongly recommend that you begin your preparation with the TEST*ware*® practice exams**. The software provides the added benefits of automatic scoring and enforced time conditions.

ABOUT THE EXAM

Who takes the CLEP Principles of Management and what is it used for?

CLEP (College-Level Examination Program) examinations are typically taken by people who have acquired knowledge outside the classroom and wish to bypass certain college courses and earn college credit. The CLEP is designed to reward students for learning—no matter where or how that knowledge was acquired. The CLEP is the most widely accepted credit-by-examination program in the country, with more than 2,900 colleges and universities granting credit for satisfactory scores on CLEP exams.

Although most CLEP examinees are adults returning to college, many graduating high school seniors, enrolled college students, military personnel, and international students also take the exams to earn college credit or to demonstrate their ability to perform at the college level. There are no prerequisites, such as age or educational status, for taking CLEP examinations. However, because policies on granting credits vary among colleges, you should contact the particular institution from which you wish to receive CLEP credit.

There are two categories of CLEP examinations:

1. **CLEP General Examinations**, which are five separate tests that cover material usually taken as requirements during the first two years of college. CLEP General Examinations are available for English Composition (with or without essay), Humanities, Mathematics, Natural Sciences, and Social Sciences and History.

2. **CLEP Subject Examinations**, which include material usually covered in an undergraduate course with a similar title. The CLEP Principles of Management is one of 28 subject examinations.

Who administers the exam?

The CLEP tests are developed by the College Board, administered by Educational Testing Service (ETS), and involve the assistance of educators throughout the United States. The test development process is designed and implemented to ensure that the content and difficulty level of the test are appropriate.

When and where is the exam given?

The CLEP Principles of Management is administered each month throughout the year at more than 1,300 test centers in the United States and can be arranged for candidates abroad on request. To find the test center nearest you and to register for the exam, you should obtain a copy of the free booklets *CLEP Colleges* and *CLEP Information for Candidates and Registration Form*. They are available at most colleges where CLEP credit is granted, or by contacting:

CLEP Services
P.O. Box 6600
Princeton, NJ 08541-6600
Phone: (800) 257-9558 (8 a.m. to 6 p.m. ET)
Fax: (609) 771-75088
Website: *www.collegeboard.com/clep*
E-mail: clep@info.collegeboard.org

Military personnel and CLEP

CLEP exams are available free-of-charge to eligible military personnel and eligible civilian employees. The College Board has developed a paper-based version of 14 high-volume/high-pass-rate CLEP tests for DANTES Test Centers. Contact the Educational Services Officer or Navy College

Education Specialist for more information. Visit the College Board website for details about CLEP opportunities for military personnel.

SSD Accommodations for Students with Disabilities

Many students qualify for extra time to take the CLEP Principles of Management exam, but you must make these arrangements in advance. For information, contact:

College Board Services for Students with Disabilities
P.O. Box 6226
Princeton, NJ 08541-6226
Phone: (609) 771-7137 (Monday through Friday, 8 A.M. to 6 P.M. ET)
TTY: (609) 882-4118
Fax: (609) 771-7944
E-mail: *ssd@info.collegeboard.org*

Our TEST*ware*® can be adapted to accommodate your time extension. This allows you to practice under the same extended-time accommodations that you will receive on the actual test day. To customize your TEST*ware*® to suit the most common extensions, visit our website at *www.rea.com/ssd*.

HOW TO USE THIS BOOK

What do I study first?

Read over the course review and the suggestions for test-taking, take the first practice test to determine your area(s) of weakness, and then go back and focus your study on those specific problems. Studying the reviews thoroughly will reinforce the basic skills you will need to do well on the exam. Make sure to take the practice tests to become familiar with the format and procedures involved with taking the actual exam.

To best utilize your study time, follow our Independent Study Schedule, which you'll find in the front of this book. The schedule is based on a four-week program, but can be condensed to two weeks if necessary by collapsing each two-week period into one.

When should I start studying?

It is never too early to start studying for the CLEP Principles of Management. The earlier you begin, the more time you will have to sharpen your skills. Do not procrastinate! Cramming is *not* an effective way to study, since it does not allow you the time needed to learn the test material. The sooner you learn the format of the exam, the more time you will have to familiarize yourself with it.

FORMAT AND CONTENT OF THE CLEP

The CLEP Principles of Management covers the material one would be taught in an introductory course in management and organization. The exam requires knowledge of human resources as well as operational and functional aspects of management.

The exam consists of 100 multiple-choice questions, each with five possible answer choices, to be answered within 90 minutes.

The approximate breakdown of topics is as follows:

15-25%	Organization and Human Resources
10-20%	Operational Aspects of Management
45-55%	Functional Aspects of Management
10-20%	International Management and Contemporary Issues

ABOUT OUR COURSE REVIEW

The review in this book provides you with a thorough recap of the facts, theories, and terminology related to management. It will help reinforce the facts you have already learned while better shaping your understanding of the discipline as a whole. By using the review in conjunction with the practice tests, you should be well prepared to take the CLEP Principles of Management.

SCORING YOUR PRACTICE TESTS

How do I score my practice tests?

The CLEP Principles of Management is scored on a scale of 20 to 80. To score your practice tests, count up the number of correct answers. This is your total raw score. Convert your raw score to a scaled score using the conversion table on the following page. (**Note: The conversion table provides only an estimate of your scaled score. Scaled scores can and do vary over time, and in no case should a sample test be taken as a precise predictor of test performance. Nonetheless, our scoring table allows you to judge your level of performance within a reasonable scoring range.**)

When will I receive my score report?

The test administrator will print out a full Candidate Score Report for you immediately upon your completion of the exam (except for CLEP English Composition with Essay). Your scores are reported only to you, unless you ask to have them sent elsewhere. If you want your scores reported to a college or other institution, you must say so when you take the examination.

PRACTICE-TEST RAW SCORE CONVERSION TABLE*

Raw Score	Scaled Score	Course Grade	Raw Score	Scaled Score	Course Grade
100	80	A	48	49	C
99	80	A	47	49	C
98	80	A	46	48	C
97	79	A	45	48	C
96	79	A	44	47	C
95	78	A	43	47	C
94	78	A	42	47	C
93	77	A	41	47	C
92	77	A	40	46	D
91	76	A	39	46	D
90	75	A	38	45	D
89	74	A	37	45	D
88	73	A	36	44	D
87	73	A	35	44	D
86	72	A	34	43	D
85	72	A	33	43	D
84	71	A	32	42	D
83	70	A	31	41	D
82	70	A	30	40	F
81	69	A	29	39	F
80	69	A	28	38	F
79	68	A	27	37	F
78	67	A	26	36	F
77	66	A	25	35	F
76	66	A	24	34	F
75	65	A	23	34	F
74	64	A	22	33	F
73	63	A	21	33	F
72	63	A	20	32	F
71	62	A	19	32	F
70	61	A	18	31	F
69	61	A	17	31	F
68	60	A	16	30	F
67	59	A	15	29	F
66	59	A	14	28	F
65	58	B	13	28	F
64	57	B	12	27	F
63	57	B	11	27	F
62	56	B	10	26	F
61	56	B	9	25	F
60	55	B	8	24	F
59	55	B	7	23	F
58	54	B	6	22	F
57	54	B	5	21	F
56	53	B	4	20	F
55	53	B	3	20	F
54	52	B	2	20	F
53	52	B	1	20	F
52	51	C			
51	51	C			
50	50	C			
49	50	C			

* This table is provided for scoring REA practice tests only. The American Council on Education recommends that colleges use a single across-the-board credit-granting score of 50 for all 33 CLEP computer-based exams. Nonetheless, on account of the different skills being measured and the unique content requirements of each test, the actual number of correct answers needed to reach 50 will vary. A "50" is calibrated to equate with performance that would warrant the grade C in the corresponding introductory college course.

Since your scores are kept on file for 20 years, you can also request transcripts from Educational Testing Service at a later date.

STUDYING FOR THE CLEP

It is very important for you to choose the time and place for studying that works best for you. Some students may set aside a certain number of hours every morning, while others may choose to study at night before going to sleep. Other students may study during the day, while waiting on a line, or even while eating lunch. Only you can determine when and where your study time will be most effective. But be consistent and use your time wisely. Work out a study routine and stick to it!

When you take the practice tests, try to make your testing conditions as much like the actual test as possible. Turn your television and radio off, and sit down at a quiet table free from distraction. Make sure to time yourself. Start off by setting a timer for the time that is allotted for each section, and be sure to reset the timer for the appropriate amount of time when you start a new section.

As you complete each practice test, score your test and thoroughly review the explanations to the questions you answered incorrectly; however, do not review too much at one time. Concentrate on one problem area at a time by reviewing the question and explanation, and by studying our review until you are confident that you completely understand the material.

Keep track of your scores and mark them on the Scoring Worksheet. By doing so, you will be able to gauge your progress and discover general weaknesses in particular sections. You should carefully study the reviews that cover your areas of difficulty, as this will build your skills in those areas.

TEST-TAKING TIPS

Although you may not be familiar with computer-based standardized tests such as the CLEP Principles of Management, there are many ways to acquaint yourself with this type of examination and to help alleviate your test-taking anxieties. Listed below are ways to help you become accustomed to the CLEP, some of which may be applied to other standardized tests as well.

Read all of the possible answers. Just because you think you have found the correct response, do not automatically assume that it is the best answer. Read through each choice to be sure that you are not making a mistake by jumping to conclusions.

Use the process of elimination. Go through each answer to a question and eliminate as many of the answer choices as possible. By eliminating just two answer choices, you give yourself a better chance of getting the item correct, since there will only be three choices left from which to make your guess. Remember, your score is based only on the number of questions you answer *correctly*.

Work quickly and steadily. You will have only 90 minutes to work on 100 questions, so work quickly and steadily to avoid focusing on any one question too long. Taking the practice tests in this book will help you learn to budget your time.

Acquaint yourself with the computer screen. Familiarize yourself with the CLEP computer screen beforehand by logging on to the College Board website. By waiting until test day to see what it looks like in the pretest tutorial, you risk experiencing needless anxiety during the test. Also, familiarizing yourself with the directions and format of the exam will save you valuable time on the day of the actual test.

Be sure that your answer registers before you go to the next item. Look at the screen to see that your mouse-click causes the pointer to darken the proper oval. This takes less effort than darkening an oval on paper, but don't lull yourself into taking less care!

THE DAY OF THE EXAM

Preparing for the CLEP

On the day of the test, you should wake up early (hopefully after a decent night's rest) and have a good breakfast. Make sure to dress comfortably, so that you are not distracted by being too hot or too cold while taking the test. Also plan to arrive at the test center early. This will allow you to collect your thoughts and relax before the test, and will also spare you the anxiety that comes with being late. As an added incentive to make sure you arrive early, keep in mind that no one will be allowed into the test session after the test has begun.

Before you leave for the test center, make sure that you have your admission form and another form of identification, which must contain a recent photograph, your name, and signature (i.e., driver's license, student identification card, or current alien registration card). You will not be admitted to the test center if you do not have proper identification.

If you would like, you may wear a watch to the test center. However, you may not wear one that makes noise, because it may disturb the other test-takers. No dictionaries, textbooks, notebooks, briefcases, or packages will be permitted, and drinking, smoking, and eating are prohibited.

Good luck on the CLEP Principles of Management exam!

INSTALLING REA's TEST*ware*®

SYSTEM REQUIREMENTS

Pentium 75 MHz (300 MHz recommended) or a higher or compatible processor; Microsoft Windows 98 or later; 64 MB Available RAM; Internet Explorer 5.5 or higher.

INSTALLATION

1. Insert the CLEP Principles of Management TEST*ware*® CD-ROM into the CD-ROM drive.
2. If the installation doesn't begin automatically, from the Start Menu choose the RUN command. When the RUN dialog box appears, type d:\setup (where D is the letter of your CD-ROM drive) at the prompt and click OK.
3. The installation process will begin. A dialog box proposing the directory "Program Files\REA\CLEP_Principles_Mgmt" will appear. If the name and location are suitable, click OK. If you wish to specify a different name or location, type it in and click OK.
4. Start the CLEP Principles of Management TEST*ware*® application by double-clicking on the icon.

REA's CLEP Principles of Management TEST*ware*® is **EASY** to **LEARN AND USE**. To achieve maximum benefits, we recommend that you take a few minutes to go through the on-screen tutorial on your computer. The "screen buttons" are also explained here to familiarize you with the program.

TECHNICAL SUPPORT

REA's TEST*ware*® is backed by customer and technical support. For questions about **installation or operation of your software**, contact us at:

> **Research & Education Association**
> **Phone: (732) 819-8880 (9 a.m. to 5 p.m. ET, Monday–Friday)**
> **Fax: (732) 819-8808**
> **Website: http://www.rea.com**
> **E-mail: info@rea.com**

Note to Windows XP Users: In order for the TEST*ware*® to function properly, please install and run the application under the same computer administrator-level user account. Installing the TEST*ware*® as one user and running it as another could cause file-access path conflicts.

CHAPTER 1

The World of Management

Chapter 1

THE WORLD OF MANAGEMENT

Every organization with more than one person has at least one manager. Someone is in charge and has more to say about what and how things happen. Managers typically make decisions about what will get done, oversee progress on those tasks, and then determine how well those results or objectives were achieved. Those who aren't designated managers work with and for managers. Increasingly, non-managerial employees are being asked to self-manage or to think and act like managers. Hence, an understanding of the work of managers is critical for organizations to succeed. Effective management is very important.

MANAGING TODAY

Managers have functioned for thousands of years. We know that there were overseers or managers among the Egyptians, in the tribes of Israel, and in the Roman Empire. In any social structure there is some form of rank and order. Given that the practice of management is thousands of years old, you would think that we know a great deal about management and what managers do. Yes, we have accumulated a number of facts, but there is also an art to the practice of management. We can identify principles, practices, and guidelines, but each manager will follow them somewhat differently. Some are very good, some less capable, and a few belong in Scott Adams's cartoon, *Dilbert*. Different approaches may even achieve the same goal. Why? Although there is a science to managing, there is also an art. Some managers have better instincts or reactions.

In this dynamic world, an effective manager must know the science and history of management. In addition, she or he must also have good reactions as they practice and implement knowledge. Both science and art are components of good management. What does science provide that art does not? Some may ask, "Why bother with science if I have good instincts?"

First of all, there are too many things happening at the same time, and second, changes occur very quickly. New products are created by competitors, new regulations established by governments, and new knowledge is developed by business professors and other managers. Think about walking around in a crowded place trying to find someone. Science gives managers clues about to where to look. Managers familiar with the science can see things more quickly and react faster, almost like having a global positioning system (GPS). Relying on instincts alone is like being able to see only a few feet because a bubble surrounds you. Not knowing the science of management limits your vision as you practice the art of management.

In today's rapidly changing business environment, not seeing things fast enough also impacts performance. Agility or quickly adapting to change is key. Science and experience help in adapting more quickly. Performance is at the heart of any manager's job. Their authority stems from the owner, who expects them to get things done. Each manager is accountable for the performance of her or his unit. Yet there is a paradox in this performance-driven world. Managers cannot do the work alone; they are dependent on subordinates to accomplish results. Figure 1.1 illustrates the need for managers to work with subordinates to accomplish results. Ancient managers used threats (e.g., many subordinates were slaves), but contemporary managers need to use better tools to elicit support and cooperation. Thus managers are often involved in working with subordinates and other managers. People are important for every manager's success.

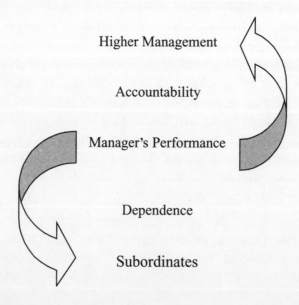

Higher Management

Accountability

Manager's Performance

Dependence

Subordinates

Figure 1.1: The accountability-dependence paradox for managers.

CRITERIA OF SUCCESS

Given the importance of performance, how do you know whether a manager is doing a good job and achieving results? Some may cite the number of products made or sold. Is volume or quantity a sufficient criterion? Performance is more than volume. We will use two different terms to characterize how well managers do their jobs. They represent our criteria of managerial success. The first term is *effectiveness*. **Effectiveness** involves *achieving the right goals*. All managers must achieve results. Products are produced and services are delivered, employees are hired, trained, and evaluated, and budgets are developed and followed. Effectiveness involves the extent to which intended goals are achieved.

Another word is key in this definition. The goals selected must be appropriate, or "right." For some managers the right target is a volume number with a quality level. Effectiveness is not just producing products, but producing products of high quality in a timely manner. For senior managers the choice of which products to make and sell is part of effectiveness. If the wrong products are manufactured, and few consumers buy them, then the company may fail. The late management guru Peter Drucker defined effectiveness as "doing the right job."[1]

The second term used to characterize or assess managerial success is **efficiency**. Efficiency is related to the amount of resources expended in accomplishing goals. It is often referred to as the ratio of inputs to outputs. An efficient process uses relatively few resources to achieve each unit of output. Drucker termed this "doing the job right."[1] If too many resources are used to accomplish a goal, then fewer resources are available for other efforts. This limits effectiveness as well as efficiency. For example, if extensive resources, such as the advertising budget, are devoted to one product, then fewer resources are available to promote other products. This advertising campaign is inefficient in its use of resources.

You can also think about efficiency on a personal level. Each student and employee is a manager of his or her time and other resources. A student's goal is to obtain a high score on the CLEP test for Economics. He devotes most of his time to studying for that test, and he does not get much sleep in the weeks prior to the final exam. The student achieves the goal of obtaining a high score, but he fails a second test, the CLEP test for Principles of Management. He also gets sick and develops a skin rash due to the stress. Achieving the economics test goal has come at a high cost, and other goals are missed. Similarly managers must make sure that they use resources efficiently across multiple goals as they strive to be effective.

Both effectiveness and efficiency must be considered simultaneously in assessing managerial or personal success. Some critics have noted that companies may be narrowly focused on efficiency to the exclusion of effectiveness. During the 1970s, General Motors was very concerned with efficiency. They controlled and costed many resources, even down to each paper clip. At the same time, Japanese automakers were eating GM's market share because Japanese cars were more suited to consumer needs. Managers at GM were doing the job right, but the wrong goals had been chosen. Although they were efficient, their low effectiveness contributed to their overall performance decline.

In striving to be effective and efficient, managers pursue multiple goals. Multiple people have an interest in their performance as well. *Stakeholders* is the term used to describe those with a vested interest in the performance of a manager or organization. Some of the multiple stakeholders of an organization are investors, suppliers, and customers. Members of the community in which the company operates are also stakeholders, as is the government. The local government is concerned because it receives tax revenue, and the jobs created by the organization benefit the local economy. Regulatory agencies of the state and federal government are also stakeholders because they are concerned with the enforcement of regulations for such issues as air and water pollution. These multiple stakeholders make the manager's job more complicated. Balance should be struck among different goals, rather than maximizing the performance of just a few.

SKILLS AND LEVELS OF MANAGEMENT

The explanation of these two terms for managerial success also noted that there are different types of managers. Management is typically viewed at three different levels: first line, middle, and top. Different demands, expectations, and skills are required at each level. As managers move across levels, they need to be aware of shifting demands. What is responsible for success at one level may not work at the next.

To help illustrate, consider why individuals are promoted from worker to manager. Most commonly, promotions to manager occur because an employee has demonstrated the capability to do the job well. He or she has demonstrated technical expertise in performing his or her job. He or she may also have shown an ability to get along well with co-workers. Thus promotions occur due to demonstrated proficiency at technical and human skills.

Technical skills require the application of specific, learned knowledge. The knowledge could be acquired through education, as with a business degree in accounting or a course in database management. Technical skills are also acquired on the job. Cardboard boxes emerge from a folding and gluing machine misaligned in a carton manufacturing plant. The experienced worker uses technical skill to fix the machine so the boxes come out square and evenly glued. In this example technical skills were used in the analysis of a situation and diagnosing problem causes related to the product. Technical skills are similarly used in service firms to improve customer service. If a customer calls with a complaint, the experienced customer service representative knows some possible events that lead to the complaint and asks appropriate questions. He or she identifies the problem and informs the customer and the manager.

Human skills relate to the ability to work with others, communicate well, and make requests in a manner that will motivate employees rather than offend them. Human skills also include the more recent term *emotional intelligence*, the ability to read, understand, and apply emotional information in dealing with others.[2] Supervisors who are able to sense and respond to the emotional reactions of subordinates help create a better environment in which to work. A recent study indicated that employees' productivity and willingness to stay with a firm is based on their relationship with their supervisor.[3] Considerable research on leadership has found that the support of managers decreases turnover and improves satisfaction. Human skills and emotional intelligence help managers to achieve desirable outcomes.

Managers also work in a larger organizational context. They have to coordinate with other managers and think about parts of the organization that they cannot see or feel directly. **Conceptual skills** give managers a mental map of the organization and what impacts it. A manager thinks abstractly about "big picture" issues that workers may not consider. First-line, or lower-level, managers need some conceptual skills, but senior-, or top-level, managers make extensive use of conceptual skills. They need to have a vision of where the organization is going to evaluate competitors and critical changes that could impact the products and services offered by the company. On the other hand, senior managers need relatively few technical skills compared to lower-level, or first-line, managers. Middle-level managers need moderate levels of conceptual skills. Some of these managers do not develop the conceptual skills needed at higher levels. Educational programs, such as an MBA degree, help to develop conceptual skills required for middle and senior management levels.

To summarize and compare, view Figure 1.2 where the distribution of skill areas across management levels is presented. The three skill areas are relatively even at middle management, whereas the percentages of human and conceptual skills are reversed in comparing top to first-line management. The constant factor across all levels is human skills. They are equally important at each level of management. Not all managers will move from lower to senior levels. As mentioned earlier, lower-level managers were promoted based on technical and human skills. They may not develop the conceptual skills required for higher levels, thus limiting their promotions in the organization. The different skill demands at each level require that managers continue to develop their skills if they wish to progress. Top-level managers may also possess technical and conceptual skills but not have adequate human skills for further promotion. The president and chief operating officer of Coca-Cola was not chosen for the top job of chief executive officer because of his abrasive style, which did not fit with the more genteel culture of Coca-Cola.[4]

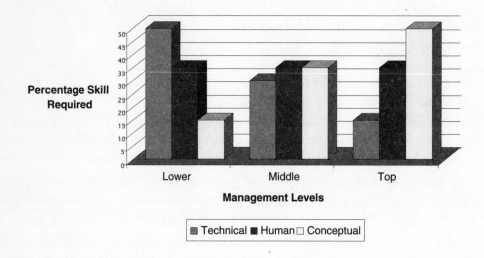

Figure 1.2: Skills needed across management levels.

In addition to the skills required, levels of management also differ in other ways. Senior-level managers use their conceptual skills to look outside the organization at factors that may affect their company. They forge external relationships, examine trends, and assess the impact of factors in the business environment. Specifics of the business environment are discussed in more detail in chapter 4. Although senior managers work with many different functions and departments across the organization, much of their work is focused outside of the organization, dealing with investors, regulators, and senior managers in other companies. Middle- and lower-level managers are focused more internally and deal with a narrower range of functions; they deal with problems that arise in their units. Middle-level managers have lower-level managers reporting to them and lower-level managers have nonsupervisory employees reporting to them. Differences in the activities that managers perform by level are summarized in Table 1.1.

Another difference between the levels of management is the time frame. The activities that involve lower-level managers tend to have a short-term or immediate quality. Problems arise that must be dealt with right away. Middle-level managers have an intermediate time frame. They look further into the future in performing their duties. For example, the marketing manager oversees advertising expenditures, sales forecasts, and new product development. This time frame is often twelve months or next year. Top-level management has the longest time frame. Managers at the top level have a three- to five-year view of where the company should be and how to get there.

Table 1.1: Differences in Managerial Activities by Level

Activities	Top	Middle	Lower
Internal vs. external focus	Primarily external	Mostly internal	Internal
Scope of activities	Broad	Intermediate	Narrow
Subordinates	Middle managers	Lower managers	Employees
Time orientation	Long	Intermediate	Short

FUNCTIONS OF MANAGEMENT

To give a conceptual view of what managers do, the manager's jobs are organized around functions. Most courses and textbooks are structured into the functions of management. A function is a dimension or broad grouping of work activities. Similar activities are grouped into functions to make them easier to recognize and retain. Today we view management work in terms of four functions: planning, organizing, leading, and controlling. These categories are based on the writings of a French manager named Henri Fayol. After spending many years as a senior manager in a French mining company, Fayol wrote down his views on management,[5] which he first published in 1916. He believed that managers performed five functions: planning, organizing, commanding, coordinating, and controlling. As you can see, his five functions are fairly close to our contemporary version.

Figure 1.3 presents the four functions and their interrelationships. The functions of management begin with planning. The **planning** function identifies the direction and purpose of the organization. Planning thus represents the starting point. The basic direction and purpose of the organization influences the remaining functions. Once the direction and purpose are established, the organization must be structured to attain these goals. The second function, **organizing**, is the pattern of relationships among workers. At lower levels it is the layout of work and hiring employees. Organizing also refers to the grouping of people into larger units and departments. Within this structure there is also an authority structure, or chain of command. Once the goals and structures are determined, leading is then considered. **Leading** involves making the plans and structures work as designed. Employees must be motivated, directed, and encouraged to follow the plan and structure to reach the desired outcomes. Finally, **controlling** is assessing whether work has been done in a manner that is consistent with the previous functions. Managers need to measure performance in different ways to determine the degree to which goals are being attained. If things go wrong, then corrections need to be made. Feedback and change are important components of the controlling function. Controlling helps to ensure that resources are not wasted. As performance is compared to the goals set in planning, the controlling function helps to close the loop in the functions of management.

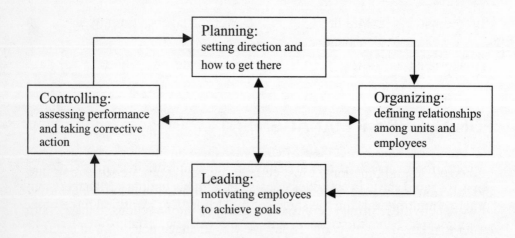

Figure 1.3: Four functions of management.

AN ALTERNATIVE VIEW OF MANAGING ROLES

Fayol's functional view of management is quite logical and has guided managers for more than eighty years. It is surprising that his reflections have held up so well. How does it fit with the science of management? The functional approach to management represents a contemplative approach. Managers sit down to plan, organize, lead, and control. Henry Mintzberg, however, took a scientific approach to studying what managers do. He observed managers, studied their mail, and analyzed their contacts. Mintzberg's findings presented a very different picture. He found that managers engage in many brief, fragmented activities at an unrelenting pace.[6] They are frequently interrupted and often switch tasks in what is now commonly called "multi-tasking." The pace is fast and hectic with a large volume of work. If you ask managers today what their workday is like, many will tend to agree with Mintzberg's description.

Do Mintzberg's findings invalidate the functional approach that is so widely written about and followed? Not really, but his research does suggest some modifications. Managers should still plan, organize, lead, and control; however, they need to realize that their plans may be disrupted or changed. With frequent interruptions, staying focused on the overall plan is a more difficult task. Organizing of work relationships may require adjustments in response to shifting goals or new feedback data from the control function. In short, Mintzberg's work tells us that functional guidelines may need to be somewhat flexible as they are implemented. Don't abandon the functions but be prepared to adapt as changes unfold. Here science can help improve the art of management.

Another result of Mintzberg's research is a different model of managerial work. In analyzing the volume of contacts and activities engaged in by managers, Mintzberg asked why the work was done. A different picture emerged of what managers do. He characterized managerial work in terms of roles or organized clusters of behavior. Viewing work in terms of roles allows for rapid shifts in activities consistent with his findings. Managers may practice multiple roles in the same setting. Mintzberg identified three broad categories of behaviors: processing of information, establishing interpersonal contacts, and making decisions. He also described ten more specific roles within the informational, interpersonal, and decisional categories, as presented in Table 1.2.

Table 1.2: Mintzberg's Roles of Management

Informational roles	Interpersonal Roles	Decisional Roles
Monitor	Leader	Entrepreneur
Disseminator	Liaison	Disturbance handler
Spokesperson	Figurehead	Resource allocator
		Negotiator

Managers spend a great amount of time dealing with information. They are the nerve center for the unit they manage. Information comes in from a variety of sources. Thus *monitor* is an important informational role. Managers take in information and prioritize it. Is this important enough to require action? How soon? If it is important, then with whom should it be shared? This leads to the second aspect, the *disseminator* role. Valuable information should be shared with others. The third informational role is that of *spokesperson*. Some of the information is shared with people outside of the organization. Especially at higher levels, managers in the spokesperson role often give statements to the press in an emergency or crisis.

Interpersonal roles, as the name suggests, involve the application of human skills in interacting with others. Some of the interpersonal roles are similar to the leading function, and others are more unique. Mintzberg's *leader* role is virtually the same as the leading function. Managers engage in activities to motivate, develop, and direct subordinates.

The other two interpersonal roles enhance our understanding of what managers do beyond the functional perspective. Mintzberg identified a *liaison* role. Given the importance of communicating with other managers and employees in an organization, the liaison role establishes networks of contacts. This role may sound similar to the informational roles but the liaison builds the contacts and relationships with others for future use. Once established, the informational roles, such as monitor, can be used later. The third interpersonal role is *figurehead*. Mintzberg found that managers engage in symbolic roles. They meet with visitors, sign documents, and preside over celebrations and ceremonies. These activities involve others from within and outside of the organization. Diplomacy and etiquette are required at these events. Senior- and middle-level managers tend to practice the symbolic figurehead role more than lower-level managers.

Managers spend much of their time making decisions about various issues and concerns. Mintzberg identified four decisional roles: entrepreneur, disturbance handler, resource allocator, and negotiator. The first decisional role of *entrepreneur* involves the initiation of new activities or planned change. New projects are developed and implemented, and existing systems and procedures are improved and changed. The manager may not be involved in all phases of the development or change; however, they may have short bursts of activity designed to spur others to complete the revisions. These short interventions are especially characteristic of senior managers.

The second decisional role, *disturbance handler,* deals with resolving problems. It is less planned and proactive than the entrepreneur role. One study found that managers in general spend about 20 percent of their time dealing with conflict—up to 26 percent for middle-level managers.[7] As this study shows, effectively managing problems that arise is an important activity.

The third decisional role is *resource allocator*. Resources in organizations are in scarce supply. Managers decide who will get what resources and if some will be diverted from one activity to another. There may be a shifting of resources as priorities and disturbances emerge, linking roles together. Part of the allocation decision involves a manager's own time; this is partially related to the planning function. Many decisions in this role category involve the authorization of resources to certain purposes or people.

The final decisional role category is *negotiator*. Managers' authority is limited. They often have discussions to balance conflicting concerns and priorities among groups. Negotiations about work standards, deadlines, staffing projects, and budgets occur for all managers. Higher-level and specialized managers, like purchasing, negotiate contracts with vendors, customers, and other companies. As the legal representatives, senior-level managers may negotiate joint ventures with other firms. This will also involve the spokesperson and resource allocator roles. Different role categories may be combined in accomplishing a set of activities.

In conclusion, this initial chapter lays the foundation for what managers do. They practice the four functions of management and the ten managerial roles. They also develop and apply technical, interpersonal, and conceptual skills. The focus of these conceptual schemes is to help managers perform their job well. The two criteria of success, effectiveness and efficiency, serve as indicators of how well a manager is performing. Subsequent chapters will provide additional details on how to implement these multiple approaches to managing.

Chapter 1 Endnotes

1. Peter Drucker, *The Effective Executive* (New York: Collins, 2002), 2.

2. Daniel Goleman, *Emotional Intelligence* (New York: Basic Books, 1997), 43.

3. A. Zipkin, "The Wisdom of Thoughtfulness," *New York Times*, 31 May 2002, C1.

4. Eric Dash, "Coke's President to Quit After Being Passed Over for Top Job," *New York Times*, 10 June 2004.

5. Henri Fayol, "Planning," in *The Great Writings in Management and Organizational Behavior*, ed. L. E. Boone and D. D. Bowen (New York: Random House, 1987), 26.

6. Henry Mitzberg, "Managerial Work: Analysis from Observation," *Management Science,* 18 (1971): 101.

7. Kenneth W. Thomas and Warren H. Schmidt, "A Survey of Managerial Interests with Respect to Conflict," *Academy of Management Journal,* 19, no. 2 (1976): 315.

CHAPTER 2

Development of Management Thought

Chapter 2

DEVELOPMENT OF MANAGEMENT THOUGHT

WHY LOOK BACK?

In chapter 1 the world of a manager was described as hectic and rapidly changing. If things are changing so rapidly, why look back at events in the development of management history? Can perspectives that are 100 to 3000 years old impact the practice of management today? Surprisingly many historical methods are still in practice. Although we have come a long way, it is useful to examine some of the prior conditions to appreciate and understand the foundations of the current approaches to management. Knowing the conditions in which early practices developed provides an understanding of when they can be useful and when they can not. Some problems reoccur and reinventing the wheel is not necessary.

ANCIENT CONTRIBUTIONS

Without knowing much about them, one would nonetheless conclude that the Egyptians, Chinese, Romans, and Israelites had fairly good forms of management. Whenever large building projects or movements of people are undertaken, management is critical. Ancient people were grouped into clusters, such as the twelve tribes of Israel. Within these organizational sub-units individuals were directed and supervised. Harsh management techniques were frequently used in ancient times. It has long been rumored, for example, that in the building of the 1500-mile-long Great Wall of China, hundreds of workers who died were buried in the wall. In many of these endeavors there was undoubtedly a division of labor where some workers performed tasks that were different from others. It is also likely that procedures or rules were established to guide leaders and managers in performing common activities.

Armies were perhaps one of the most frequently used large organizations in ancient times. "The army of the Roman Empire was highly professional and well organized including standard procedures manuals and drill books."[1] Armies had a strict chain of command for issuing and following orders. Soldiers were organized into units whose commanders served as the coordinating links during battle. More recently, the success of the Prussian army in the Franco-Prussian War of 1870–1871 encouraged students of war and business to study the Prussian methods. The Prussians employed planning and scheduling, a division of labor between line and staff, and a focus on efficiency in executing tasks.[2] Many early management writers admired components of the Prussian army and applied them to business.

Much of the language for work and business reflects its military heritage. Business strategy was adopted from "military strategy." Other common phrases adopted from the military include "in the trenches," "outflank the competition," advertising "campaign," market "penetration," and even "bullets" in a presentation. "Sending up a trial balloon"[3] was an action taken by the military in the nineteenth century to view enemy troops before an attack (well before satellites were available to transmit pictures).

EARLY WORK AND ORGANIZATIONS

Although early advances in management were made in the military and government, much of the work in ancient times was agricultural or commerce-based. Food was grown and traded for other goods. Thus, business organizations were small and simple. Products were craft-like, made one at a time in the home, small workshop, or palace, and then sold in the market. Kings and wealthy individuals employed a number of craft workers who made pots, armor, furniture, and clothing. These workers largely labored as individuals with little coordination. Near the end of the dark ages cottage industries emerged in the home. In the cottage industry the family was the organization. Raw materials were acquired, products were made in the home, and family members took them to the marketplace for selling.

Real changes in the nature of work came with the Industrial Revolution in the latter part of the eighteenth century in England and the nineteenth century in the United States. Power sources—first water and then steam—allowed for the concentration of people in factories. In the United States, the early 1800s manufacturer was a talented craftsman or small mill operator with a shop in or adjacent to his home.[4] By the latter part of the nineteenth century, large factories were in operation. The transition from small, craft-oriented businesses to large-scale enterprises brought a number of changes. One change was the separation of ownership and labor. Cottage industries were owned and operated by families. Large factories now had separate classes of owners and hired employees, who offered their labor in exchange for wages. The separation of capital and labor brought with it problems and led to criticisms that workers were exploited by owners and not fairly compensated for their labor. The concentration of workers also led to a need to organize and manage work. In the earlier craft and cottage eras, workers made and brought their own tools to work. Individualized processes resulted in wide variability in the quality and quantity of the product. Manufacturing companies were in need of a more systematic approach to the design and management of work in this industrialized era.

CLASSICAL SCHOOL

The response to the dramatic changes that occurred during the Industrial Revolution constitutes the classical school of management history. The first response was scientific management, followed by Weber's bureaucracy. The administrative school spanned a longer time frame and contributed additional notions about what managers should do.

SCIENTIFIC MANAGEMENT

The Industrial Revolution contributed to the increase in the size of companies, and it also increased the speed of manufacturing. Power replaced human labor, reducing the time needed to produce goods and therefore improving efficiency. As costs went down, the added profits were often used to purchase smaller companies and further increase the size and complexity of organizations. Managers were not equipped for this dramatic increase in scale and complexity. For many years the first-line foreman autocratically determined the procedures and practices. However, different foremen used different procedures and there was little standardization. Foremen also used the "drive" system to motivate workers. This involved screaming, pushing (and other physical methods), and threatening workers. Although these practices would not be tolerated today, they were common in the late nineteenth and early twentieth centuries.

Scientific management proposed studying work in a systematic manner in order to find a more rational way of conducting work. To illustrate the need for better procedures, Frederick W. Taylor described a situation he encountered in a steel factory.[5] In one area he noted that workers were busy shoveling rice coal (the smaller sized pieces that sifted to the bottom of a coal bin), of which the average weight of a load was 3¾ pounds. The same workers would then head off to another part of the factory and shovel iron ore weighing an average of thirty-eight pounds. "Why the great discrepancy?" Taylor asked. Typically the foreman had set the amount based on his own experience. Which is the proper weight to shovel and how should this be determined? Scientific management advocated the observation and measurement of work. The process of studying tasks to find the best way became known as time and motion studies. The motions of a worker were first analyzed and broken into components, then timed with a watch to determine the most efficient movements in completing a task.

The application of scientific principles to the work environment brought further improvements in productivity, as well as a reduction in costs. In the steel plant Taylor reported a 50 percent reduction in costs over three years. The shoveling workforce was reduced from 400 to 140 men.[6] The remaining workers also earned more money.

Scientific management made significant contributions to the science and practice of management. In addition to time and motion studies, Taylor also advocated hiring workers more suited to the tasks they performed. Stronger workers were hired for jobs requiring greater strength, fostering selection based on worker-job matches. He also advocated training workers in proper methods so as to maximize productivity. Once jobs were analyzed and broken down into components, it was easier to train workers to perform the component tasks. Finally he advocated paying workers more for greater performance. He was concerned about worker-management cooperation. A common problem at that time was "soldiering," where workers intentionally slowed down and feigned effort. Incentives were a tool used to reduce soldiering and increase cooperation. His incentives paid workers a higher rate once their performance exceeded an established standard, what is now called a differential piece rate. Piecework pay systems were used prior to Taylor, but he advocated paying at a higher rate for exceeding the standard.

Taylor also encouraged the establishment of specialized departments to record cost information and process analyses. The planning department was one of the first staff units designed to support the line managers or foremen. The intent was to transfer some of the knowledge from supervisors to this office. The planning department eventually accepted more responsibilities and became the early forerunner of personnel, or human resource, departments.[7]

Taylor was a public figure who frequently spoke to audiences and individuals about his ideas. By sharing these ideas with managers, he became one of the first consultants. These changes were, however, not without controversy. At the time of his innovations, foremen and skilled workers rebelled because the new planning department took away their discretion and influence. Strikes and walkouts occurred. In the mid- to late-twentieth century, Taylor and scientific management remained somewhat maligned. Taylor and scientific management are associated with job simplification and taking the skill and "soul" out of work. These were unintended consequences of scientific management but Taylor was not against the worker. His focus was on improving the work so greater productivity and efficiency could be realized.

As mentioned earlier, Taylor was a public figure and the most well-known from this school of thought. Other contributors included Henry Gantt, who developed a tool known as the Gantt Chart for planning and tracking progress on different tasks in a project. Frank Gilbreth, Jr., and Ernestine Gilbreth Carey wrote the book *Cheaper by the Dozen* (made into a 2003 movie), chronicling their lives growing up as two of twelve children of efficiency experts Frank and Lillian Gilbreth. Frank and Lillian developed procedures for making work more efficient and applied them to their large family.

BUREAUCRACY

About the same time as scientific management, another approach to more systematically organizing office work was being developed in Europe. Max Weber was a German theorist who advocated a set of principles to solve the problems that were being experienced at the time. In late nineteenth-century Germany, work was also informal and chaotic. Personal relationships were critical in hiring and assigning workers to jobs. Positions were obtained through personal connections and family ties with loyalty shown to those who secured the job, rather than the organization. To overcome this patronage approach, Weber proposed principles of bureaucracy that were designed to make office work more professional. He emphasized the creation of files to provide written documentation of actions taken and rules to govern all routine office functions. Furthermore, employees should be trained in these procedures. In addition, employees should be hired based on their qualifications for the job rather than personal connections.

Weber also encouraged the concept of a vocation or career.[7] There should be a hierarchy so that employees can advance over time as they demonstrate competence and learn new tasks and procedures. Increased compensation should occur as they move up the hierarchy. Thus rewards were given for efficiency and competency instead of favoritism or personal ties.

Weber brought order and systems to the office environment as Taylor had to the factory. Like Taylor, Weber has also been criticized. A dependence on rules and procedures has proved to be counterproductive. "Bureaucrats" emerged as a negative term for those who blindly follow the rules without regard to purpose. The human aspects of the workforce were given less attention by both of these early management theorists.

ADMINISTRATIVE SCHOOL

While scientific management and bureaucracy focused primarily on changes in the immediate work environment and the way that jobs were performed, the administrative school advocated broader administrative practices, typically for higher levels of management. Many of the contributors to the administrative school were experienced managers who retired and wrote about their insights. This section will describe the contributions of Henri Fayol, Chester Barnard, and Mary Parker Follett.

Henri Fayol. As mentioned in chapter 1, Henri Fayol, a French mining executive, was instrumental in the development of the functions of management. He also identified fourteen principles of management[8] that remain the bedrock of administrative practice. Table 2.1 lists and provides an explanation of each principle, many of which form the foundation for the organizing function described in greater detail in chapter 7. Several prominent ones will be discussed here.

Principle 2, the dual importance of authority and responsibility, remains critical today. Increasingly, lower-level employees are given responsibility for accomplishing tasks but they are not always given the authority to execute the tasks effectively. Both authority and responsibility are needed for effective performance. Unity of direction (5), remuneration (7), equity (11), and team spirit (14) also remain critical. Fair rewards, teamwork, and "being on the same page" are important in rapidly changing organizations that depend on a degree of employee self-management. The issue of which decisions to centralize (8) and which to decentralize also continues to be a challenge for managers. Decentralization also helps to encourage initiative (13), which is also important in today's fast-paced world of business.

Table 2.1: Fayol's Administrative Principles

Principle	Explanation
1. Division of Labor	Divide tasks and increase specialization to improve efficiency.
2. Authority & Responsibility	Responsibility = Authority. Authority is needed to sanction and encourage obedience. Managers also assume responsibility for their actions.
3. Discipline	Obedience in following and honoring agreements made between firm and employee.

4.	Unity of Command	A single voice or superior is essential so that authority is not undermined.
5.	Unity of Direction	For coordination of effort, unity of action is essential.
6.	Subordination of Interest to General	Individual interests must be subordinated to the interests of the greater corporate good.
7.	Remuneration of Personnel	Pay should be fair and satisfying for all employees. Remuneration includes bonuses, piece rates, profit-sharing, and non-monetary incentives.
8.	Centralization	Centralization or decentralization varies in proportion in each firm over time. Some decisions are best centralized and others decentralized.
9.	Scalar Chain	All individuals are linked vertically in a chain of command for communication and authority.
10.	Order	Materials and people should be organized. Good selection is part of this order.
11.	Equity	Equity and equality of treatment are key principles of administration.
12.	Personnel Stability	Time on the job is required for good work; stability in the job is important for effectiveness.
13.	Initiative	The freedom to propose and initiate action is important at all levels.
14.	Esprit de Corps	Team spirit should be fostered and not abused by written communication. Verbal explanations help maintain spirit.

Chester Barnard. Another member of the administrative school was Chester Barnard. Like Fayol, Barnard wrote his views about management after retiring; however, he wrote in the 1930s, considerably later than Fayol. Barnard had served as president of New Jersey Bell Telephone Co. Barnard was concerned with the cooperation and willingness of employees to contribute to the overall organization. He believed that the organization had to create positive inducements and minimize negative inducements in order to encourage cooperation. Since he was less concerned with formal organizational procedures and policies, his approach became known for its emphasis on the *informal* organization.

Besides inducements, another aspect of the informal organization was the acceptance of authority. Bernard did not assume that employees would automatically accept whatever directives they received from superiors. He believed that each worker had a zone of indifference that encompassed the issues on which employees were willing to accept authority. If an employee was asked to do something outside the zone of indifference, the authority would have no influence. He believed that employees had the free will to make choices.

Mary Parker Follett. The final writer presented in the administrative school is Mary Parker Follett. Follett was trained in psychology and was not a former manager like Fayol and Barnard. She applied psychological principles to understanding workers and their reactions to management. Her views were close to Barnard's in that she did not believe that orders would be blindly accepted; persuading and even reasoning with workers is not sufficient. The attitudes of the workers, such as taking pride in work or accepting responsibility,[9] were important. She recognized that managers influence workers' attitudes.

She was also an early advocate of empowering workers. Managers should share power and facilitate tasks for workers rather than control and order. Her views are considered very modern for someone who wrote in the 1920s.

Her work, plus that of Barnard, nudged managers toward the human aspects of managing. Scientific management, bureaucracy and the administrative school focused primarily on planning and organizing. In the 1920s and 1930s, management thinkers began to realize that the leading function was important. The worker would not robotically follow the plan and organizational scheme; management was more complicated than that. Hence the human perspective began to emerge.

HUMAN PERSPECTIVES

Many consider the rise of human issues to be due to an unlikely source—a series of scientific management experiments. Three contributions will be highlighted in this section. First the Hawthorne studies will be described, then the contributions of Abraham Maslow and Douglas McGregor.

HAWTHORNE STUDIES

The first study was an investigation of the impact of lighting on productivity in a manufacturing plant in suburban Chicago. The site was the Hawthorne Works, part of Western Electric. Researchers from Harvard believed that lighting had an impact on worker productivity so they conducted a series of experiments with varying levels of illumination. They found that no matter how they changed the lighting, productivity improved. Counter to their expectations, lowered lighting levels even raised productivity and production also improved in the control group where lighting stayed constant. They asked, "Why?"

Subsequently an extensive set of interviews were conducted along with two other experiments, one with a group of female workers and one with a group of male workers. Although some question the explanations, the legacy of the Hawthorne studies is twofold. The first conclusion has been labeled the Hawthorne effect; as a result of studying something the researcher interacts with and changes it. The groups that were studied received added attention, with some having specialized work conditions, including breaks, food, and work environment. These special treatments impacted performance more than changes in lighting. The second finding was the effect of the informal system of group dynamics to sanction some behaviors and limit others. The reactions of individuals and work teams impacted the managers' ability to obtain results. This knowledge is represented in Figure 2.1, where the classical approach represents scientific management, bureaucracy, and the administrative school. These classical perspectives held that the proper design of work and sound organizational procedures would lead to effective performance. Scientific management experiments did yield improvements in productivity, but the Hawthorne studies showed that human and group dynamics were equally important. The supervisor also impacts the attitudes and motivations of the workers and workgroup. Employee issues can enhance or undermine productivity. Here, the leading function emerged as a significant management factor. Workers and teams must be encouraged to use the procedures as designed.

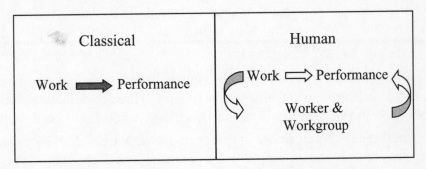

Figure 2.1: Comparing classical and human approaches to work.

Following the Hawthorne studies, the human relations movement developed, focusing the managers' attention on worker satisfaction and the impact of supervision on the worker. The "drive" system was losing favor among reformers prior to these studies, but now research supported coop- eration with the workforce, as suggested by Barnard and Follett. The focus of human relations evolved into "keeping the workers happy." Underlying this approach was the assumption known as the "pet milk theory," namely that contented cows give better milk. Questions were raised as to whether happy workers were really more productive. The classical school viewed worker motivation simply in terms of compensation and incentives. The hu- man relations approach also had a somewhat narrow view of worker motiva- tion; it assumed that treating workers nicely and humanely was important for motivation. This approach proved to be too naïve.

ABRAHAM MASLOW

Several authors in the 1950s and 1960s specifically examined employ- ee motivation in greater detail to yield a more complex but realistic picture of the workforce. Abraham Maslow proposed five categories of need that influence human motivation. These were arranged in a hierarchy with lower order needs more influential or prepotent than higher order needs. Maslow's lowest need was physiological. These needs were focused on survival and basic drives. Safety needs were second. Workers need to feel secure and comfortable. Social needs came next. Prior to the 1950s, most approaches to management were based on these three categories of needs. Maslow's top two categories have been recognized as higher order needs. His fourth category was esteem needs. People need a sense of pride and worth in what they do. Recognition for work well done is important. The final need was self-actualization, or being the best that a person can be. These higher order need categories suggest that workers can take pride in the performance of their tasks and strive for development. Just treating workers pleasantly does not appeal to higher order needs or influence the drive to improve. More details on Maslow's theory are presented in chapter 11.

DOUGLAS McGREGOR

Another influential writer in this period was Douglas McGregor. Mc- Gregor questioned the assumptions that managers held about workers. He labeled one set of attitudes as Theory X. Managers with the Theory X atti- tude believe that workers are lazy and shirk responsibilities (like Taylor's soldiering). In contrast, Theory Y managers believe that workers will ac- cept responsibility and strive to improve themselves. McGregor explained that workers responded to the attitudes of their managers, creating a self- fulfilling prophecy. If a manager held Theory X attitudes, then he treated the workers in a harsh and controlling manner and they responded accordingly. However, if a manager expected responsibility and self-motivation from workers, then they too acted as expected.

As with Maslow's lower order needs, Theory X was a feature of the classical perspectives. Modern views of employees show that many workers want pride, esteem, and self-development. McGregor's contribution was that the manager or supervisor's treatment affected the worker's response. In contrast to the "be nice to workers" approach of the human relations movement, the idea that workers can be motivated to accomplish goals and seek development has been labeled as the "human resource" approach. It reflects a more complex view of worker motivation that is consistent with contemporary practice.

SYSTEMS THEORY

Another limitation of the classical schools of management is that they viewed organizational success in terms of internal features. If the work was designed well and workers were treated properly, then the organization would be effective. The focus was on activities performed within the boundaries of the company, termed a *closed systems approach*. From biology we learn that living organisms require food and other things from the environment in which they live. The systems theory was developed in science to define the boundaries for the phenomena that were studied. For example, the circulatory and nervous systems are components within the body that could be defined as distinct and studied. However, they must interact with the environment to survive or be a part of an open system. Open systems require inputs from the environment. They act on or transform the inputs and then return outputs, or byproducts, back to the environment. Open systems are represented in the cycle of organic and organizational life.

Though developed in the natural sciences,[10] systems theory can be applied to a range of phenomena. Organizations are also open systems. They require energy, people, ideas, raw materials, capital, and information as inputs from the environment. Organizations transform the inputs into products, services, knowledge, profits, and trained employees. Isn't it logical to assume that companies were always viewed as open systems? Although logical, most of the early classical writers treated organizations as closed systems. Scientific management believed that efficient design of work and proper supervision lead to effectiveness. For example, a number of very efficient buggy whip companies went out of business. Why? Not because they weren't efficient in terms of closed systems, but because they did not look outside of the organization. New ideas and new means of transportation were being invented. New vehicle accelerators (as buggy whips were) emerged, such as the carburetor. Today, fuel injectors have even replaced carburetors.

Effectiveness in the long term entails adapting to the environment. One of the benefits of the systems theory approach is realizing that long-term success requires looking into the environment for developments. Chapter 3 will address the different elements of the environment to which managers need to pay attention. Dependence on the environment is also an important element in strategic planning, covered in chapter 5.

Daniel Katz and Robert Kahn wrote an influential book that further delineated the principles of a systems approach to organizations.[11] They identified ten principles, as presented in Table 2.2. The first three were inputs, throughputs, and outputs, as discussed earlier, and the other principles involved feedback. By comparing input to output, the system can assess the efficiency of the transformation process. Feedback is a necessary element in the good use of resources and is the basis of the control function. Without adequate feedback control, a system uses up its inputs. A furnace will continue running and burning fuel without a thermostat to provide a control. Negative entropy is another system principle. We know that biological systems wear down over time. More energy needs to be imported to sustain the system and maintain homeostasis, or balance. For organizations this means that they have to devote extra resources to overcome the natural tendency to decline. The field of change management and organizational development (covered in chapter 14) is an effort to put resources into improving organizations so they do not decline and atrophy over time.

Differentiation and integration are important aspects of organizing that will be covered in more detail in chapter 8. Systems grow and become more complex over time, requiring more connections or integration among the parts. Finally, the principle of equifinality asserts that different paths exist to achieve effectiveness. Different organizations may be successful using different means to achieve goals. There is more than one way to be successful.

Table 2.2: System Theory Principles for Organizations

Principle	Description
1. Input	Dependent on the environment to survive by taking in energy and other resources.
2. Throughput	Inputs are processed and transformed.

3.	Output	Products, services, and knowledge go out into the environment.
4.	Cycles of Events	Cycles of exchanges occur to define the boundaries of the system.
5.	Negative Entropy	Systems wear down unless they import energy to reverse this tendency.
6.	Negative Feedback	Feedback is important to using resources efficiently.
7.	Steady State & Homeostasis	Systems need to maintain a steady state, or balance, both among internal parts and between the internal and external environments.
8.	Differentiation	Systems become more elaborate and differentiated over time through growth.
9.	Integration & Coordination	Differentiation increases the need for integration to maintain homeostasis.
10.	Equifinality	Different paths to the same outcome. Multiple routes to success.

CONTINGENCY VIEWS

Many early approaches to management would be classified as universal today, meaning that they would work in all situations or be universally effective. One of the outcomes of the systems view of management is that organizations must adapt and that there are different routes to the same endpoint. Organizations adapt to different situations in different ways. Thus some approaches to management are not universal. The science of management has discovered that some principles do not hold in all situations. For example, Joan Woodward found that different types of organizing were effective depending on the type of technology that an organization used. Fred Fiedler found effective leadership required a match between the leader's style and the situation. No style was universally effective. Both of these examples are referred to as the *contingency approach* to management. What is effective is contingent upon the situation. Situational features determine what works best.

CONCLUSION

What can we take from these various approaches and use today? First, scientific management taught us that the flow and design of work should be studied to find the most efficient layout or process. Business process reengineering is a modern version of eliminating wasteful motions and steps to save money. Care must be taken not to oversimplify jobs. The humanistic movement taught us that worker and workgroup reactions and attitudes are important. The supervisor's role is key. Records of decisions should be kept and positions should be linked and coordinated (administrative and bureaucratic schools). Organizations must be aware of the external events to which they must respond and adapt. Efforts must be devoted to renewing and improving organizational processes (systems theory). Finally, examine the situation to see what works best in that context. Don't expect to apply what someone else did in a different context and expect it to work universally (contingency). Even today these are valuable lessons to retain and apply.

Table 2.3: A Summary of Historical Contributions to Management

Source	Specific Contribution	Contemporary Function
Ancient	Hierarchy, division of labor, procedures	Organizing
Military	Hierarchy, language, planning & scheduling, line-staff distinctions	Planning, Organizing
Scientific Management	Division of labor, specialization, standard procedures, worker-job matching, training, incentives for performance, personnel	Organizing, Leading
Administrative School	Functions of management, chain of command, responsibility & authority, giving direction, accepting authority	Organizing, Leading
Human Perspectives	Informal organization, human reactions to work, employee motivation	Leading
Systems Theory	External environment's impact on performance, feedback	Planning, Controlling,
Contingency Views	Situational determinants of performance	Planning, Organizing, Leading

Chapter 2 Endnotes

1. Morgan Witzel, "The Art of Management and Military Science," *European Business Forum* 17 (2004): 67.

2. Ibid., 67.

3. William Safire, "The Way We Live Now: Balloon Going Up?" *New York Times*, 23 February 2003.

4. Daniel Nelson, *Managers and workers: Origins of the new factory system in the United States 1880–1920* (Madison, WI: University of Wisconsin Press, 1975), 3.

5. Frederick W. Taylor, "Bulletin of the Taylor Society," reprinted in *Classics of Organization Theory,* 4th ed., ed. J. M. Shafritz and J. S. Ott (Belmont, CA: Wadsworth Publishing, 1996), 73.

6. Ibid., 76.

7. Max Weber, "Bureaucracy," reprinted in *Classics of Organization Theory,* 4th ed., ed. J. M. Shafritz and J. S. Ott (Belmont, CA: Wadsworth Publishing, 1996), 82.

8. Henri Fayol, "General Principles of Management," reprinted in *Classics of Organization Theory,* 4th ed., ed. J. M. Shafritz and J. S. Ott (Belmont, CA: Wadsworth Publishing, 1996), 52.

9. Mary Parker Follett, "The Giving of Orders," reprinted in *Classics of Organization Theory,* 4th ed., ed. J. M. Shafritz and J. S. Ott (Belmont, CA: Wadsworth Publishing, 1996), 160.

10. L. Von Bertalanffy, "General System Theory," *General Systems* (Yearbook of the Society for General Systems Theory) 1 (1956): 4.

11. D. Katz & R. L. Kahn, *The Social Psychology of Organizing* (New York: John Wiley & Sons, 1966), 23–30.

CHAPTER 3

The Environments
of Business

Chapter 3

THE ENVIRONMENTS OF BUSINESS

PalmOne is the company that originally developed the personal digital assistant (PDA) as a hand-held scheduler. PDAs became popular in the 1990s as a convenient way for busy business people to keep track of their calendars, agenda, and lists of business contacts. The Palm operating system is also used in hand-held computers made by other manufacturers. The functions of PDAs have expanded over the years but so have other products. New technologies have emerged that may impact the sales and success of PalmOne's products. The business environment is rapidly changing for PalmOne managers; they need to be aware of trends affecting their products and find ways to adapt.

All texts in the management field now include a chapter on the environment of business. This late twentieth century practice can be attributed to the development of systems theory. Chapter 2 described the ten principles of the systems theory presented by Katz and Kahn. Among the principles were the cycles of exchange between the organization and its environment and the need to overcome entropy, the tendency of systems to wear down over time. For senior managers concerned about long-term success, knowledge of the environment is critical. A multitude of changes outside of the organization will influence a firm's ability to achieve unit and organizational goals. For example, when Sony, a major customer of PalmOne, decided to stop using the Palm operating system, the performance of PalmOne was impacted. Also, cell phones are now developing the technology to perform many new functions, including some that compete with PDAs.

Today firms are also very concerned about competitive advantage. Part of a firm's success is driven by the actions of other firms in their industry. Hence competitive advantage also relates to the environment.

This chapter will discuss two different components of the external environment: the general environment and the task environment. Mere knowledge of these forces and trends is not sufficient; businesses must also have strategies to more effectively interact with these environmental components. Strategies for adapting and influencing the environment will be presented. The chapter will close with a discussion of an additional environmental issue, the culture, or internal environment, of the firm.

EXTERNAL ENVIRONMENT

GENERAL ENVIRONMENT

The environment of business refers to the relevant issues external to the organization. It is not about the atmosphere or ecology, but rather the information, trends, and emerging issues. The **general environment** is the broadest category of issues in the environment to which managers must pay attention. In chapter 1 the importance of science and theory was described. Science and theory enable managers to respond and focus their attention more quickly. Similarly with the environment, knowledge of categories or sectors of the environment helps managers in the search process. It narrows the search to those issues or components that are most likely to impact them. Forces in the external environment include the economy, technology, and legal-political and socio-cultural issues. Each force, along with examples, is presented in Table 3.1.

Table 3.1: Forces in the General Environment of Business

Force	Example
Economy	General economic downturns cause firms to reduce spending on materials and parts, impacting suppliers.
Technology	New and shifting technologies create new opportunities and threats, generating new businesses and closing others.
Legal-Political	Regulatory guidelines change business practices, impose fines, and pose barriers to starting businesses in other countries.
Socio-Cultural	General consumer trends, such as healthy life styles and concern for the environment, impact product development and marketing.

The **economy** is one of the most obvious impacts on firm performance. For some time, managers have known that general economic trends, such as inflation, impact their organization. Economic markets around the world impact other countries as well. Economic trends can affect the cost of capital and interest rates for firms to borrow, potentially increasing costs. As the cost of borrowing increases, firms buy fewer supplies and make less capital investments thereby reducing sales for suppliers and other firms with which they do business. At the end of World War II, there was so much pent-up demand for consumer products that many firms, even those without good management, were successful. Thus both upward and downward economic trends impact the performance of companies. Some larger firms that are particularly dependent on the economy hire economists or economic consultants to track the economic trends of interest to them.

A second force in the general environment that is important to firm success is **technology**. A new wave of technology can make a product obsolete, as evidenced by the example in the last chapter with buggy whips being replaced by carburetors and carburetors by fuel injectors. New technology, such as fuel cells, may eliminate other components in the automobile. In chapter 6 on planning, the impact of developing technologies, like cell phones versus PDAs, will be discussed. Some senior managers consult with experts who will attempt to forecast the next wave of technology in a particular business. Technology can play a large role in creating new businesses and shutting down older ones.

Technology can also change the nature of work. Offices today can be very mobile. Cell phones and small computers allow some people to work out of an automobile. A claims adjustor for an insurance company can go to the scene of an accident or disaster, assess the damage, and immediately file a report electronically. Such mobility speeds up claims processing and gives the customer better service. Wireless networks are now in operation in restaurants, airports, and bookstores, enabling professionals to check and respond to e-mails around the world. These technological innovations enable work to be done more efficiently but also blur the line between work and non-work, adding to worker stress.

Another important set of forces in the general environment is the **legal-political** issues. All companies function within a legal and political context. Each country has standards of regulation that impact business. As an example, in the United States the Environmental Protection Agency (EPA) regulates standards for emissions into the atmosphere or waterways. In some countries the environmental standards are lax, or if they exist, not enforced.

The EPA may conduct investigations of alleged violations and bring charges against polluters, as it did in the case of an Alabama pipe manufacturer who dumped huge quantities of polluted water into a creek near Birmingham.[1] Managers need to be aware of these guidelines and make decisions to limit a company's liability for fines and sanctions.

New laws can be passed that impact trade, affect the ability to lay off workers, or require equal pay for males and females. For example, the Americans with Disabilities Act set up guidelines that required employers to make their facilities more accommodating to wheelchair-bound employees. The Sarbanes-Oxley Act specifies guidelines for reporting financial information and is supervised by a federal regulatory agency, the Securities and Exchange Commission (SEC).

Internationally, the overthrow of a leader in a country can change the receptivity of the government to foreign business overnight. For a U.S. business moving into a new country, the legal-political environment is critical. In some countries a foreign company must partner with a domestic company before it can sell or produce products. With the growth of the European Union (EU), the standards which are set by the EU impact many other countries and firms. European standards regarding confidentiality in the transfer of employee data drove a revision of U.S. guidelines. Companies around the world were required to conform if they wished to continue trading with EU members.

Some of these economic and legal examples demonstrate that many environmental issues are also international. Business is truly international today, with a global interdependency among companies. If the Japanese economy is slumping, as it has been for a number of years, then Japanese consumers buy fewer products from companies around the world. It is better for all economies to be healthy. Each country also has different values and preferences that impact the design and marketing of products and services. This chapter has not identified a specific international component of the environment because international issues are intertwined with each of the general environment forces.

Finally, **socio-cultural** issues represent general values and consumer trends that managers need to be aware of and address. Shifts in consumer attitudes and beliefs need to be recognized. In the U.S. there is a growing focus on healthy foods and beverages. The growing demand for non-carbonated drinks was a trend that soft drink companies, such as Pepsi and Coca-Cola, anticipated in acquiring water bottling and sports drink companies. The addition of these new products enabled their sales to remain strong across all products lines. Packaging is another trend. With landfills reaching capacity in some towns, a reduction in packaging is desired by many consumers. Most deodorants are now sold without any paper boxes as packaging. Values, like a concern for the environment, are also emerging. There is a three-month waiting list for the Toyota Prius, whose engine gets fifty-plus miles per gallon of gasoline. As gas prices soar, more fuel-efficient cars are sought. At the same time, some automobile makers are introducing larger trucks and sport utility vehicles (SUVs) that have higher pollution levels and use more gas, indicating that different values and preferences exist in the marketplace. Demand for SUVs fell with rising gas prices after hurricanes Katrina and Rita hit the U.S. Gulf Coast and interrupted oil refining in 2005.

The automotive example just discussed indicates that some domestic markets may be divided into nearly diametrically opposed attitudes. Likewise, consumer attitudes vary around the world; trends in Asia may not be the same as in South America or the Middle East.

Embedded in the socio-cultural sector are demographic issues that could be important to a business. Latinos have become an important market segment in the U.S., and their numbers are growing. Latinos represent a significant market for many companies. Having knowledge of the values and preferences of demographic groups also helps in adapting to the environment. In the past, teenagers were targeted as an important demographic group for some manufacturers. More recently, the pre-teen group has emerged as a significant demographic group for companies to watch and target.

These four factors represent forces in the general environment. They are represented in the outer ring in Figure 3.1 Broad trends in these areas have a diffuse and long-term impact on business. Another set of factors is closer to the heart of each business and is labeled the immediate environment of business. The immediate environmental factors are represented in Figure 3.1 by a ring inside of general factors.

IMMEDIATE ENVIRONMENT

The components of the immediate environment have a specific and direct impact on the business, and may also be categorized as **stakeholders** of a company. Each has a specific interest in the well-being of the organization and the organization is in turn influenced by stakeholders. Forces or components of the immediate environment to discuss include customers, competitors, suppliers, labor organizations, and the community. They are presented in Table 3.2.

Figure 3.1: The environments of business.

Table 3.2: Forces in the Immediate Environment of Business

Force	Example
Customer	Changing customer needs or dissatisfaction with a product can lead to loss of sales revenue.
Competitor	Important competiter introduces new products or services and eats into your market share.
Suppliers	Companies that provide inputs in terms of materials and information.
Human Capital	Human skills and capabilities in the environment that a firm needs to operate its business.
Community	The relationship and goodwill that a company and its employees have within the community where they reside.

One of the most important stakeholders is the **customer**. Retaining customers has become an important topic for many managers. Why? One website devoted to customer retention provided some calculations on the cost of losing customers. If a firm loses one customer per day and that customer spends only $50 per week, the firm has a loss of nearly $1 million in revenue for the year ($989,000 precisely).[2] In contrast to the socio-cultural component of the general environment where broad consumer trends were noted, this customer element of the immediate environment requires a more specific knowledge of current customers. Managers strive to stay in touch with customers. Some will visit key customers regularly. Retail organizations give consumers special discounts if they use a card with a barcode when making purchases. Each consumer transaction is then tracked, giving retailers more information about the habits and preferences of consumers. Some companies send surveys to customers to assess the level of satisfaction with products or services. A sense of dissatisfaction often precedes a decision to switch to another product or service company.

For PalmOne, Sony's decision to quit using its operating system was not necessarily due to product dissatisfaction. The decision was driven by technology and market changes. Sony used the Palm operating system in its Clio PDA but then decided not to market Clio in North America anymore. Declining markets for the Clio, presumably because cell phones are replacing them, drove the decision; nonetheless this decision adversely impacted PalmOne. The technological force in the general environment impacted the customer force in the immediate environment.

Competitors are equally as important as customers. In some industries key competitors closely observe and follow one another. The rivalry between Coca-Cola and Pepsi is legendary. In recent years both have introduced sodas with lemon and then lime flavoring. Both have acquired bottled water and sports drink lines. Not all industries have two such dominant and competitive players. In these other industries it is also useful to track several key competitors and to watch for new competitors entering the industry. Trade magazines and newsletters are one set of tools to help keep managers abreast of competitor developments, but personal networks may provide more detailed information that is more current.

One of the systems principles from chapter 2 was inputs. To survive and flourish, a company needs inputs from its environment. **Suppliers** provide the material and informational inputs that a company needs. These include paper, office equipment, and machines for manufacturing. A financial services firm may need a Bloomberg terminal, which provides information for analysts on the financial markets. Similar to those with customers, the relationships that a firm has with suppliers are important. The favored customer of a supplier may receive price discounts or special consideration on a rushed order. Some suppliers provide Internet access so customers can place an order directly into the system resulting in faster delivery.

Another type of input is **human capital**. Employers need people with key skills to make the business work well. A number of companies have developed a list of competencies that are viewed as critical to the success of the firm. People are either hired with these competencies or are hired with the potential and then the competencies are developed after hiring. Some of the human capital comes from agencies that supply people on a temporary basis. Some agencies specialize in temporary employees for specific professional positions, such as accounting or information systems. The human resources department, when described in more detail in chapter 8, plays a critical role in assessing the extent to which key competencies are available in the environment. They may even coordinate a program where employees visit college campuses to interview prospective employees.

A final factor in the immediate environment of a business is its **community**. The topic of social responsibility, to be covered in the next chapter, relates to managing relationships with the local community. The community has expectations of employers. Employers contribute taxes and their employees spend money in the community, enhancing the local economy. However, more than these basics is typically expected. Managers visit area schools to talk about careers in their industry. Members of the organization may offer volunteer services at food pantries or reading programs at the local library. A company needs to maintain a good reputation within the area in which it operates. Non-profit institutions also need to manage relationships with the community. A wealthy and prestigious institution like Yale University needs to be perceived by the city of New Haven as contributing. If they are not, then the city could move to tax Yale's extensive property holdings.

RESPONSES TO ENVIRONMENTAL FORCES

Being aware of the environmental forces helps an organization, but the real benefit from awareness is in taking action. If there are adverse conditions or forces in the environment, a company wants to limit their impact inside the organization. If there is a positive force, then the organization needs to find ways to leverage that force within the organization. Strategic planning, discussed in chapter 6, provides a framework for planning based on environmental trends. Here we identify two broad strategies or responses that organizations follow to adapt to forces in the environment to ensure long-term survival. These strategies can be viewed in terms of the directionality of the effort in reference to the environment. Adapting to the environment takes a force or issue and brings it inside the organization as the company adjusts to that force. This strategy is illustrated in Figure 3.2 by the arrow moving from the environment into the circle, which represents the company. The second strategy is illustrated by the arrow moving from inside the company out into the environment. Influencing the environment is an attempt by the organization to modify or influence some aspect of the environmental force.

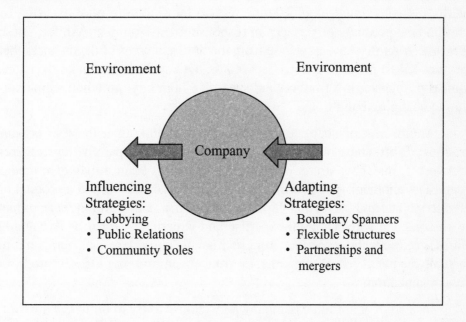

Figure 3.2: Company responses to environmental forces.

One set of responses to environmental forces is to **adapt** to the forces. This strategy represents an adjustment. One way to adjust is through **boundary spanning roles**. As the term implies, boundary spanners are viewed as being on the periphery of the organization. They spend a portion of their time looking out into the environment. To a limited extent, all managers are boundary spanners. They are expected to read business or industry publications and go to professional meetings. These activities can inform managers of some general trends and even competitor actions. Some positions or roles involve a higher percentage of boundary or external activities. Lawyers and corporate counsels study new laws and court cases that could impact the organization, accountants monitor tax regulation changes, and human resource managers note changes in compensation and discrimination guidelines. As can be seen by some of these examples, structures can be added with virtually entire departments engaged in boundary spanning activity, that is, monitoring the environment.

Another structural response to environmental forces is to create **flexible and adaptive structures**. Chapter 7 on organizing describes several types of organizational structures. Some structures, like the functional structure, make it harder for a company to change and adapt. More flexible or organic structures can more readily adapt to changing conditions in the environment. A product- or customer-based structure is more decentralized and oriented to a component of the immediate environment. Team-based structures with cross-functional membership are also more able to pool expertise to design new products or services in response to environmental shifts. These flexible structures have expertise from the different areas of the business that are needed to make decisions, as well as the capability to make decisions quickly. Relevant information and speed are both key ingredients in adapting to changing conditions.

Another set of adaptive measures involves linking with other organizations. **Joint ventures or partnerships** involve cooperative agreements between firms. This strategy could be used when Firm A has identified a trend that another organization, Firm B, has already developed a product or service to address. A partnership will allow Firm A to develop that product with someone who has both expertise and experience, Firm B. Eventually Firm A acquires this expertise. A more dramatic and expensive approach is to actually acquire Firm B via a merger or takeover, bringing Firm B into Firm A's organization.

Instead of adapting, a company may choose to try to influence the forces in the environment. As with the adaptive strategies, some of the **influencing strategies** relate to individual roles and departments. One traditional way to gain influence is through lobbyists. Companies pay a fee to someone who meets with legislators and regulators to influence the nature of laws and regulatory guidelines. Some companies pool their resources in a trade group, like the American Flower Importers Association or the National Retail Federation, who speak for many firms in the same industry.

Another influencing strategy is through **public relations**. Companies release information to the public, often coordinated through a media campaign, to influence public opinion on a particular issue. Public relations campaigns may address issues in a local community or on a broader industry scale. Community-service roles are another way that firms seek to influence the environment. Assigning employees to service roles and paying them for their time spent in community activities, like the United Way or a reading program, seeks to create a favorable impression for the firm, primarily in the local community.

These two sets of strategies, influencing and adapting, provide actions that companies can take to better interact with their environments, thus assuring some degree of long-term survival.

CORPORATE CULTURE

The final environmental issue to discuss is corporate culture, the innermost ring of Figure 3.1. This topic refers to the internal environment of an organization. Have you ever walked into a company and sensed something different about it? Perhaps the employees were eager and energized, or perhaps the opposite: employees were listless and somewhat hostile to strangers. These experiences reflect the culture of the organization. The **culture** is defined as the set of values and beliefs shared by members about how work should be done and what is important. The culture embodies the informal processes in a company rather than official statements or procedures. It reflects what is actually done rather than what managers say or profess. Consultant Martin Bowers referred to it as "the way we do things around here."[3] Managers who are both aware of the culture and act consistently with the culture are termed, "walking the talk."

The concept of culture comes from the fields of anthropology and sociology where the cultures of different peoples and their societies are studied. To survive, a group of people like the Yanamamo Indians of Central America had to share their beliefs with their children and socialize them into that culture. Values, customs, and attitudes are taught to newcomers. The same principles apply to organizational culture. New employees learn "the company way" of doing things. They attend ceremonies such as a recognition luncheon, where all the employees of a manufacturing firm celebrate a unit that set a record for the length of time worked without a lost-time accident. The company here is identifying and rewarding the values of safety in the workplace. It is stressing the importance of safety and trying to get all employees to embrace this attitude.

How do values and attitudes develop in the workplace? Where does culture come from? Some elements are historical. DuPont is a major chemical company that emphasizes safety as part of its culture. Few may know that DuPont began as a gunpowder manufacturer, experiencing frequent explosions. This dangerous industry required safe practices to survive. That historical legacy is embedded in the current culture of DuPont today. The prescribed practices of a company's culture represents accumulated wisdom.

What has worked well in the past often continues in the present. Edgar Schein[4] theorized that culture reflects a company's patterns of adaptation to external events, as well as patterns of internal cooperation or integration in response to environmental events. These patterns become priorities and are taught to others. Eventually they become more deeply held attitudes and values.

Why is culture important? These practices and values can impact performance. In the last fifty years many companies have established quality as a key part of their goals and strategies. Customers around the world demand quality. Jim Fairfield-Sonn[5] wrote a book describing the critical role of culture in continuous improvement. Sometimes the culture must be changed for quality to improve. Senior managers need to assess the culture to determine if it supports the goals and strategies. The actions of senior management are also important in establishing or changing the culture of an organization.

If a manager wants to assess the culture, what should he or she look for? Although someone can recognize the feel of a workplace, culture is not real easy to see. Certainly values and beliefs are not openly visible. As anthropologists look for artifacts of an ancient culture, a manager can also find artifacts of corporate culture. Signs, slogans on the walls, and posters can reflect some of the values of the culture. These visible objects are symbols of the underlying culture. Symbols impart meaning beyond the mere object itself. Some companies ask employees to wear uniforms as a means of demonstrating team spirit and building loyalty to the firm. The physical environment also makes a difference. Some offices have expensive furniture and wall coverings to reflect the status of their occupants while other companies have simple and uniform offices. These differences reflect the values about status and equality. However, recent research by Jeff Pfeffer[6] has found that successful companies tend to de-emphasize status differences.

Table 3.3: Visible Manifestations of Culture

Cultural Component	Example
Symbols	Objects, uniforms, physical environment
Language	Slogans, jargon
Narratives	Stories, myths
Practices	Ceremonies, rites, rituals

In addition to symbols, Table 3.3 presents other visible manifestations of culture.[7] Some of the language used in an organization represents the common meaning that members share. Key phrases, or jargon, can impart meaning. Official slogans such as "quality is job one" may reflect a marketing campaign that is part of the mission and values of a company. Repeating these key phrases is one way to instill values in members.

Narratives represent a longer type of language that is an element of culture. In some corporate cultures, stories are told about overcoming past problems; sometimes the events have been distorted or embellished and take on elements of myth. Whether true or just tall tales, a lesson is taught. They remind them of key values and may even suggest a procedure for addressing a customer problem. The nature of the stories told tells much about the culture. The stories can be constructive or they may be like Scott Adams' cartoon *Dilbert*, describing poor management or worse (e.g., sexual harassment). People tend to remember vivid, interesting stories.

Another visible element of corporate culture is termed the practices of the organization. Practices include ceremonies, rites, and rituals. Rituals are the smallest cultural unit. A ritual for a morning meeting may involve arriving early for coffee and donuts in order to socialize and build informal bonds. Most organizations hold rites and ceremonies to acknowledge and reinforce values. Rites are dramatic, planned sets of activities carried out for the benefit of an audience; ceremonials are systems of several rites connected with a single occasion. The commencement ceremony of colleges extols the virtues of education. Rites involved in this ceremony include the conferring of degrees, procession of faculty, and the awarding of honorary degrees. The annual sales meeting draws attention to highly successful salespeople, hoping to encourage others to join the platinum club of high sales volume.

Experts like Fairfield-Sonn encourage leaders to review the visible manifestations of their culture and assess what values are being expressed. Leaders should evaluate the degree of fit between the culture and the goals of the organization. To take the DuPont example, if safety as a value is inconsistent with entrepreneurship and product innovation, the DuPont managers should try to move the culture in different directions. New stories, rites, and ceremonies should be developed. What ultimately gets rewarded also plays a role in the development and evolution of the corporate culture. Culture changes slowly. It may be more appropriate to think of changing culture using a topiary metaphor. Introducing new practices and modifying old ones is like shaping an evergreen by careful pruning here and there. It takes time, but eventually a recognizable new shape emerges.

CONCLUSION

This chapter described several aspects of the environment of business that are important to managers. Forces in the general and immediate environment can impact the current and future success of a company. Managers need to not only be aware of these trends, but to also know strategies for adapting to and even influencing these forces. Finally, the internal culture of a company influences worker behavior and should be assessed with regard to whether these informal beliefs support the goals of the firm.

Chapter 3 Endnotes

1. David Barstow, U.S. Brings New Set of Charges Against Pipe Manufacturer, *New York Times,* 26 May 2004, A19.

2. *The Coleman Chronicles* 1, No. 4, http://www.coleman.bc.ca/publications/chronicles/vol1issue4.html.

3. Martin Bowers, quoted in *Corporate Cultures: The Rites and Rituals of Corporate Life*, Terrence E. Deal & Allan A. Kennedy (Reading, MA: Addison-Wesley, 1982), 4.

4. Edgar H. Schein, *Organizational Culture and Leadership* (San Francisco: Jossey-Bass, 1985), 52.

5. James W. Fairfield-Sonn, *Corporate Culture and the Quality Organization* (Westport, CT: Quorum Books, 2001), 3.

6. Jeff Pfeffer, *Human Equation: Building Profits by Putting People First* (Boston: Harvard Business Press, 1998), 90.

7. Harrison M. Trice & Janice M. Beyer, *The Cultures of Work Organizations* (Englewood Cliffs, NJ: Prentice-Hall, 1993), 78.

CHAPTER 4

Managerial and Group Decision-Making

Chapter 4

MANAGERIAL AND GROUP DECISION-MAKING

Barry is the local manager of a store that is part of a drugstore chain. An employee from one of the stores contacted you, alleging sexual harassment by Barry. He had been touching her on the hips and making suggestive comments, even after she asked him to stop. As the district manager, you hired Barry and occasionally play golf with him. You have heard him make suggestive comments about female golfers but thought that he was professional with his employees. You remember from newspaper articles that sexual harassment cases can cost the company a great deal of money. What would you do?

Much of the manager's job involves decision-making. Not all of it is as serious as Barry's dilemma. Workers frequently come to managers with procedural questions and simple problems. The first-line supervisor is expected to examine the issue and make a decision. At other times the supervisor may decide that the issue is "big" enough that higher levels of management should be consulted before making the decision. The issue may be considered "big" because it impacts more than one department, has major cost implications, or because the supervisor feels that how this decision is handled may set a precedent for future decisions or impact policy. **Decision-making** is the process of evaluating alternate options in order to take action steps to address perceived problems or issues in organizations. Managers are also expected to be able to work with groups to make good decisions. This chapter will be divided into sections on managerial and group decision-making.

MANAGERIAL DECISION-MAKING

When managers make decisions, it is not a single event but a process that involves multiple steps and analysis of the context in which the issue arises. This section first details the typical steps in the decision-making process and then describes several characteristics of decision situations, or contexts. Several theoretical models are then examined that have viewed decision-making in different ways. The managerial section will also describe several different patterns or styles of decision-making used by managers.

A MODEL OF DECISION-MAKING

A series of steps are presented in Table 4.1 that describe the typical process used in making decisions. Before anything can happen, a manager needs to be aware that there is a need to make a decision. Something has to trigger awareness of a decision issue or problem. As described in the opening paragraph, there are instances when an issue is brought to a manager's attention (someone complains about alleged sexual harassment). A subordinate or superior does not necessarily have to create problem awareness. Managers scan data from information systems to detect quality problems, budget shortfalls, and competitive threats. They are looking for a break or deviation from the expected standard as part of the control function. One of the primary purposes of information systems is to provide feedback about issues that need managers' attention. The challenge is that, with the large capacity of today's computers, there is too much information stored for managers to actually review and study. John Rockhart of the Massachusetts Institute of Technology suggests that organizations define up to seven critical success factors that are carefully measured and monitored.[1]

Once an issue has been identified that requires a decision, the next step is to formulate the problem. Defining the problem is not as simple as it sounds. A misleading formulation of the problem can misdirect the subsequent search for information. One aspect of defining the problem is putting boundaries around it. What is the context or situation in which the issue arose? Social scientists refer to this as **framing**. Think about a picture frame without the picture. If you hold it up and ask someone to look through it, you are directing their attention to a narrow range of all possible issues. This focused attention is framing.

Table 4.1: Steps in the Decision-Making Process

Decision-Making Steps
1. Awareness of need for a decision.

2. Formulation of the problem.

3. Diagnosis and information gathering.

4. Generation of alternatives.

5. Evaluation of alternatives and selection of best option.

6. Implementation of solution.

7. Feedback and evaluation of decision.

Some managers may define the problem too narrowly and miss potential causes and solutions. For example, a supervisor observes that an employee's performance has dropped. If the manager defines the situation too readily as a motivation problem, then the process is already cut short. Performance can be impacted by equipment in the work environment, coworkers, health, or even home factors. Other ways to define the problem include stating the nature of the deviation, where the problem was observed, when it occurred, and what the extent of the problem or issue was.[2]

Another part of defining the problem is the recognition of impact, urgency, or priority. If the problem is found to have a large impact, the amount of research and involvement of other individuals might be different. Charles Ford found that "elite" decision-makers were able to assess the effect or impact of the problem quickly.[3] Knowledge and experience are key factors in assessing impact. With time, managers learn what factors influence impact. If a new manager has difficulty in determining impact, then he or she needs to do more information gathering, perhaps consulting with other managers.

Once the problem and its potential impact have been defined, the next step is diagnosis and information gathering. Efforts are made to determine the cause of the problem. If the decision is an interpersonal dispute between individuals (as in the opening scenario), then both versions of the story must be examined. Another aspect of this step may be to consult with experts. The human resources department is a staff area with expertise in this area. Legal staff may also be consulted. The company may also have a policy that dictates how sexual harassment reports should be handled. These outside sources can reduce uncertainty for a manager and help in reaching the best decision for the company and persons involved. Decision tools are available to help in diagnosis. For example, fishbone analysis is a tool for identifying root causes of quality problems.

Once the background and causes have been identified, the focus shifts to what can be done and alternatives are identified. It is important not to do too much censoring of options early in this phase. Group techniques, like brainstorming and nominal group technique, explicitly separate option identification from evaluation of the value, or worth, of options. Some options may not have equal likelihoods of success but it is important to generate a broad list of choices from which to choose.

Once an adequate list of options is identified, the choices are more critically judged on several criteria. One criterion may be cost. Another is ease of implementation, or likelihood of solving the problem. Time needed to implement may be another factor in assessing which option best addresses the decision issue presented. This stage of option evaluation can also be quantified. Each criterion can be given a weight of 1, 2, or 3. Then the choices are rated on a one-to-five scale in terms of the degree to which the option meets that decision criterion. The weights are then used and the rating is multiplied by the weight. These products are summed up for each decision option. The option with the highest total sum is chosen. This quantification is a version of the decision matrix developed by the consulting firm of Kepner-Tregoe, Inc., which specializes in rational managing.[4]

Upon choosing the best option, the manager then moves to implementation. Some decisions can be implemented quickly while others may need a process of systematically informing others. Some managers have implemented decisions poorly. You may have heard horror stories about employees who received an e-mail informing them that their job was terminated. A decision of this nature needs to be implemented via face-to-face communication. There is a sense of timing and fairness that needs to be considered in implementing decisions. If a decision is made to eliminate a unit within a department, it would be appropriate for the senior manager to inform the unit head before the announcement was made public. Some managers have better common sense and emotional intelligence when it comes to implementation.

When decisions are broad in scope and involve multiple individuals, a strategy for implementing change may be appropriate. Employees need communications about the change. If resistance is anticipated, then consulting with employees beforehand may be part of the change strategy. Participation in reaching the decision leads to greater acceptance of the outcome. Individuals have a sense of justice or fairness. In fact there are two types of justice. *Distributive justice* is a sense that the decision outcome is fair—that is, that the outcome of the decision was reasonable in terms of what the individual expected to receive. The other type of justice is *procedural*; individuals may accept a less than favorable outcome (i.e., low distributive justice) if the procedures used to reach the decision were fair. Some procedures that are viewed as fair include participation and having a grievance or appeal process. Giving individuals a voice in the process enhances procedural justice perceptions.

The final stage in the decision-making process involves feedback and evaluation of the decision and the processes used to reach it. Not all decisions are made correctly. Some review of the procedures and criteria may be useful in improving future decisions. Other changes can also be made. For example, a manager finds that subordinates keep bringing a similar problem to his attention. A procedure can be created and shared with subordinates that specifies how that problem should be handled. The creation of new procedures guides employees in their decision-making and frees the manager for other higher priority tasks.

DECISION SITUATIONS OR CONTEXTS

In addition to seriousness or importance, decision situations vary in other ways. Sometimes the manager knows the answer and other times he/she does not. Uncertainty is something that managers learn to live with when making decisions. **Certainty** is defined as a situation where the manager has full information about goals, options, and the outcomes associated with each alternative. A sales agent may present his manager with a request for reimbursement. The company has clearly defined policies and procedures about reimbursement. The manager consults the guidelines and approves the request because it falls within the policy. There were two options available, and the manager had the information needed to make the decision.

Many decisions, however, do not fall into this category. Another type of situation is termed *risk*. **Risk** is defined as a situation where the goals and options are known but the outcomes are not. There may be several outcomes, each with a certain level of probability. A product manager notices that revenues from her main product have leveled off. She has data that products in her division tend to have a three-year cycle or run; her plateaued product has been on the shelves for sixteen months. About the same time, a cross-functional design team has proposed a new product. She looks at her decision in terms of risk. She knows that 60 percent of new products that are successfully test marketed become successful within fifteen months. She has to meet her revenue and profit targets. She has several options. She can stay with the current product (option #1). To meet her targets she would have to invest more in promotions and advertising and/or offer discounts (hoping that volume will make up for reduced profit margins on each product). She can drop the current product and go with the new one (option #2). She can also phase out the old and phase in the new product (option #3), spending promotional money on both. Each choice has a projected level of cost and probability. She knows her options and the outcome associated with each has a certain probability.

Situations labeled as uncertain have less information than risk and certainty. **Uncertain** situations involve known goals but incomplete option information and the likelihood or probability of outcomes is not known. The manager does not have all of the information needed to make the decision. In uncertain situations, managers may create a task force of people from different areas (e.g., a cross-functional team) to gather more information. Sometimes in uncertain situations managers make assumptions and use hunches and intuition. For example, a chief rival firm launches a new product. The division president convenes a group to reduce uncertainty. They may define options and try to set some estimate of the likelihood of each event. They attempt to move the situation from uncertainty to risk. Sometimes they make assumptions that are correct and sometimes they are wrong. There is more room for error in uncertain situations.

PERSPECTIVES ON DECISION-MAKING

Classical Approach. With over 100 years of writing about management, different perspectives have emerged regarding what decision-making is about and what is best to do. Most approaches offer prescriptions for making good decisions. As economics was the first discipline in business, it had an early influence on decision-making. The **classical approach** is grounded in the view that the manager operates in the best economic interests of the organization. A series of assumptions underlie the classical approach to decision-making.[5] The first assumption is that problems can be clearly defined. Implicit in this assumption is the fact that the decision-maker knows and understands the goals of the organization. This seems straightforward, but it is not always the case. A second assumption is that all relevant information can be obtained and used in making decisions. The third assumption is that the criteria for evaluation of the decision are definitely economic in nature. Finally, this approach believes that the decision-maker is logical and rational, fully using the information and applying the criteria appropriately. These assumptions represent ideal conditions but rarely are the case. The classical approach assumes that much of the decision-making occurs under the conditions of certainty. The next model questions some of these assumptions.

Administrative Model. In sharp contrast to the classical approach, the **administrative model** of Nobel laureate Herbert Simon viewed decision makers as less rational. Simon's approach, although somewhat cynical, is more grounded in the reality of decision behavior. Simon introduced two concepts that challenged the classical approach. *Bounded rationality* asserts that decision makers have limited time and mental capacities with which to make decisions. They do not thoroughly evaluate all alternatives, nor do they apply decision criteria consistently in the rational manner proposed by economists. People are inconsistent and take shortcuts. He coined another term, **satisficing**, to define the fact that people search for a minimally acceptable, not optimal solution. They are not exhaustive in their search and quickly settle for the first option that meets the minimum criteria of acceptance. In your own experience, which approach is more common, the classical or the administrative?

Political Model. A third approach moves further from the classical approach of rationality. The **political model** of decision-making states that decision contexts do not have an objective set of criteria and priorities. The determination of what is valued and viewed as important is based on political processes. There really are no objective decision problem definitions and decision criteria. Informal groups of managers form coalitions and these subgroups support certain alternatives[6]. Consensus and bargaining determines what is "right" and what gets implemented. The dominant coalition's view becomes reality.

What can the new manager gain from these approaches? Strive to gather information in making decisions but realize that at times, satisficing decisions are made with bounded rationality. In critical situations, managers need to guard against satisficing, but, on the other hand, they should also not try to spend too many resources gathering all possible information. When a certain level of risk is attained, then movement and action are required. At other times, be aware that political, rather than rational criteria, determine what is accepted and implemented. In short, use selected portions of all models.

DECISION STYLES

Some individuals make decisions without a great deal of deliberate thought while others may thoroughly contemplate each decision. Decision-makers vary in the styles and the criteria that they use to make decisions.

One area of decision-making in which people differ is in the tolerance or propensity for **risk**. Some people are willing to take bigger chances. In studying his elite decision-makers, Charles Ford found that positive thinkers were willing to take calculated risks because they saw opportunities on the upside of a decision.[7] Negative thinkers were prone to look at threats and not take risks. From research in negotiations we also know that some situations encourage risk. In general, people tend to be risk-seeking in situations where a loss is involved.[8] Where gains are involved, people are risk-averse. For example, given a choice between an option of losing $5,000 versus a 50 percent chance of paying nothing or paying $10,000, people tend to choose the second, more risky option. If the choices were rephrased to include gaining $5,000 or a 50 percent chance at $10,000, people would go with the sure thing, which is less risky. What are the implications for decision-makers? Be careful in loss situations that you do not choose excessively risky options. The converse rule is to not be too cautious about gains.

Another way to look at differences in decision-making styles is to look at categories of preferences which people exhibit. The Myers-Brigg Type Indicator (MBTI) is a self-assessed instrument for categorizing differences. Two of the four MBTI dimensions relate specifically to decision-making and will be presented here to help understand differences in decision behavior[9]. One MBTI dimension looks at how people gather information and how they evaluate it. In terms of perceiving or information gathering, some people prefer to take in detailed information directly through the senses. Sensing (S) types prefer and enjoy fine detail work such as computer programming or accounting. Fictional detectives Sherlock Holmes and Adrian Monk are classic S's, perceiving things that others miss. The other perceiving type is intuition (N). People who are classified as N's rely more on hunches and intuition than the senses. They are able to see the "big picture," see patterns in a mass of data, and look ahead into the future. Those who are N's focus on new issues and developments and tend to become bored with the present, though they may also miss some of the small details.

Once information is gathered, a second dimension involves how people evaluate, or judge what they have gathered. One aspect of judging is thinking (T). Decision-makers who prefer thinking use facts in a logical rational approach to decision-making. They evaluate costs and benefits as the classical model of decision-making stipulates. In contrast, an alternate way of judging is to use feelings or values (F). Those who prefer using an F-style approach consider the human consequences, values, and ethics in reaching a decision.

Relying exclusively on one approach to making decisions can cause problems. More managers tend to use thinking rather than feeling when making decisions. Business schools emphasize analytical tools and cost–benefit analysis. When these are the sole criteria for decisions, problems arise. The recent problems experienced by Enron, Adelphia, and WorldCom illustrate managers who focused too much on economic issues and not enough on values and ethics. Conversely, managers who make all decisions only with people in mind are not successful either. Sometimes it may be better for the company and the individual to give critical feedback to an employee or even fire him or her. Managers need to balance the logical/analytical criteria with the human/ethical.

These two dimensions can be combined into a two-by-two model, as shown in Table 4.2. This model depicts four decision styles and some of the occupations chosen by those styles. The occupations chosen by ST's tend to involve a lot of detail and cost elements. In contrast, the NT occupations are longer range and development-oriented, but also logical and rational. The SF's tend to choose detailed occupations that involve people. The NF's choose broader, longer-range occupations that focus on the development of people and values.

Table 4.2: Myers-Briggs Type Indicator Decision Styles and Choices of Occupation[10]

| | | Judging | |
		Thinking	Feeling
Perceiving	Sensing	ST: accountants, finance	SF: sales, education, nursing
	Intuition	NT: science, law	NF: creative writers, clergy, trainers

In terms of decision-making, which style is best? As you might expect, all four styles are useful in making decisions. Thus differences in how decisions are made should not be viewed as obstacles or problems. It is important to have different "angles" on a decision. Given that there are relationships between style preferences and occupations, it is also helpful to have a decision team with different backgrounds. A group of accountants or engineers who are prone to details (S) and analytical procedures (T) may miss broader implications or human issues in a decision. Thinking types help in analyzing the financial costs and benefits while feeling types examine the human and ethical implications. All four perspectives are useful in coming to balanced, well thought through decisions, as suggested in Table 4.3.

Table 4.3: Use of Myers-Briggs Dimensions in Decision-making[11]

MBTI Style	Value in Decision-making
Sensing	Identify relevant facts in situation, focus on details.
Intuition	Explore the implications of decision.
Thinking	Use relevant facts to examine logical consequences of decision.
Feeling	Consider values and human impacts of decision.

GROUP DECISION-MAKING

Given the prevalence of using groups and teams to complete tasks in today's organization, additional information will be presented about decision-making in a group context. You might begin by asking why groups are used so often to gather information and make decisions. We have alluded to several advantages already, one of the most obvious being that more information can be brought to bear on the decision, especially if decision-makers come from different functional areas, as shown in Table 4.4. Secondly, different styles may also be present so that details, future implications, ethical issues, etc., can all be considered.

Table 4.4: Advantages & Disadvantages of Group Decision-Making

Advantages of Group Decision-making	Disadvantages of Group Decision-making
Additional informational resources	Greater time spent in decision-making
Different decision styles	Additional information to weigh
Greater understanding of underlying issue	Group process loss (e.g., groupthink)
Greater acceptance of decision outcomes	Riskier decisions
Group synergy effects	Social loafing

By examining and discussing the problem, individual team members come to understand the issues related to the decision. They are also more likely to accept the outcome (procedural justice). Both understanding and acceptance improve the success when implementing a decision. A final benefit of using groups is what has been termed a **synergy effect**. The theory is that when individuals share thoughts, one person's ideas stimulate another to think of issues that would not have arisen working alone. The common phrase is "the whole is greater than the sum of the parts." More information is generated via synergy than would be generated by all of the same individuals working alone.

Group decision-making has some drawbacks. Groups require more time to reach decisions. The information potential that is present in groups needs to be shared and this takes time. This additional information also needs to be assessed and evaluated. Some members may dominate the discussion, causing others to withhold valuable information. **Process loss** is defined as a sub-optimal decision process whereby the available information is not shared and used in the decision-making process. When process loss occurs not only is there no synergy effect, but only partial information is used to make a decision. Thus process loss, when it occurs, is a major detractor in group decision-making. Groups also tend to make riskier decisions and take greater chances. The reason for this risky trend is that the sense of responsibility for the decision is not held by any one person, but is diffused throughout the group. Finally, when groups reach a size of five or more, it becomes easy for some members to sit back and let others do the work. Social loafing occurs when some members do not participate, instead allowing others to do the work for them.

The pragmatic question is how can the advantages of group decision-making be leveraged while minimizing the disadvantages? Several techniques or procedures will be discussed to encourage the benefits and limit the drawbacks.

Most group decision-making occurs in meetings. Meetings can be the traditional face-to-face type or can be virtual, mediated by technology with members distributed geographically. Some managers are good at running meetings while others are horrendous.

A few guidelines, shown in Table 4.5, can help meetings run better. The first is to consider the purpose of the meeting. Groups can be effective tools to make decisions. A meeting is not a good use of time to share routine information or announcements; a manager should use memos, e-mails, or a bulletin board to distribute routine communications on new procedures. The meeting is best used to bring together information uniquely held by different members or to answer questions that multiple individuals have. Meetings are also useful in making sense of uncertain information. Getting different interpretations and building consensus is helpful.

Most people who attend meetings work better if there is some preparation; therefore, sharing an agenda in advance is useful. Members know what is expected to happen and can prepare and bring relevant support information. If specific individuals have responsibilities for leading a portion of the meeting, they should also be informed and designated on the agenda. Sometimes meetings can be sidetracked by trivial events; therefore the construction and timing of the agenda is important. Time limits should be placed on routine items or they can be left until the last ten minutes. It is very frustrating for members to prepare work and then never get a chance to discuss or present it because minor issues took too long. Many managers allocate a fixed amount of time for each item on the agenda. If they go over, then the issue is raised and decided by the group as to whether they will continue with this important item and save others for a subsequent meeting or stick to the agenda.

Table 4.5: Guidelines for Effective Group Meetings

Guidelines
1. Use meetings for the right purpose.
2. Distribute an agenda in advance.
3. Start on time and follow the agenda.
4. Control participation.
5. Push for decisions.
6. Assign responsibility for follow-up.
7. Appoint a process observer or seek feedback.

Another simple point related to the agenda is to start on time. If you ask important people to come to a meeting, be sure that it starts on time. Late arrivals are thieves who steal valuable resources from the group. As the meeting progresses, it is also important for the manager to follow the agenda. One factor that can sidetrack meetings is domination by certain members. The leader of the meeting has the responsibility to see that all get a chance to speak and to inform some members that they are taking more than their share of the meeting.

As the title of the chapter suggests, meetings are for more than sharing information. The leader may need to push the group to decide because some may want to over-analyze and try to reduce all uncertainty. Group meetings need to reach conclusions—that is, make decisions. Once decisions are made, steps are taken to assure decisions are implemented; follow-up is important. A manager may note who has responsibility for subsequent actions and when they are expected. A more formal way of managing follow-up is through responsibility chartings. A table is constructed (and shared) of what tasks are to be done, by whom, and by what time and date. The chart can then be used in the next meeting to track implementation.

Just as feedback is the last step in decision-making, some feedback should be gathered periodically at meetings. Several options are available for managers. In organizations where many have been trained in meetings and group dynamics, a process observer can be appointed. The process observer watches how the group interacts rather than participating in the content of the meeting. Near the end of the meeting, the process observer shares her or his observations with the group. A less formal way of obtaining feedback is for the manager to ask members for suggestions on improving subsequent meetings. Things may have happened of which the manager was not aware. Open discussion of the group process can help future meetings.

Several specific techniques have been developed for getting the most out of group decision-making. Most people have heard of **brainstorming**; however, not all groups follow the principles properly. Brainstorming is a method of rapidly throwing out ideas with the goal of generating more ideas using the principle of synergy (presented earlier in the chapter). Ideally, stating the purpose and the ideas the group is expected to generate will begin brainstorming. Brainstorming can be used to identify causes or generate alternative options in making decisions. The key step is to separate generation from evaluation. For brainstorming to work as intended, options are generated. One member's comment may elicit a response from another. The important ground rule is to not criticize as ideas are generated. Evaluation comes in a subsequent stage. Once the group has exhausted its ideas, then the leader asks the group to identify overlap among suggestions and to comment on the degree to which the suggestions address the problem. By withholding critical comments in the generation phase, group process loss is minimized. The weakness of brainstorming is that some members may dominate and quieter members may not get a chance to speak. When a cross-functional team is formed with members from different levels in the hierarchy, the lower-level members may be reluctant to speak out.

Nominal group technique (NGT) addresses these shortcomings. The word "nominal" means in name only. NGT does not use a spontaneous brainstorming phase to generate information or options. The generation stage is done individually. Members are given the problem to address and are asked to generate responses in writing. Once all individuals are finished, then the ideas are posted; the leader goes around the group and asks each member to list one of their ideas and this round-robin procedure continues until all ideas are posted. Like brainstorming, no critical comments are allowed as ideas are generated, and only clarification questions may be asked. Once posted, overlap is then identified and ideas are evaluated (step four is the same for both techniques).

Table 4.6: A Comparison of Brainstorming and Nominal Group Technique

Brainstorming	Nominal Group Technique
1. Issue presented to group.	1. Issue presented to group.
2. **Group generation** of ideas spontaneously.	2. **Individual generation** of ideas in writing.
3. Posting of ideas as generated.	3. Ideas posted in round robin fashion.
4. Evaluation of ideas by group.	4. Evaluation of ideas by group.
5. Best option chosen for implementation.	5. Best option chosen for implementation.

The two group techniques are compared in Table 4.6 above. The major difference lies in how ideas are generated, step 2. NGT is more structured in the generation of ideas by giving each member a chance to present ideas. NGT can be superior to brainstorming in groups where cultural differences may cause some to speak less or when there is a wide variation in the hierarchical level or status of members. Each member has an equal footing when presenting their ideas, helping to minimize group process loss.

By being mindful of the advantages of groups, and using a few of the techniques discussed, managers can help make groups more effective decision-making bodies, yielding better decisions and wasting less time.

Chapter 4 Endnotes

1. John F. Rockhart, "The changing role of the information systems executive: A critical success factors perspective," *Sloan Management Review* 24, no. 1 (1984): 4.

2. Charles H. Kepner & Benjamin B. Tregoe, *The Rational Manager:A Systematic Approach to Problem Solving and Decision Making* (Princeton, NJ: Kepner-Tregoe, 1965), 47.

3. Charles H. Ford, "The "Elite" Decision Makers: What Makes Them Tick?" in *Readings in Management*, Max D. Richard (Cincinnati, OH: 1986), 150.

4. William R. Daniels, *Group Power: A Manager's Guide to Using Meetings* (San Diego, CA: University Associates, 1986), 43.

5. Richard L. Daft & Dorothy Marcic, *Understanding Management* (4th ed.) (Mason, OH: Thomson/South-Western, 2004), 191.

6. Richard M. Cyert & James G. March, "A Behavioral Theory of Organizational Objectives." in *Classics of Organizational Theory* (4th ed.), ed. Jay M. Safritz & J. Steven Ott (Belmont, CA: Wadsworth Publishing, 1996), 140.

7. Ford, 155.

8. Leigh L. Thompson, *The Mind and Heart of the Negotiator* (3rd ed.) (Upper Saddle, NJ: Pearson/Prentice-Hall, 2005), 17.

9. Isabel Briggs Myers & Peter B. Myers, *Gifts Differing* (Palo Alto, CA: Consulting Psychologists Press, 1980), 3.

10. Ibid, 207–208.

11. Ibid, 205.

CHAPTER 5

Ethics and Social Responsibilty

Chapter 5

ETHICS & SOCIAL RESPONSIBILTY

Army recruits at Fort Benning, Georgia, are required to take a class in personal finance during basic training. The course is designed to help naïve nineteen-year-olds, who are living on their own for the first time, better manage their finances. A number of soldiers in that course signed up for what they thought was an Army-approved savings plan or mutual fund. They were told to initial a large stack of forms without reading them. It turns out that they purchased an expensive life insurance policy with a one hundred dollar-per-month payroll deduction. The military offers a life insurance policy for substantially less. Financial experts say that these policies (that the soldiers purchased) represent a poor option for members of the military,[1] because the high premiums go mostly to agent commissions in the first few years without generating much cash value for the soldiers.

Are these sales legal, ethical, or moral? Pentagon rules prohibit solicitation of military personnel while on duty, making the sales pitch a violation of rules. The real problem with the sales approach is that boot camp teaches new soldiers to "question nothing."[2] Recruits believed that the Army endorsed the program; some of the agents were former military officers. The president of a lobbying group, the American Council of Life Insurers, who is also the former governor of Oklahoma, did not feel that there was anything wrong with the sales, as he believed that people who are mature enough to fight and die should be able to make decisions about life insurance. Several weeks after the first report of these sales, Congress began hearings to investigate these practices, and perhaps to propose new legislation.

If there were ethical violations, who was unethical and who is responsible? Are the insurance agents at fault? Is the insurance company responsible? Do senior military officers at Fort Benning bear some of the responsibility for allowing the agents on the base? This chapter will discuss a variety of issues related to what can be called "doing the right thing." It sounds easy, but ethics are not a simple matter.

Should managers really care about ethics? What are the costs of ethical violations? The costs can be outlined at three different levels.[3] The first type of cost is fines imposed by the courts and regulatory agencies. These fines can exceed $500,000. Another type of costs involves legal, administrative, and investigative costs associated with an ethics violation. Remedial actions, such as training, may also be mandated by the courts, incurring additional costs. The final category of costs is less obvious. Loss of reputation, customer defections, lower employee morale, and eventually employee turnover can further damage a company's performance. Ethical violations can be very costly.

Most of the time ethical dilemmas occur in situations with more than one difficult option. To resolve these dilemmas, managers need guidelines for assessing and interpreting situations. Different ethical frameworks will be presented that can be used to evaluate ethical dilemmas and reach decisions. Another related issue, social responsibility, will also be covered. What is the role of organizations in their communities? Should they share time and resources? Are these actions also part of "doing the right thing"? Are there problems associated with devoting time and resources to community issues?

ETHICS

CLARIFYING TERMS

Before proceeding further, some definitions of terms are needed. **Business ethics** is defined as *the beliefs about appropriate behavior in the workplace*. Both managers and employees are expected to act ethically. People differ in their standards or beliefs about appropriate behavior. Some may verbalize one thing and do something else. Ethics help to create a sense of community in that they often reflect the collective good. If employees' behaviors were only guided by their narrow self-interests, then the world would not be a very nice place. People would lie and cheat to get what they want without concern for others. Some have presented ethics as the golden rule, treating others as we would prefer to be treated. Professional education for such occupations as accounting or law has courses or subject matter on ethics. Professional societies often present codes of behavior that reflect members' shared beliefs about appropriate behavior and serve as guidelines for new members.[4]

A term related to ethics is *morals*. **Morals** are *fundamental values that societies impart to their members about right and wrong*. Respect for human life is a value that is part of the morals of many societies. Morals are broader than ethics but can influence them. Native Americans have strong morals about the environment and relating to the natural world. These morals could influence their business ethics in that they would be less prone to engage in business activities that would damage or destroy the environment.

The ethical dilemmas in the workplace tend to be between financial and social outcomes. If I maximize my personal gain or that of the company, is someone else harmed? For example, a product designer is paid a bonus for creating a working prototype at a certain cost by a certain time. Suppose that the designer is working on a new infant car seat prototype. Motivated by a bonus that rewards production at or under budget by a specific date, he cuts down on the cost of materials and doesn't do all of the tests on the seat that he could have. He tested forward-impact collisions but not lateral impact as the time deadline was looming. Subsequently several infants die in accidents when the vehicles in which they were riding were hit from the side. The restraining straps did not hold up to lateral impacts. He received a bonus for delivering the prototype under cost and on-time, but the social consequences were severe. To conduct additional tests and use higher quality straps would have delayed the presentation of the prototype and added to the costs. A series of choices were made, not all deliberate. Is the designer solely to blame? Do the company and his manager play a part for setting and rewarding these objectives?

Table 5.1: Comparing Laws, Morals & Business Ethics

Laws	Morals	Business Ethics
A limited set of minimal rules for living, maintained by external controls	Fundamental values about what is right and wrong	A set of internal beliefs about appropriate behavior in the workplace

Laws also provide guidelines for the greater good of the community. Laws are compared with morals and ethics in Table 5.1. Laws are different, however, in that the rule of law is a system of externally imposed controls. These controls *provide a minimum standard for not doing harm in society*. Not stealing, physically harming someone, or selling defective products are examples of minimal standards for living in society. In democratic countries, duly elected representatives approve laws; hence the laws are presumed to reflect society's collective interests. Laws often require enforcement to be effective. Obeying stop lights and speed limits benefits the citizenry in general, but we have all observed speeders and persons running red lights. Periodic enforcement of law violators is necessary to maintain the controls over time.

As laws provide minimal standards for not harming others, a question to ask is whether acts that do not violate the law are ethical. Some legal acts are not ethical, so there is a gap between the rule of law and ethics. A person who acquires a handicapped-parking sign for an aging grandparent parks in the handicapped zone even when the grandparent is not present in the car. The action is legal, but many would consider it unethical because the grandchild was able and denied the spot to someone who may have needed it. Community interests were not served. Self-interest or free choice provides no restrictions or controls. Ethical standards take an intermediate position, attempting to provide internal controls. Individuals with ethical controls think about the implications of their actions on others.

Sometimes laws are created when too many individuals act without internal controls or unethically. The demise of Enron was the result of both illegal and unethical actions. Senior managers misrepresented the financial performance of the company to a variety of stakeholders. They did not follow the ethical guidelines established by the accounting profession. Following ethical problems at Enron, Tyco, Arthur Andersen, WorldCom, and others, new laws were created on financial reporting. The Sarbanes-Oxley Act of 2002 was a legal response to unethical behavior. In addition, the law protects whistle-blowing employees who report these actions to public officials.

Ethical guidelines are important because laws cannot be written for every possible situation or circumstance. Some laws are created by a majority but are not viewed as moral, as were the old laws limiting voting to land-owning males and other segregation practices. It is important for employees and managers to have internal standards about right and wrong. One guideline frequently given is the front-page standard: how would you feel about your choice if it were published on the front page of your local newspaper? How would your family feel about your decision? If the choice made stands up to public scrutiny and many others find it acceptable, then it is likely to be ethical.

ETHICAL FRAMEWORKS

Since many of the dilemmas that face managers and employees are not simple decisions, several common frameworks will be presented that are often used to analyze decision choices and provide guidance with options.

Each framework provides a different approach to defining what is right and sometimes what is right in a given situation or circumstance.

Utilitarian. The utilitarian ethical framework is based on microeconomic theory. It focuses on the *outcomes or consequences* of decisions and is based primarily on costs and benefits. Simply stated, a utilitarian approach examines which alternative would do the greatest good for the greatest number of people. With the focus on outcomes, this framework can also be interpreted as "the ends justify the means." Managers act to bring about the best possible outcomes for themselves and their companies. This reasoning provides the justification for layoffs. Some unfortunate individuals lose their jobs so that a firm can save costs and preserve jobs for a greater number of remaining employees. Although those receiving "pink slips" may feel unfairly treated, this action saves the jobs of other employees, the greater good. Conversely, the habits of Dennis Kozlowski, CEO of Tyco, spending corporate resources on a lavish birthday party for his wife, served only his interests, not those of the corporation, its managers, or its shareholders. His expenditures were unethical in that few benefited, and he has subsequently been convicted of fraud, sentenced to prison, and ordered to pay $97 million in restitution and $70 million in fines.

There are some problems with this framework. The implication is that profit optimization leads to the greatest social benefit.[5] The reasoning behind utilitarianism is that the presumed efficiency of economic markets provides for the best distribution of resources for all. "The problem—and the essence of the ethical dilemma for management—is that sometimes improvements in economic performance—increases in sales or decreases in costs—can be made only at the expense of one or more of the groups to whom the organization has some form of obligation."[6] Sometimes not all costs are included in the evaluation of choices. A company may reason that by eliminating healthcare benefits to a segment of employees it saves money to benefit other employees and shareholders. However, if the disenfranchised employees must rely on emergency services for medical treatment, the local healthcare system is overloaded and is unable to provide critical care for those who need it. Essentially the company did not consider the costs to the greater community. It transferred its costs to others who may be less able to afford them. Similarly, a retailer demands and receives tax abatement for ten years to build a new store in the inner-city area. As a result of that abatement, city residents' taxes remain high. A tax-paying retailer may have enabled the city to lower taxes or offer more services to residents. If the outcomes of only the corporation are included, the decision looks appropriate. The costs were too narrowly defined, ignoring the lower-income citizens of the community.

If the means do not matter, then is bribery an acceptable tactic to win a contract? Is it acceptable to exaggerate the virtues of a product or service in order to make the sale? Is it acceptable for a manager to describe a job in very positive terms, failing to note the long hours and stress that are typically required? Means do matter. In fact, the focus on outcomes assumes that managers act in legally appropriate ways.

Given the importance of winning, some Olympic athletes have resorted to performance-enhancing drugs. Is this ethical? New rules and tests (an enforcement procedure) have been set up to monitor drug use. Several athletes lost medals at the 2004 Olympics because they used unfair means (performance-enhancing drugs) to reach their goal, disadvantaging those who did not. The preoccupation with ends can lead to unfair means. Similar reasoning can be applied to cheating on a test. Not only is it not fair to others taking the test without cheating, but the individual cheater does not learn. Here both the outcomes and the means are undesirable.

Universalism. If focusing solely on the ends is not an adequate ethical perspective, then should one focus on the means? Universalism looks at the means and intentions, stating that the ends are not most important but rather the duties and obligations followed in getting there. The obligations that we owe are to treat others as we would prefer to be treated. Faced with the same set of circumstances, would we treat all others the same way? The term "universalism" is applied because our response is universal, treating all the same way. Consistency in behavior is a key element of this approach. Examples of unethical behavior tend to occur when people exempt themselves from the guideline, leading to inconsistency; it is not appropriate for sales agents to accept gifts, but I can because I don't make as much money as the more experienced sales staff.

This consistency approach to ethics treats people as ends, not means. You should be as engaged and polite to the custodian as you are to the CEO of the company. Applying universalism means all employees are treated with dignity and respect, regardless of rank. You would not "use" a relationship with someone to further your ends if it took advantage of them, thus you act as you wish others to act, as the golden rule suggests.

Applying this perspective, employees should be informed of a plant closing because each of us would want prior information about such an event so we could begin to look for other employment. However, the company would have a difficult time completing its work prior to closing if numerous employees left. The means are just, but the ends present problems for managers. This example again illustrates the difficulty in making choices. The utilitarian approach might suggest that the costs and benefits to the company are greatest by not giving much notice, while the universalism view would dictate giving as much notice as possible. The law has become involved in this issue through the Plant Closing Act of 1988, requiring employers to provide employees with sixty days notification of a plant closing.[7] This law again shows how legislation can be formulated in response to perceived unethical behavior on the part of businesses and managers.

Universalism advocates treating all people well. This is usually a good philosophy. So what are the shortcomings of this approach? One problem that it shares with utilitarianism is that it can be subject to individual interpretation. What does it mean to treat others with respect? Can it always be possible to treat others as ends and not means? In addition, LaRue Tone Hosmer[8] points out that this perspective often does not provide priorities or a means of ranking choices. Does the truly ethical manager need to fill in the missing areas with utilitarian reasoning? Before answering this question there are several other frameworks to review.

Moral Rights. To fill in some of the vagueness regarding treating others with respect, morals rights have been identified that provide absolute categories of treatment. The absolute rights that people have include:

- Freedom of consent
- Freedom of privacy
- Freedom of conscience
- Freedom of speech
- Right to due process[9]

To be ethical, these rights should not be violated. Individuals should freely and knowingly give consent to actions. They should do so with full information. Hence in the opening illustration, Army recruits were not given full information about the life insurance policies and did not freely consent. They were misled into thinking that the policies were endorsed by the government. They should also have the right to refrain from activities to which they object. Being in the military, they may not have felt that they could reject the offer, as it would be like refusing an order from a superior.

Justice. The justice approach assumes that all should be treated with fairness and impartiality. Rules and procedures should guide actions. Decisions related to distributing outcomes should not be arbitrary. In this way it is similar to the rule of law, but it can extend further to other reasonable rules established by the organization for fair and impartial treatment, such as seniority-based decisions. Those last hired are the first to be released. Human resource management practices tend to be based on this approach to ethics. Decisions should be based on a system—like merit—not race, religion, or personal relationships. The justice perspective also does not hold individuals responsible for actions over which they have no control.[10] It also attempts to be consistent with all employees, which is a feature of universalism.

Table 5.2: Applying Ethical Frameworks to the Sale of Life Insurance to Soldiers

Ethical Framework	Interpretation
Utilitarian	What are the costs and benefits and to whom? The soldiers gain no advantage and incur high cost. The sales agents gain and the insurance company gains. Agents in general lose as their image is further tarnished by these actions.
Universalism	There is no respect shown for soldiers and they are not treated according to the golden rule.
Moral Rights	Several rights were violated. They did not knowingly consent with knowledge of the consequences. The insurance was misrepresented as government endorsed. Soldiers may not have felt that they had the free conscience to decline in this situation.
Justice	The soldiers were not treated fairly and equitably, and rules were not followed.

Follow-up. It was announced on September 23, 2004, that refunds were offered to soldiers at Fort Benning, Georgia, by American Amicable Life Insurance Company. Furthermore, three agents involved in selling the policies were fired and a fourth resigned. These actions were taken after the state insurance commissioner of Georgia exerted pressure on the company. Regulations and external enforcement again help to re-assert ethical guidelines and punish unethical actions. As I write this, there are no reports of disciplinary actions taken against the military officers who allowed the agents on base to conduct the classes.

SOCIAL REPONSIBILITY

Like ethics, social responsibility involves choices between financial and social outcomes. Today we acknowledge that the typical company has numerous stakeholders, including the community in which the organization operates. Does the organization have responsibilities to the community as a citizen or is the primary obligation only to one stakeholder, the shareholders? Milton Friedman succinctly stated the latter position:" . . . there is one and only one social responsibility of business—to use its resources and engage in activities designed to increase its profits as long as it stays within the rules of the game, which is to say, engages in open and free competition without deception and fraud."[11] Friedman argues that social responsibility dilutes shareholder value and hence is not good. His approach is based on the utilitarian philosophy that the greater good is served by increasing shareholder value. In the long term this outcome is of the greatest benefit to society as a whole. Profit maximization leads to the fair distribution of wealth for society. The interests of shareholders are similar to property rights; they should not have these rights infringed upon by expectations of sharing resources with non-shareholders.

Others disagree, saying that increasing shareholder value often benefits only a small class of wealthy members of society. Companies operate in urban areas with people living nearby who may never own stock. The question then becomes, What obligations or duties do firms have to society? At one extreme, Friedman argues that a firm should operate lawfully and ethically, doing no harm. It should maximize shareholder value by "playing fairly" and maximizing its profits. Some also say that companies are not obligated to be good citizens, only individuals are. Philanthropically inclined employees may therefore be encouraged to donate their money and non-work time to charities, not corporations.

CATEGORIES OF RESPONSIBLE ACTION

Attempting to resolve these discrepancies, Carroll[12] described four different categories of social responsibility for corporations, each with a different set of obligations, as shown in Table 5.3. Consistent with Friedman, the first category of social responsibility is economic. This obligation is most fundamental, as the survival of the firm supports many stakeholders. Identifying the right products and services and delivering them efficiently benefits many. Without these obligations, the firm cannot survive.

Similarly firms are expected by society to obey the laws and follow the guidelines established by federal, state, and local agencies. Both economic and legal responsibilities must be simultaneously attained. Such is the expectation of society. Society, however, often expects more than these minimal responses. Corporations and their employees are expected to act in an ethical manner, adhering to principles of behavior beyond the mere legal minimum. Many corporations follow the justice framework in dealing ethically with employees, trying to be fair and consistent with all.

Table 5.3: Responsibility Categories of Corporate Social Responsibility

Economic	Legal	Ethical	Discretionary
Produce goods and services desired by society to earn a profit.	Operate lawfully in conformance to laws and regulations.	Actions beyond the law that are expected, such as fair treatment of employees.	Activities beyond the prior categories.
Example: Eliminate a product line that has declined in sales and introducing new ones based on market research.	Example: Follow established accounting practices for reporting income and expenses.	Example: Have an appeal and review process for disciplinary violations.	Examples: Provide job training for the unemployed, daycare services, and have employees serve as mentors in area schools.

Discretionary responsibilities are those for which society has no clear set expectations. The term *discretionary* suggests that these are not requirements, but are activities that firms engage in to provide benefits for the greater good of society. Increasingly, communities and other stakeholders are exerting pressure on firms to fulfill discretionary responsibilities at some level. When employees are laid off, many firms fund outplacement services to help employees get new jobs. Daycare centers are established on-site for employees. These activities benefit internal stakeholders and also help to improve morale. Allowing employees to mentor urban grade school children on company time represents a discretionary activity that benefits community stakeholders.

Discretionary activities are not necessarily solely altruistic. Companies may gain economic benefit from discretionary activities. Increasingly, mutual funds are offered to investors containing only companies who are judged to be ethical and socially responsive. Some consumers seek to buy products from companies that are socially responsible, even if it costs more. Recently,

Paul Godfrey[13] suggested that discretionary acts also protect shareholder wealth. Discretionary corporate philanthropy generates positive moral capital in communities and in turn acts as insurance to protect some of the firm's intangible assets. Thus there are several arguments to counter Friedman's narrow view.

A good question to ask is, What is the range of activities that firms engage in to be more responsible? The Haas School of Business and the University of California at Berkeley have established the Center for Responsible Business[14] to foster social responsibility and ethical behavior. Figure 5.1 illustrates some of the areas that are considered good business.

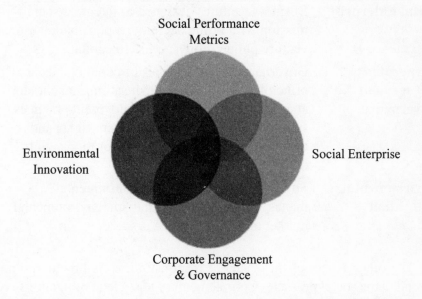

Figure 5.1: Content areas for corporate social responsibility.

These four areas could be considered in both the ethical and discretionary categories of social responsibility. Social performance metrics help build public trust by freely reporting standards and measurement issues. For example, oil companies are encouraged to publicly report violations of guidelines and the associated fines. This openness allows for the establishment of benchmarks and the tracking of performance over time. Chevron-Texaco publishes an annual corporate responsibility update.[15] This level of openness builds trust in the organization.

The four areas of performance are detailed in Table 5.4. Social enterprise actions are more solely discretionary in nature, involving social missions and philanthropy. Corporate engagement and governance focuses on ethical issues, such as executive compensation and labor issues. The final content area of environmental innovation relates to the external environment. Firms strive to manage, and not exploit, the environment.

Table 5.4: Content or Performance Areas of Social Responsibility

Social Performance Metrics	Trust and transparency, reporting and standards, measurement and metrics
Social Enterprise	Business ventures designed to integrate social mission with profit, socially responsible investing, venture philanthropy, access to capital
Corporate Engagement & Governance	Governance models, codes of conduct, business principles, executive compensation, stakeholder engagement, responsible employment practices, supply chain management, human rights and labor issues, cross-sector collaborations, global responsibility
Environmental Innovation	Sustainable development, environmental management, natural capitalism, environmental market opportunities

The other aspect of these sets of responsibilities is how corporations respond to the social pressure. Complementary to societal obligations is corporate responsiveness. Carroll also identified four categories of responsiveness. The reaction category represents the highest level of resistance. Those whose response is reaction are likely to meet only economic and legal responsibilities. Defense companies are likely to add some ethical categories of responsibility. The accommodation category adds some discretionary activities to its obligations. These actions often involve the social performance and social responsibility expectations. Though relatively rare, corporations in this response category practice social responsibility using metrics, corporate governance and engagement, and social enterprise content areas.

Table 5.5: Corporate Reactions to Responsibility Pressures

Reaction	Defense	Accommodation	Proaction
Fight the pressure all the way.	Do what is required.	Be progressive, going beyond the minimum.	Lead the industry, far exceeding expectations.

Proactive, or leading, companies do more than strive not to do harm. They may go beyond the legal minimums in cleaning outputs before discharging them into the environment. They may refrain from testing products on animals. They may give a percentage of profits to needy groups or organizations in the community. These are highly responsive organizations. Corporations in the proaction category will engage in activities in all four content areas when applicable. You can go to their websites and explore the pages that deal with the environment and society. Responsible firms: Ben & Jerry's *http://www.benjerry.com/our_company/about_us/*, Tom's of Maine *http://www.tomsofmaine.com/about/statement.asp*; The Body Shop *http://www.thebodyshopinternational.com/web/tbsgl/values.jsp.*

WHAT CAN COMPANIES DO?

Thus far, categories for analyzing and describing both ethics and social responsibility have been described. A new or senior manager may still be uncertain about how to proceed in these areas. For social responsibility, a logical place to begin is with an assessment of the current status. In which responsibility categories from Table 5.3 is the company involved? Presumably all companies are engaged in economic, legal, and, to some extent, ethical activities. What is the desired response of the company from Table 5.5? Decisions can be made about defending, accommodating, or being proactive. Choices can then be made about additional ethical and discretionary activities. Also, which performance or content areas should be added to support the firm's position on social responsibility? Once decisions are made about positions, then communication of these positions is important. Statements should be placed in newsletters, on websites, etc.

Ethical applications tend to focus more on individual employees. Generally the first step is to establish codes of conduct for ethics. These statements should also be well publicized in corporate documents and displays and communicated to all employees. Training programs should be established to guide managers in making ethically appropriate decisions.

Frameworks beyond the utilitarian model should be covered. In addition, provisions should be made for reporting ethical violations. A hotline can be created for employees to anonymously ask questions and report observed violations. When all of these elements are in place, there is a greater likelihood that ethical violations will be reported.[16]

As noted earlier in this chapter, ethical violations are costly and damage performance. Without programs, ethical problems are likely to ensue. Beyond ethics, social responsibility imposes further obligations on managers and corporations. Both ethics and social responsibility represent efforts to balance the financial performance of the firm with the greater social concerns of the community. In a civilized world, goals in both domains need to be reached with neither maximized to the other's exclusion.

Chapter 5 Endnotes

1. Diana B. Enriques, "Basic Training Doesn't Guard Against Insurance Pitch to GIs," *New York Times*, 20 July 2004.

2. Ibid.

3. Terry Thomas, John R. Schermerhorn Jr, and John W. Dienhart, "Strategic Leadership of Ethical Behavior in Business," *Academy of Management Executives* 18, no. 2 (2004): 58.

4. For several examples of professional codes of ethics, examine the following websites: http://www.imanet.org/ima/ and http://www.shrm.org/ethics/.

5. LaRue Tone Hosmer, *The Ethics of Management*, 3rd ed. (Chicago: Richard C. Irwin, 1996), 35.

6. Ibid, 85.

7. Alok K. Bohara, Alejandro Islas Camargor, Therese Grijalva, and Kishore Gawande, "Fundamental Dimensions of U.S. Trade Policy," *Journal of International Economics* 65 (2005) 93–125.

8. Hosmer, 95.

9. G. F. Cavanaugh, D. J. Moberg, and M. Velasquez, "The Ethics of Organizational Politics," *Academy of Management Review* 6, no. 3 (1981): 366.

10. Ibid.

11. Milton Friedman, "The Social Responsibility of Business is to Increasd its Profits," *New York Times Magazine*, 13 September 1970: 126.

12. Archie B. Carroll, "A Three-Dimensional Conceptual Model of Corporate Performance," *Academy of Management Review* 4, no. 4 (1979): 500.

13. Paul C. Godfrey, "The Relationship Between Corporate Philanthropy and Shareholder Wealth: A risk management perspective," *Academy of Management Review* 30, no. 4 (1995): 777.

14. The University of California at Berkeley, Haas School of Business Website. http://www.haas.berkely.edu/responsiblebusiness/.

15. Rick Jurgens, "Chevron Touts Social Responsibility," *Knight Ridder Tribune Business News*, 29 September 2004: 1.

16. Linda K. Trevino and Michael E. Brown, "Managing to be Ethical: Debunking five business ethics myths," *Academy of Management Executives* 18, no. 2 (2004): 78–80.

CHAPTER 6

Planning

Chapter 6

PLANNING

What do you do when you question whether your business can survive? Palm originally developed the personal digital assistant (PDA) as a hand-held scheduler. As we said earlier, PDAs became popular in the 1990s as a convenient way for business people to keep their calendars and business contacts at their fingertips. After a few years, several managers left Palm to form a competing PDA manufacturer, Visor. Both were successful for a period of time. As business declined for both, they merged into one company to be more efficient in producing and selling PDAs. Nevertheless, the combined company, PalmOne, is still struggling, with declining sales.

Managers at PalmOne and stock analysts are questioning why. Part of the problem comes from the environment of this technological industry. As described in prior chapters, a number of factors in the environment, such as competitors and changes in technology, impact business. In terms of technology, laptop computers have become smaller and lighter, can do more than PDAs, and are approaching them in size. Another product, the cell phone, has evolved so that it is also competing with PDAs. Cell phones are becoming "smarter" and more versatile; they can be used to play games, send messages, and take pictures, performing some of the functions of computers and more. The marketplace in which PDAs compete is becoming more competitive, thus cutting into the market for PalmOne products.

PalmOne is now wondering what business they should be in and in what direction they should head in the future. Such a fundamental question as "Should we continue making PDAs?" may be under consideration. In short, planning is a major issue for them.

PLANNING TERMS

Planning is defined as specifying desired organizational results, or outcomes, as well as identifying the means for achieving those results. **Goals** are statements of desired results. **Objectives** are specific statements of intended outcomes. While goals and objectives specify outcomes, **plans** specify the means, or activities, that are chosen to reach them. A 6 percent increase in sales for the coming year is an example of a goal. Developing improved marketing communication materials is part of the plan, or means, to increase sales by 6 percent.

Planning is the first of the four functions of management because organizations need to have a sense of where they are going before they set up other business operations. It is the starting point. Planning provides several benefits. One is that it provides a sense of direction, or focus, for managers and employees. With so many things to do, priorities are needed. Planning also helps to unify efforts, encouraging members to "pull in the same direction." Planning further helps to define the organization for stakeholders outside of the company, such as customers and investors. Planning requires managers to think ahead and anticipate the future. Thus planning can help in reacting to unexpected events by providing guidance to managers. For example, a disaster plan specifies steps and actions to follow if a disaster occurs. It enables an organization to respond more quickly and effectively to these events.

Planning is also important because the other functions of management emerge from it, as depicted in Figure 6.1. The second function of *organizing* specifies how work and workers are arranged in order to execute the plans. Knowing the plan, employees coordinate efforts and work together, achieving better organization as well. *Leading* is encouraging employees to execute the plan and use the organizing design. As part of the leading function, top managers create and distribute a vision statement, which provides motivation among employees to achieve objectives. The fourth function, *controlling,* is also based on planning because the assessment of the degree to which the plan was achieved is based on the goals and objectives. Corrective action is taken in controlling and then new goals and objectives are established. Planning provides the standards for assessing the extent to which the job was done right, as originally intended. Thus each of the other three functions is linked to planning.

The process of planning begins by identifying the results, or end points, desired. In chapter 1, effectiveness and efficiency were identified as two general criteria that tell managers how well they are doing. Some goals cover topics related to efficiency, or how well resources are used. Reducing costs by 10 percent is an efficiency-oriented goal. This goal provides feedback on the use of a critical resource. Other goals are related to effectiveness, or doing the right job. As discussed in an earlier chapter, efficiency goals alone are not suf-

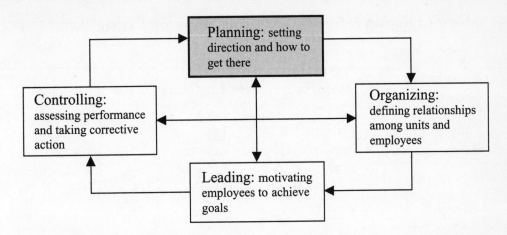

Figure 6.1: Four functions of management and their inter-relationships.

ficient measures of success. Effectiveness relates to areas of the business that indicate whether the right choices have been made about what to do. Growth is not a reasonable or good goal in a declining industry because it would be very hard to attain.

GOALS AND OBJECTIVES

A variety of goals should be established to cover different areas of the business. Robert Kaplan and David Norton developed the notion of a balanced scorecard.[1] Based on their research, they suggest that goals should be established in four distinct areas: human, customer, financial, and internal business processes. To neglect any one area would lead to an incomplete or inaccurate measure of performance. They further suggest that these four areas are linked and should be considered in order, beginning with human skills, as reflected in Table 6.1. Financial goals will not be achieved unless goals are first set and attained in human, business process, and customer areas. Thus, goals may be developed in terms of the number of training hours per employee (human), time to fill an order (business process), customer returns (customer), and finally profits (financial). In addition to advocating a range of goals for a business, Kaplan and Norton's approach also supports the human resource notions that investing in people up front is critical for organizational success.

Table 6.1.: Kaplan & Norton's Balanced Scorecard Causal Chain

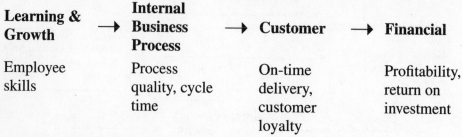

Learning & Growth →	Internal Business Process →	Customer →	Financial
Employee skills	Process quality, cycle time	On-time delivery, customer loyalty	Profitability, return on investment

Adapted from Kaplan & Norton (1996), p. 31.

Goals are set for each level in the organization. Corporate-wide goals are set for revenue and profits, for example. In larger corporations with multiple business units, goals are also set within each unit, often termed strategic business units (SBUs). At each lower level in the organization, the goals and plans become more specific, as reflected in Figure 6.2. Each unit takes the goal from the higher level and in turn sets increasingly more specific goals and objectives. Within each SBU, functional goals are established that may include a new marketing communication program and revised training program for the sales force. The marketing and human resource strategies support the strategic plan and are key components of planning to achieve goals and objectives. Furthermore, goals may be set for each unit and eventually objectives set for each employee.

Corporate Goals

Strategic Business Unit Goals

Functional Goals

Unit Goals

Individual Goals and Objectives

Figure 6.2: Goals by levels in the organization.

Objectives are more specific targets. The acronym SMART is frequently used to define the desired qualities of objectives. SMART objectives are specific, measurable, attainable, relevant, and time-based, as shown in Table

6.2. Objectives should first be *specific*. "Do your best" is not a specific objective. The lack of specificity can lead to inaction or the wrong action. Employees need to be clear on what is required of them. "Increase the number of claims processed each week by 5 percent" is specific.

Table 6.2: Examples of SMART Objectives

Objective Feature	Poor example	SMART Objective
Specific	"Do your best."	"Increase productivity by 7 percent."
Measurable	"Improve worker relations."	"Reduce grievances by 10 percent."
Achievable	"Double output."	"Reduce customer returns by 10 percent."
Relevant	"Increase profits."	"Reduce scrap rate by 6 percent."
Time-frame	"Improve your work in the future."	"Improve the number of claims processed by 5 percent during the next quarter."

Good objectives should also be *measurable,* as is the claims processing objective of 5 percent. Insurance companies measure the number of claims processed and keep records. Measurement is essential to assess whether the goal has been attained. "Improve communication with customers" is neither specific nor measurable. "Meet with each customer twice a year" can be counted and is thus measurable. A manager can tell if the subordinate has accomplished the objective. Measurable objectives have the quality that allows you to say clearly "yes, it was achieved" or "no, it was not."

Objectives also should be viewed as achievable, or attainable. A vast amount of research on goal setting[2] has found that people are highly motivated to achieve moderately challenging goals. When the objectives are viewed as too difficult, no effort is expended to reach them. In most work instances, "doubling output" is not feasible. Increasing sales for PalmOne in a shrinking market is also not feasible. It takes knowledge and experience to determine what a reasonable but challenging goal should be for a unit or individual employee.

The relevance of objectives is also important. Goals that are not relevant or pertinent to a work unit have no impact on performance. The goal of "increasing profits," though relevant for a corporation, would not be relevant for a machine shop, as their contribution to profit is limited. Costs or scrap rates would be relevant areas in which to establish goals.

Time deadlines are also important. Most people are multi-tasking, that is, performing more than one task during a give day or hour. Deadlines provide a sense of priority and clearly communicate when an objective should be achieved. Without set deadlines, employees may shift their efforts to other tasks on which they prefer to work, but which are viewed as less pressing by managers.

PLANS AND STRATEGIES

Having defined the end results, managers then use planning to develop a set of activities used to attain these end results. These "means to the ends" are strategies and plans. There are many different types of plans operating at different levels in the organization, helping managers and employees accomplish goals and objectives.

Organizations develop and use two broad categories of plans, as shown in Table 6.3. One is termed **single-use** plans and the other is called **standing** plans. Standing plans are used over and over; they could also be called recurring plans. A large part of the manager's job is to respond to subordinates' questions. Over time, different employees repeat the same questions. A manager could spend a great deal of time dealing with these repetitive questions. A way for him or her to use time more efficiently is to specify policies and procedures for handling these events. Thus, standing plans involve guidelines for handling recurring events. Policies are general descriptions of expected behavior. A company creates a policy about attendance and professional behavior. The policy informs employees as to the importance of these areas of conduct. Procedures, in turn, are steps to be taken in these circumstances. For example, if an employee misses work, then the procedure is to contact the supervisor and human resources. For each day of absence, the employee's sick time is reduced until the limit specified in the policy is reached. Basic procedures that are frequently used are termed standard operating procedures, or SOPs. SOPs may involve cleaning equipment or handling customer complaints. Policies and procedures guide both supervisor and employee in how to respond in various situations.

Table 6.3: Types of Plans

Single-Use Plans	Standing Plans
Strategies	Policies
Project Plans	Procedures

Although standing plans are reused, single-use plans may only be used once. Single-use plans specify activities to achieve a specific purpose. A project team specifies a plan to achieve its objectives for that project. The plan involves steps, interim deadlines, and other things that have to be done in order to attain the goals of the project.

Another type of single-use plan has become very important to organizations. **Strategy** is the set of activities designed to help an organization or business achieve its goals. *Strategy* is a term borrowed from the military. Generals developed broad plans (strategies) to win the war. Similarly companies have strategic plans for long-term success. Developing or formulating the strategy for a business is also a process of examination and analysis. Companies take a look at who they are, who they compete against, and what they should do in the future. Strategy and strategic planning are now critical for PalmOne, as described in the opening paragraphs of this chapter. To effectively compete, organizations must be different in some ways from their competitors. The process of developing or formulating strategy helps a company to come up with these distinctive qualities.

STRATEGIC PLANNING

As the example with PalmOne demonstrates, competitive forces in the environment play an important role in a company's long-term success. Therefore before beginning to look at strategy, managers need to understand the competitive forces in their industry.

Porter's Competitive Forces. Michael Porter identified a set of five competitive forces in a firm's industry that impact its strategy and success.[3] They are presented in Table 6.4.

Table 6.4: Porter's Competitive Forces

Force	Explanation
Potential New Entrants	Ease with which a new business can be established to compete
Threat of Substitute Products	Alternative products available
Bargaining Power of Buyers	How informed customers are and how they wield their knowledge
Bargaining Power of Suppliers	Concentration of suppliers and their ability to dictate terms
Rivalry among Competitors	A few powerful competitors means intense rivalry

Potential new entrants represents the degree to which new businesses can enter the market and compete with your product. Capital-intensive businesses, like steel or automobiles, are very difficult to establish today. In comparison, a pottery business is easy to set up in a garage and sell through the Internet. Where new business are easy to establish, the forces are much more competitive.

A second threat comes from substitute products. As we saw with the PalmOne example, cell phones have become substitute products for PDAs. Computers can now serve as audio players and televisions. When substitutes are readily available, then a firm loses market share and the industry is more competitive.

Buyers can acquire power, often through information, to exert pressure on businesses. The Internet is a great provider of information for consumers. The purchase of new automobiles has become very competitive because consumers can find information about dealer costs and bargain more assertively for lower prices. Many automobile dealers have adapted by shifting their focus to service because they make more money on parts and service than on new car sales.

Suppliers can acquire power through concentration. When there are only a few sources for supplies, then the supplier can demand more in terms of price. Again, with the Internet, businesses can find more suppliers, potentially reducing the power of those in the region of the business.

The fifth, and final, force in the industry is rivalry among competitors. In some ways this summarizes, and then goes beyond, the other forces. For some industries, several dominant players exist. Each firm watches the others carefully and reacts to competitive moves. Pepsi and Coca-Cola are two intense rivals in the soft drink industry. When one introduces a new product, like cherry-flavored soda, the other also does. Both have bottled water products and sports drinks. Products and services are matched as one strives to beat the other. Each monitors the other and matches initiatives. This competitive external force drives the internal choices.

Strategic Planning Process. Once a firm understands its competitive environment, the strategic planning process begins at the highest level in the organization, where senior managers define a mission statement. The mission statement is the organization's basic reason for existing. It is also a tool to set it apart from other companies. To compete effectively, companies must be viewed as offering something distinctive and of value to consumers. It is useful to think about strategy in terms of degrees of separation from the competition. The more degrees of separation that exist, the more customers will buy the product or service, and the more they may be willing to pay. Products that are highly distinctive tend to have big price tags.

Most plans start with a mission statement. GlaxoSmithKline's mission statement is "to improve the quality of human life by enabling people to do more, feel better, and live longer."[4] The mission statement provides a broad sense of purpose for employees and informs investors, regulators, and other stakeholders as to the reasons for the company's existence. Lower-level plans should all be directed toward achieving the mission statement.

The strategic planning process goes through a number of stages, as outlined in Figure 6.5. It begins with a review of the current mission, goals, and strategy. Past performance may also be taken into account. If profits have declined and competitors are reducing market share, then the company has to consider an alteration in strategy. PalmOne is in this position.

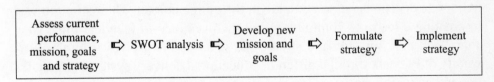

Figure 6.3: Steps in the strategic planning process.

The next stage involves conducting a SWOT analysis. The letters stand for *strengths, weaknesses, opportunities,* and *threats.* This is a critical portion of strategic planning. The first two components, strengths and weaknesses, refer to internal features of the company. Managers need to think about what the company's strengths are. Each company has developed some set of skills, or competencies, that enable it to succeed. For some, it may be a highly skilled workforce that can quickly adapt to customer requests for changes in product features. PalmOne's strengths may be the efficiency of its Palm operating system and the dedication of its workforce. The identified strengths and weaknesses are then compared with factors in the external environment. The environment provides opportunities and threats. Clearly the expanding functionality of cell phones represents a threat to PalmOne. The challenge for managers is to find new opportunities for their products or find ways to adapt the products to be able to succeed.

The SWOT analysis emphasizes the importance of fitting within the environment. The company cannot just be good at certain things. Those particular strengths must fit with opportunities in the environment. Great buggy whip companies died when other forms of vehicle acceleration were developed for the automobile. Threats in the environment, like different types of competitors, that come from areas of weakness are particularly problematic. The relative inflexibility of PDAs, when compared to laptops and cell phones, poses real problems for PalmOne.

Following this analysis, the mission statement is revised and new goals established. Then new activities for achieving the goals are developed as part of strategy formulation. In the education field, the University of Phoenix is the fastest-growing higher education institution in the world. It delivers online programs to learners any place in the world where the Internet operates. It has lower costs because it does not have tenured faculty as a fixed cost like many of the traditional universities with which it competes. Some colleges felt that they needed to address this threat and develop strengths in the area of online, virtual courses. Other institutions realized that they did not have the resources to compete (i.e., a weakness matched with a threat) and made deliberate decisions not to compete in the online market. Their strength was in creating a learning community that involves face-to-face learning. They sharpened their mission and strategy to separate themselves from the University of Phoenix through different educational delivery systems (e.g., talking and engaging learners face-to-face).

Returning to PalmOne, its analysis may determine that it does not have internal assets to match-up against environmental opportunities. It needs a strategy to acquire resources. Recently, it announced an agreement with software giant Microsoft to use a Windows interface in its Treo organizer. This partnership gives PalmOne additional resources and opens new opportunities to compete with BlackBerry, the leader in mobile phone/organizers among business people. The partnership strategy may prove to be a valuable addition to PalmOne's plans.

Effective strategic planning does not stop with formulation. In fact, how the plan is implemented, or put into effect, is, perhaps, most important. A company can copy the strategy of another, but it may not be able to pull it off. Why? Each company has a culture and set of strengths that impact performance. Copying only one piece (i.e., a portion of the strategy) will not ensure success. Another aspect of good implementation is managing change. People resist change. Companies that effectively implement strategy know how to help people to change (more in chapter 14) and provide support, like additional training, to help in adjusting to the new strategy.

Competitive Strategy Categories. In striving to find ways to separate themselves from the competition, Porter also suggested that companies adopt three types of strategies. A **differentiation** strategy finds some basis for being different. The differences can be based on product features or organizational qualities. BMW, for example, differentiates itself from the rest of the automobile market with its fine handling and driving experience. New cars, like the Acura TL, are often referenced in comparison to a BMW product that has set the standard. Internal differentiation can be in innovation. 3M encourages employees to set aside time for new product and idea development, resulting in the expanding Post-It line of products. Because products and services are viewed as unique, a differentiation strategy usually commands higher prices and profit margins.

A second strategy of separation is **cost leadership**. This strategy is based on price. Wal-Mart is the best example of low-cost leadership. Its organization is built around low costs. It finds ways to be more efficient at buying and distribution. As the world's largest retailer, it also has enormous buyer power. Wal-Mart also runs a controlled organization that seeks to prevent unions from forming. These internal practices help control costs and maintain its leadership position.

The third type of competitive strategy is niche, or **focus**. This strategy identifies a specific consumer group, or niche, in the market place that the company will serve. The University of Phoenix has become the largest university in the world by developing online courses for busy students who wish to pursue their education whenever they have time to do it, not when classes are scheduled in physical classrooms. Enterprise Rent-A-Car has also gained ground by going after a different segment of its industry. Instead of catering to business travelers, like Hertz and Avis do, Enterprise aims to serve those whose cars are damaged in accidents or stolen. They even deliver the car to the customers' homes.

Thus, strategy involves understanding the forces in the environment and doing careful analysis, comparing the company's past practices and competencies with factors operating outside of the firm. A strategy or means of separating or distancing itself from the competition is then formulated.

Henry Mintzberg of McGill University suggests that strategy formulation and implementation is not as linear or sequential as suggested.[5] Mintzberg presents evidence that strategies emerge, sometimes without careful planning. Some new strategies may be experimented with in different parts of the organization. Then a crisis or new environmental threat is recognized. In these crisis times, the experimental strategies are brought forth and given a broader chance for success. In short, Mintzberg argues that both formal and informal emergent processes operate to develop strategies. As he showed us in chapter 1 with the roles of managers, emergent strategy is an informal process. The practice of strategic management is different than the theory. Unexpected, informal strategy supplements formal, strategic planning.

OTHER PLANNING TOOLS

Earlier in the chapter we referred to disaster plans. These represent another type of plan, usually termed a **contingency plan**. A contingency is an unexpected event. Having a plan for various types of contingencies enables the organization to respond quickly and decisively. Managers do not need to hold meetings to figure out what to do in a situation, they simply pull out the plan and implement it. The contingency plan may not dictate all actions to be taken, but having gone through the process of anticipating these types of events, many of the pieces are in place for responding to them. New Orleans had disaster plans in place in the event of hurricanes but may not have acted quickly enough as Katrina approached in 2005.

Another process that is often used in planning is **benchmarking**. Companies do not need to spend a lot of time developing what others have already done or learned. Benchmarking involves a manager or team of employees going to other companies and observing their processes. If the goal is to reduce costs by reducing the number of steps in the billing process, then why not go to a company that has a reputation for outstanding billing or information technology? Adopt some of their practices, termed **best practices**, and incorporate them into plans and goals.

CONCLUSION

Planning is the first function of management. By setting clear objectives, planning provides a sense of purpose and direction for the organization. As plans are developed and linked at each level in the organization, coordination is also achieved. Strategic management is critical today. A company's ability to analyze competitive forces and develop a plan to address them is another element in long-term success.

Chapter 6 Endnotes

1. R. S. Kaplan and D. P. Norton, *The Balanced Scorecard* (Boston: Harvard Business Press, 1996), 21–29.

2. E. A. Locke and G. P. Latham, "Building a Practically Useful Theory of Goal Setting and Task Motivation," *American Psychologist* 57, no. 9 (2002): 750–716.

3. Michael E. Porter, *Competitive Strategy* (New York: Free Press, 1980).

4. GlaxoSmithKline, "Overview." http://www.gsk.com/about/about.htm.

5. Henry Mintzberg, "Crafting Strategy," *Harvard Business Review* (July–August, 1987).

▼

CHAPTER 7

Organizing

Chapter 7

ORGANIZING

The panel created to analyze the September 11, 2001, terrorist acts issued its report on July 22, 2004. One of the most prominent recommendations was the creation of a cabinet-level post to oversee U.S. intelligence efforts, much like the Homeland Security position created earlier. This new post would consolidate intelligence activities formerly done in separate agencies, such as the CIA, the FBI, the National Security Council, the Pentagon, and other agencies. The rationale for the change is that putting authority and responsibility for intelligence in one agency concentrates the information in one office, leading to better sharing and coordination of intelligence. The report found that the failure to share information among existing agencies was one factor that allowed the terrorist acts to occur. Combining resources from multiple agencies into one may also yield cost savings and improved efficiency.

This recommendation illustrates some of the advantages and drawbacks of the organizing function. Like the federal government, companies strive to find the "right" form of organization—one that will concentrate information and allow for coordination, but also provide adequate control of operations and costs. Organizing can be complicated. Authority and responsibility must be designated. Yet, firms also want to allow a certain amount of flexibility and freedom so units can be creative and effective, not just efficient. In designing organizational structures, trade-offs are often made among features. The suitability of organizing systems also changes over time as the company grows and shifts its goals, necessitating altered forms of organizing.

The 9/11 Commission's organizing recommendation is likely to meet serious resistance. Why? This proposed reorganization takes power away from the agencies that formerly operated autonomously. Changes in organizing often impact power and influence. Some individuals may lose jobs when redundant positions are eliminated. One key issue is who has budgetary control. Budget also relates to authority and power. Without the clout of budgetary control, a new agency might be weak and without the desired impact.

This chapter examines the principles of organizing. Organizing is the second function of management and is linked to planning. To achieve the goals of reducing terrorism, the 9/11 Commission has recommended reorganization. The organizing system is designed to achieve goals and so the connection to planning is direct, as shown in Figure 7.1. Some of the administrative guidelines for organizing are based on Henri Fayol's principles, while others are more recent. Organizing principles tend to be more abstract and conceptual as they relate to the entire organization. No one can directly see and experience the complete organization. Related to chapter 1, the senior managers who choose design features are using conceptual skills in re-designing features of the organization. The organizing function also provides managers with guidelines for linking the efforts of employees to achieve the goals and strategies of the organization.

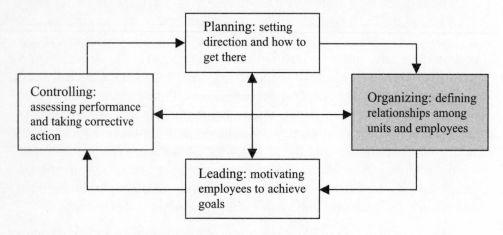

Figure 7.1: Organizing function of management.

There is also a practical side to organizing. The organizational scheme impacts the way people work and interact with others. A poor organizing system leads to frustration and conflict. When you don't get the information you need or when two units in the same company are fighting over responsibilities or turf, performance declines. Thus, organizing has behavioral consequences for individuals as well as organizational performance. The right form of organizing can minimize, but not completely eliminate, these problems.

You may recall from chapter 1 that **organizing** was defined as the pattern of relationships among employees. Employees are organized, or put in the proper organizational scheme, to achieve the goals and objectives of the organization. A secondary part of organizing involves hiring, assigning, and training employees for organizing structures, a topic covered in the next chapter. Organizing provides much of the vocabulary of management, so pay attention to the following terms that are bold and italicized.

The most concrete embodiment of the organizing function is the **organizational chart**. Most charts use rectangles to represent departments or other units, with lines showing the connections and formal authority relationships, as shown in Figure 7.2. This chart reflects several of Fayol's principles. All workers should be connected in a **chain of command** and the tasks they perform should reflect a division of labor. The chain of command links each employee to a manager who is linked to another manager until the chain reaches the most senior manager, forming a clear and distinct line of authority. Another of Fayol's principles of administration is **division of labor**; tasks are divided and employees become specialized in performing certain tasks. A section from Adam Smith's famous book, *The Wealth of Nations*,[1] first published in 1776, describes how productivity can be improved through **specialization**. By performing a small set of tasks, greater volume in productivity can be achieved. All types of organizing today have a division of labor, specialization, and a chain of command. Although these facts are well-known and practiced, there are many different patterns, or schemes, in the way that employees may be linked in the chain of command.

The organizing topics presented in this chapter are structured around a series of practical questions, as shown in Table 7.1. What is the nature of the jobs? How are the jobs grouped? How are reporting relationships structured? How does coordination occur among units and individuals? What factors or contingencies influence the choice of optimal organizing features?

Table 7.1: Organizing Questions

Question	Explanation
What is the nature of the jobs?	The level of specialization and complexity built into the nature of the tasks employees perform.
How are reporting relationships structured?	The principles for making decisions and interactions between managers and subordinates.
How are jobs grouped?	The various forms of departmentalization that reflect the grouping of jobs.
How does coordination occur among units and individuals?	The various mechanisms that are used to communicate with other units
What factors or contingencies influence the choice of optimal organizing features?	The situational determinants of organizing features are presented.

WHAT IS THE NATURE OF THE JOBS?

As we examine possible ways to answer this organizing question, we will start at the bottom of the hierarchy with the nature of the jobs that employees perform. The construction of jobs influences the overall organizing scheme. The basic building blocks determine how large or small individual jobs are. Taylor, along with other scientific management practitioners (as discussed in chapter 2), advocated studying the motions of the job to find the most rational way to perform it. Time and motion studies lead to simplification—breaking jobs into smaller, simpler parts. Weber, in his bureaucracy principles, also wanted rules and procedures for tasks to increase predictability. Some degree of specialization is useful but, when taken to the extreme, can be negative.

The effect of the historical practices of specialization, bureaucracy, and division of labor was smaller, simpler jobs. During the 1960s many companies found that very simple jobs had some serious drawbacks. Although simple tasks made it easy to hire and train workers for the low-skill jobs, quality problems emerged. Simple jobs are often boring jobs, and workers are not motivated to do good work. Besides the motivational issue, highly simplified jobs tend to create a larger overall organization. There will be more layers, or levels, in the hierarchy. More employees are assigned the task of checking others below them in the hierarchy, increasing costs and lowering overall efficiency.

If simple jobs are not very desirable, then what other options exist for organizing? One of the first alternatives to highly specialized jobs is *job rotation*. With the rotation option, the nature of the jobs does not change but employees are moved around from job to job. By moving to different jobs periodically, workers experience some variety in what they do, reducing boredom. For example, in a shipping area one person might review invoices while another moves boxed products. They could swap jobs each day or week. Given that the jobs themselves do not change—just the people who perform them—the overall structure of the organization is unchanged. The benefits are really for individual employees.

Another option is *job enlargement*. This option actually reduces specialization by giving employees additional tasks. Tasks are reapportioned as employees in a unit are given additional tasks. Thus, all get more variety much of the time, not just a periodic change as with job rotation. This alternative job design does impact the rest of the structure to some extent, as employees are given larger portions of work. The drawback is that they are given more of the same type of work. There is more variety, but the skill level does not change.

Fred Herzberg's studies and writings on motivation[2] (presented in chapter 11) observed that adding more of the same did not really improve motivation. What really needed to change in jobs was the complexity and skill level required. The option that emerged from his work has been termed *job enrichment*, or vertical job enlargement. Job enrichment adds responsibilities and requires more complex skills.

Richard Hackman[3] developed a psychological approach to work design that built into work those features that would motivate employees. The job dimensions that motivate workers are meaningfulness, autonomy, and complexity. Hackman further explained that meaningfulness can be designed by adding skill variety, task identity, and task significance. *Skill variety* is similar to job enlargement, discussed previously. *Task identity* means that workers do a whole piece of the job so that it becomes personal to them. Putting six rivets in a pair of jeans is not very meaningful, but assembling a complete pair of jeans does lead to more identity, especially if your name is placed in the pocket. *Task significance* is the extent to which a task has impact on lives. Assembling a full set of automobile brakes has more safety consequences, and thus more significance, than making ballpoint pens.

Autonomy in work involves the freedom and independence to make and implement decisions without consulting a supervisor. Employees who can stop an assembly line when they detect quality problems have autonomy. Sales clerks who can give customers a full refund on the spot have autonomy. The final characteristic is *feedback*. Does the work provide knowledge of results in a clear fashion? Some employees put their names on or in the finished product. Not only does this give them identity, but the customer may contact them, providing feedback as well. A production team may also have a conference call with a customer to get feedback.

Theorists, and some management professors, have suggested that people want and need enriched jobs. In reality not everyone does. Some prefer the routine and predictability of simpler jobs. Hackman found that workers with higher order, or growth, needs want enriched jobs, while those with lower order needs prefer simpler jobs.

Enriched jobs result in a different type of overall structure. As will be discussed in the next section, job design can lead to either a tall or a flat structure. Many job designs today also incorporate team components, as these apply the principles of variety, identity, autonomy, and feedback. Team-based structures are covered further in the "How are jobs grouped?" section.

Another aspect of the division of labor, related to the nature of the jobs, is whether the work is classified as line or staff. Some workers make a product or deliver a service; these are **line** employees. They are in a direct line of authority from producers to top management. A further distinction is between managers and employees; managers who supervise line employees are line managers. Simple enough, right? Another category of employee in the division of labor is **staff**. As organizations grow, managers cannot perform all the tasks that are required of them. They may not have the time or expertise to place advertisements for hiring new employees, answer outside phone calls, type invoices, collect job applications, or do reference checks. Those tasks have been delegated to staff positions and departments; these tasks may be performed by human resources staff (covered in chapter 10) or by clerical staff. Examples of staff positions or departments include legal staff and accountants. They do not directly assist in making the product but provide critical advice or information. Those who manage these employees are termed *staff managers*. Line managers typically have more clout and influence, as they are viewed as making the most critical contribution to the purpose of the organization. When lay-offs are required, staff areas are usually the first to experience losses.

HOW ARE REPORTING RELATIONSHIPS STRUCTURED?

The nature of the jobs has implications for how those jobs are linked together and to the relationships that employees have with supervisors. The traditional forms of organizing with simple, specialized jobs tend to result in tall, vertical organizational structures. **Tall structures** have more layers of decision-making, taking longer for decisions and communication to move up and down the hierarchy, slowing adaptability. Many feel that the middle layers of tall structures are not productive. As companies grew in the post-World War II era, they developed many layers of middle management whose primary job was controlling those below them. In the global marketplace these tall structures are very costly and inefficient because decisions are not made fast enough. Today many organizations have gone through cycles of structural changes, resulting in a flatter structure by removing layers of middle management.

In the 1950s, Sears department stores were one of the first companies to experiment with **flat structures**; they made a decisive and sudden move to flatten their structure. They wanted to push decision-making down to the floor level. Decision-making was delegated to lower levels throughout the organization. Structures where the authority for making decisions is at lower levels are termed **decentralized**. When decisions are made at high levels, the decision is **centralized**. Sears wanted to decentralize their stores. Instead of the store manager having six or eight unit managers reporting to him or her, Sears rearranged the structure so that managers would have 20–30 subordinates reporting to them. Another related organizing term is **span of management**, or how many subordinates report to one manager. By increasing the span of management, Sears was forcing decentralization and flattening the overall structure. This move proved helpful and improved the performance of stores. Decentralization forced managers to set general direction but allowed unit managers more latitude and gave them more responsibility in their jobs.

HOW ARE JOBS GROUPED?

Another aspect of organizing is how people are grouped into units or departments. This grouping is referred to as departmentalization. There are several traditional structures that are frequently used in various combinations. **Functional structures** group people according to the basic functions of the business that they perform. Common functions in a business include purchasing, sales, marketing, and accounting. The type of organizing used in many of the historical notions of Weber and Fayol was based on the functional forms of organizing.

Most small organizations start with a functional grouping. In a basic manufacturing organization, production is an important line function. Groups of workers make or assemble the product; but before they can make it, someone has to design it and lay out the manufacturing machinery appropriately. In very small organizations workers and managers make these decisions together. As the organization grows, the system becomes more differentiated and complex and more professional expertise is needed in design. The formation of another functional department—engineering—can assist in the design process, as depicted in Figure 7.2. Another important function is sales and marketing. Someone has to call on customers, encouraging them to buy the products. The sales force performs this function.

While reviewing the organizational charts, notice the position off to the side. The assistant is a staff position. It is typically drawn off to the side, not in the direct vertical line to the president. Staff positions perform tasks that support the line employees. The assistant to the president, for example, answers phone calls, types letters, maintains an appointment calendar, organizes meetings, and so forth.

Functional Structure

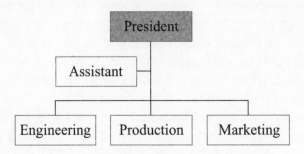

Figure 7.2: Functional type of departmentalization.

Returning to the marketing function in this company, additional tasks are performed besides sales. Other employees may do research to see if new products appeal to customers. Thus, within these functional units, other functions develop based on specialization. Marketing may also have a communications unit that coordinates advertising and writes brochures and other collateral materials designed to increase sales. Production and engineering also have subunits within those broader functional categories. Tasks within production may include machining, assembly, and shipping. Engineering may have a research unit where new products are designed and tested (different from marketing research where finished products are shown to customers). This elaborated functional structure is shown in Figure 7.3

There are a number of advantages to functional departmentalization, as presented in Table 7.2. Functional departmentalization is the common form for new organizations. With employees performing the same function within that unit, there are cost savings in terms of economies of scale. Equipment and other resources can be shared. As the volume and type of work in the same function grows, then specializations develop, as illustrated in the elaborated structure of Figure 7.3. Managers of functional departments have good preparation for managing that unit, as they have experience with that function and the subunits within it. This structure is best in new organizations and in stable environments with relatively few products or services, as shown in Table 7.2

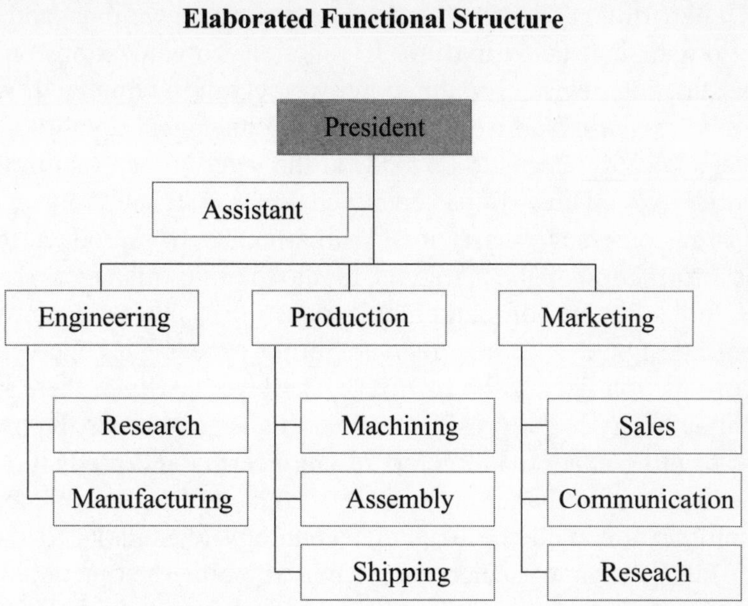

Elaborated Functional Structure

```
                        ┌──────────────┐
                        │   President  │
                        └──────────────┘
              ┌──────────────┐
              │  Assistant   │
              └──────────────┘
     ┌──────────────┐ ┌──────────────┐ ┌──────────────┐
     │ Engineering  │ │  Production  │ │  Marketing   │
     └──────────────┘ └──────────────┘ └──────────────┘
      ┌──────────┐     ┌──────────┐     ┌──────────┐
      │ Research │     │ Machining│     │  Sales   │
      └──────────┘     └──────────┘     └──────────┘
      ┌──────────────┐ ┌──────────┐   ┌──────────────┐
      │Manufacturing │ │ Assembly │   │Communication │
      └──────────────┘ └──────────┘   └──────────────┘
                       ┌──────────┐     ┌──────────┐
                       │ Shipping │     │ Reseach  │
                       └──────────┘     └──────────┘
```

Figure 7.3: Elaborated functional structure.

Table 7.2: Advantages and Disadvantages of Functional Structures

Advantages	Disadvantages
Pooling of resources, economies of scale, and cost efficiency	Limited capacity to handle information, tendency to refer decisions up the hierarchy
In-depth skill development and technical specialization	Limited coordination and communication across functions
Development of functional managers who know technical issues	Effort focus, lack of responsibility for product or service ("not my problem")
Perform best in stable environment with relatively few products	Slow response to environmental change

It sounds as though functional departments work fairly well, so why would a manager or company want to change? As we learned in chapter 3, the environment of business is rapidly changing. Technology, globalization, and customer demands push for innovation and change. To understand why functional departments become inadequate over time, we must add another aspect of organizing, **coordination**. In functional organizations one of the basic coordination devices is the hierarchy, or chain of command. When issues, termed *exceptions*, arise that lower-level managers do not know how to resolve, a decision needs to be made at the level in the organization that has authority over all areas impacted by the decision. If sales representatives report that customers are dissatisfied with a feature of a product, they will refer this information up the hierarchy, first to the sales manager who in turn reports it to the director of marketing. It doesn't stop there. A new product has to be redesigned with new manufacturing processes; hence engineering and production need to be involved. The level at which there is cross-functional authority is the president. Once this issue reaches the president, he or she has to contact the directors of engineering and production. If the number and extent of changes is modest, the chain of command can handle the communication with the help of technology (e-mails) and meetings. When the rate of change accelerates to a certain point, the functional system becomes overloaded; managers become stressed because the functional systems cannot handle the volume of information.

The functional structure is not good at sharing information across functional departments. Some critics have suggested that functional departments are like silos on a farm. They are tall, isolated tubes that have a hard time communicating and seeing the perspective of other departments. Similarly functional departments develop an "effort focus," meaning that engineers tend to only consider the engineering issue of the product. The point in this structure where someone has responsibility for all functional aspects of the product is the president; typically functional employees and managers do not own or feel responsible for the total product, only their functional component in it.

Given these drawbacks, what is the alternative? The most common change in structure when functional problems occur is a shift to a **divisional** form of structure. Part of the problem with functional structures stems from a growth in size, and the need to respond to environmental changes more quickly. A divisional structure can be based on products, geography, customers, or even materials. We will consider a product structure as one form of divisionalization. A product structure takes functional people and assigns them to product teams. Compare Figures 7.2 and 7.4. Both have employees from the same functions but they are ordered differently. The functions are reproduced in each of the three product teams. How does this arrangement solve the informational problems of the functional structure? After comparing the two figures, find the level in the organization where someone has full responsibility for the product. Is it the same as the functional? The correct answer is *product managers*, as highlighted by the shaded boxes. Now the level of cross-functional authority has moved down a level. Product managers have authority over the three functional areas in her or his department. Over time the units or teams develop some specialization based on their products and customers, so each product team, or unit, becomes more differentiated over time.

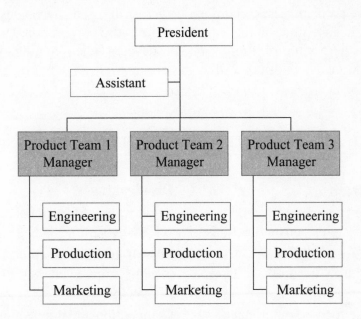

Figure 7.4: Product form of divisional structure.

The biggest advantage of this modification is greater coordination across functions. This coordinative ability leads to greater responsiveness to changes in the business environment. The product managers now have full product responsibility. If sales brings a customer problem to the product manager, a meeting of the product team can be called and changes made more quickly. The decision does not have to go through additional layers of the hierarchy. Although new managers have a more difficult initial transition, as they have to learn other functions than those they previously performed, these managers now are better prepared for higher levels of management, as they have worked with the different functional components involved in the product or service. These and other advantages of the divisional form of departmentalization are shown in Table 7.3.

All problems are solved, right? Not exactly. With any structure there are trade-offs. There is some loss of economies of scale as the functional areas are duplicated in each team, leading to reduced efficiencies. The new product teams also experience a loss of in-depth technical expertise. The engineering staff may have to perform a broader range of tasks with less specialization; they are forced to become generalists within their functional expertise. Over time the functional generalists do develop more specialization based on the product, customer, and geography, but not initially. Furthermore, the manager does not have experience in each function, making it somewhat more difficult to supervise initially. Finally, a new type of co-ordinative problem arises, coordination across divisions. Divisions focus on their goals, sometimes at the expense of the entire corporation. Duplication of efforts across the divisions can also develop when coordination is reduced and members of other divisions are unaware of activities performed elsewhere.

Table 7.3: Advantages and Disadvantages of Divisional Structures

Advantages	Disadvantages
Improved coordination and communication across functions	Duplication of functional resources across divisions
Product focus with clear responsibility for products/services	Loss of in-depth functional expertise, more generalized perspective
Expertise focused on product, customer, region	Competition and duplication of effort across divisions
Management development— managers have cross-functional knowledge	Senior management development— managers not familiar with other divisions
Adaptive to change by adding, deleting, or acquiring divisions	Focus on division goals, not corporate

The example provided for a divisional structure was a product-based organization. As mentioned earlier, divisions can also be formed based on customers, geography, or materials. Sales units are frequently organized based on geographic regions. Some retail organizations are also organized geographically, as preferences for products may vary by regional areas and climate. An example of divisions based on customers is a publishing firm. It may have separate divisions for high school books, college texts, and trade books for businesses and other organizations. Each division represents a distinct market with different customer needs and products. If this publishing company wished to add a new line of publications for another market, such as early childhood, it could form a new division. This move would be much easier within a divisional organizing scheme as opposed to a functional scheme.

The typical large organization frequently uses a combination of these two basic types. Within the marketing function, the sales force is grouped geographically and operates in a decentralized fashion. Other marketing functions such as research and communications may be centralized in corporate headquarters. As divisions grow, they have functional units within them. At some point these functional units may be broken into further divisions based on customer groupings. Thus, knowledge of functional and divisional structures is helpful, as these basic forms are combined in various ways in organizations.

The third traditional organizing scheme is a combination of the first two. If you overlay a functional design with product teams you get a **matrix**. The matrix scheme, like the instant juice product Tang, was a by-product of the space program and the Cold War. During the Cold War, the U.S. was very competitive with the Soviet Union. In 1957, the Soviet Sputnik became the first satellite to be launched into space. Prior to that point, many in the United States doubted the ability of Soviet technology and training to perform such a feat.[4] Their successful launch created doubts and fears in the U.S. Eventually a race to get the first human into space evolved, which the Soviets also won. In 1961, President John Kennedy challenged the Soviets in a race to the moon. To get humans safely to the moon and back required both new technology and rapid development. Thus, the in-depth functional specialization quality of the functional design was needed as was the coordinative and responsive abilities of product teams. TRW Systems used this organizational matrix to design and build a number of space components. In 1969, U.S. astronauts were the first to reach the moon, winning the space race. Organizing played a key role in that accomplishment.

How does a matrix design work? Employees are assigned to a functional department. Remember that functional departments allow the development of specialized technical expertise. These functional affiliations are typically drawn as the vertical component of the matrix. To speed up coordination and provide better control, product teams are drawn from the functional departments. A product manager requests participants from each functional area to form a product team. The product manager holds meetings and pushes for goal completion. Individual workers thus belong to two units, a product team with tight deadlines and a functional group with longer-term development concerns. See any problems? The matrix violates an old administrative principle, unity of command. Fayol and other experts agree that an employee should have only one boss. A matrix has **duality of command**. A worker has both a functional and a product manager. At times there may be conflicting requests from each manager to which the worker may not be able to comply. This duality is one of the major problems of a matrix. It should be used only in highly specialized conditions. Although rarely used, it is useful to understand how it operates as it actually emphasizes some of the benefits of the functional and divisional designs.

HOW DOES COORDINATION OCCUR?

Other variations on these two basic themes involve adding **integration mechanisms**. The matrix design achieves coordination but at a fairly high cost. Organizations can add other integrative mechanisms before going to full-blown matrix design. All organizations use several basic coordinating mechanisms such as the hierarchy, procedures, and the planning process.[5] All companies have the *hierarchy*, or chain of command to which decisions may be referred. Decisions and information are passed up and down the hierarchy through formal channels. As seen with the functional structure, this approach has a limited capacity to handle information. *Rules and procedures* are also used to coordinate. A rule may exist that purchase orders of a certain dollar magnitude need approval from a higher level manager. If an equipment problem arises in production, it may be standard practice to contact engineering. These procedures handle fairly routine circumstances and the occasional emergency. Also as part of the planning function, all companies use *goals and directions* to coordinate. When deciding on goals and directions, information is sought from other areas. The drawback to this approach is that it does not account for unexpected issues.

Direct contact is another approach to achieve coordination. A manager may go to another manager or worker informally. This could occur through an unplanned interaction or by e-mail, phone call, or walking over to that person's work area. This approach is also limited and can violate the chain of command principle. A manager may be upset that another manager has gone to one of his or her subordinates without discussing it first. The norms for interacting in the corporate culture may dictate whether or not direct contact is acceptable.

As the need for coordination increases, the previous basic mechanisms become inadequate. Formal positions, or roles, are designated for coordination. A *liaison role* is created. The liaison may have full or part-time responsibilities for coordinating with other units. This role adds coordinative capacity but also adds costs since this person, an engineer, for example, now spends an appreciable amount of time coordinating, rather than doing design work. *Task forces* represent a temporary coordinating mechanism involving multiple people and areas of expertise usually focused on a single problem or event.

With more frequent coordinative needs, some organizations create a *liaison department* that has responsibilities for regularly coordinating among multiple units over time. Following the 9/11 terrorism acts, the U.S. government created the Terrorist Threat Integration Center[6] as a liaison department to coordinate intelligence efforts concerning terrorism. The 9/11 Commission later deemed this unit inadequate in its ability to gather and analyze intelligence in the war on terrorism; it said a centralized intelligence agency is needed to concentrate information from multiple sources.

The method of last resort is the matrix, as described above. It is a complex means of coordinating and should only be used where both coordination and in-depth functional expertise are needed. The need for coordination has increased in many organizations; most use task forces, some use liaison roles, and fewer use liaison departments. Paralleling this need is a tendency for work to be done in teams. Cross-functional task forces, or permanent teams, are commonplace today. Some would argue that teams are a new form of organizing.

Teams are increasingly relied upon by many organizations in their organizing systems. Earlier in this chapter some of the motivational components of teams were identified. Teams in the form of task forces and committees also provide coordination. Next, different team aspects of organizing will be discussed, specifically self-directed teams and team-based virtual organizations.

Self-directed teams represent an organizing form where the team is responsible for a finished product or service. The team's focus could be a motor for a refrigerator or an insurance claim. How are self-directed teams different from other teams in the workplace? Self-directed teams tend to perform broader, more varied tasks, work independently of a supervisor (i.e., autonomous), and have team-based rewards.[7] As the role of supervision is dramatically different, this form of organizing takes time and training to implement. Jack Osburn and Linda Moran report that self-directed teams can produce more than conventional forms of organizing.[8]

Increasingly, organizations are finding that traditional forms of organizing are too slow and non-responsive. Substantial costs are tied up in the human capital in functional departments or divisions. Recently, attempts have been made to find more fluid and flexible forms of organizing, at times crossing the boundaries of the organization. Teams are a basis of this new flexible form. Some may call it a *virtual or network organization*. For some time, companies have relied on outside organizations, like staffing agencies and consulting firms, for human resources. The idea behind networked teams is that a manager assigns work to project teams based on the issues and problems that arise. The basis for organizing is work, rather than workers. Human resources are drawn from within and outside of the organization to address the problem at hand. For example, some of the teams may have a contract worker involved in designing a Web page. People from different divisions, or units, are placed on these teams. Their permanent "home" department is really only a paper designation. They move from one project to another, sometimes working on multiple projects at one time.

Networked teams have some features in common with the matrix but are more fluid. The demands on managers are greater. Managers need high levels of conceptual skills to visualize the projects and see that employees are fully occupied and contributing. Managers also need to have the organization's best interests at heart and not be concerned with empire building by creating large employee counts under them. There are substantial pay-offs for this design. It is leaner in terms of overhead costs and certainly more flexible and adaptive. It works best in a rapidly changing environment.

CONTINGENCIES FOR ORGANIZING

In chapter 2, the contingency perspective was introduced as one of the historical influences on management. A contingency approach implies that the effectiveness of a particular principle is linked to circumstances in the situation. No single form of organizing is universally effective in all situations. There are several contingencies for organizing. Some structures are effective only in certain situations. Research has identified the contingencies for organizing as size, strategy, technology, and environment.

Organizations change over time and so does their form of organizing. Growth and shrinkage are the most common forms of change. The most common form of organizing for small companies is the functional structure. As these small companies grow, this structure strains to accomplish the organization's goals as the effort focus and coordinative limitations emerge. **Size** is one contingency. As companies grow they become more differentiated, having more departments and specialized roles. With greater differentiation, there is a greater need for integration.

Along with size, companies also establish geographical units and product units. Many companies grow in global directions, so international divisions are typically established. Often these are based on continents such as Latin America, Europe, or Asia. As units within an organization grow, they increase their span of management. Some decisions that were handled informally now become more formal. Additional rules and procedures are developed and some tasks become more centralized.

Somewhat related to growth is the contingency of strategy. **Strategy** is about choices and focusing on some areas instead of others. One question raised by students of organizing is what comes first, strategy or structure? Planning was introduced as the first function of management, but the question relates more to cause and effect. Many believe that strategy should determine structure. One of the foundations for this contingency is the Alfred Sloan book that chronicled the emergence of General Motors.[9] At GM, Alfred Sloan took a loose collection of automobile firms and crafted them into a vision of the American dream. His vision was a type of car for each of life's stages, beginning with the low cost, economical Chevrolet and ending in the lap of luxury with a Cadillac. He also used this strategy to devise his organizing scheme. His structure and vision were successful for many years. His vision then became muddled in subsequent years as different divisions shared common platforms and often competed with one another. Today, General Motors' products no longer support this vision. The principle was not followed and the market place also changed as Japanese companies introduced high quality cars.

For other companies, strategy should be a significant influence on organizing. As discussed earlier, if a firm wants to develop or acquire a new business that does not relate well to existing ones, it is best to add a new division, retaining existing businesses as separate divisions. Strategic business decisions influence the choice of organizational structures.

Another contingency for organizing is **technology**. Companies can be described in terms of the core technology that they employ. The core technology is the basic system by which the business transforms inputs into outputs. Technology is important because the core technology impacts the number of exceptions and the interactions between managers and workers. Thus, technology impacts reporting relationships.

Some firms use a large assembly process while others produce customized products in small quantities. Joan Woodward found that successful firms have different structures based on the technology they use. She found three basic categories: small batch, large batch, and continuous process technologies. These three categories also form a scale of technological complexity starting from small batch and increasing up through continuous process. Small batch technologies produce small numbers of products, often with features detailed to specific customer needs. Thus, organizing is not based on efficiency but on product features. In contrast, large-batch technologies repetitively produce the same product as efficiently as possible. Continuous technologies have no discrete product. ExxonMobil uses continuous process technology. Gasoline and other chemical products are fluids. The technology keeps producing output that is stored in various containers. Process-based technologies are often sprawling plants with few people. The physical dispersion of employees results in narrow spans of control. Employees and managers need to be ready to respond quickly to disruptions in the technology. Process technologies also have the longest chains of command, with the most levels.

The final contingency for organizing is the **environment**. As mentioned in chapter 3, organizations adapt to the environment by creating specialized roles and structures. Although the environment was described as dynamic and changing, not all environments are the same. Environments are typically categorized regarding their stability and complexity. Dynamic, unstable environments are more rapidly changing. Complex environments have more features that change. For example, many retail organizations operate in dynamic environments. Customer demands change quickly and new products need to be developed. Hence the organization and its members need to monitor changes and respond to them. The environment, however, may not be very complex. The creation of a new clothing style or new breakfast cereal will not require new technologies or radically different manufacturing processes. Consequently there is a focus on change, but it is not pervasive. Liaison roles and perhaps a research department may be part of the organizing scheme to respond to environmental change.

Where environments are both dynamic and complex, greater resources must be allocated for change and adaptation. The organizing system must be flexible. More budgetary dollars may be spent on research and development. New units may have to be quickly formed to develop new products. In these environments a greater percentage of employees may be involved in boundary spanning or adaptation activities. For example, in the computer industry, products have a short shelf life and new technology emerges quickly and must be implemented in new products. Companies like Hewlett-Packard spend a great deal on product research and development. New units may be created to respond to emerging technologies. In short, the system of organizing must match the nature of the environment.

CONCLUSION

In summary, organizing is a complicated conceptual task. Conditions and structures change. Organizing systems are based on the nature of the jobs, the reporting relationships among employees, how jobs are grouped, the level of coordination required, and the contingencies facing the organization. In some ways the organizing system keeps changing because internal conditions change and the external environmental changes push for more internal responses. The well-prepared manager understands principles of organizing and knows how and when to apply them.

Chapter 7 Endnotes

1. Adam Smith, "Of the Division of Labor," in *Classics of Organizational Theory* (4th ed.), J. M. Shafritz & J. S. Ott (Eds.) (Belmont, CA: Wadsworth Publishing, 1996), 40.

2. Frederick Herzberg, "One More Time: How Do You Motivate Employees?" *Harvard Business Review* (January–February, 1968): 58.

3. J. Richard Hackman, "Work Design," in *Motivation and Work Behavior* (3rd ed.), R. M. Steers & L. W. Porter (Eds.) (New York: McGraw-Hill, 1983), 498.

4. http://ussrsputnik.homestead.com/SputnikInfo.html

5. Jay R. Galbraith, "Matrix Organization Designs," *Business Horizons* 14, no. 1, (1971): 31.

6. http://www.whitehouse.gov/response/index.html

7. Jack D. Osburn & Linda Moran, *The New Self-Directed Work Teams: Mastering the Challenge* (2nd ed.) (New York: McGraw-Hill, 2000), 12.

8. Osburn & Moran, 31.

9. Alfred P. Sloan, *My Years with General Motors* (New York: Bantam Double-day Dell Publishing, 1963), 5.

CHAPTER 8

Human Resource Management

Chapter 8

HUMAN RESOURCE MANAGEMENT

In the previous chapter, "Organizing," we learned the importance of having the appropriate structures and relationships to achieve organizational goals. Organizing forms the structural skeleton of the company but does not provide muscle and flesh to bring it to life. You can think of human resource management as those necessary enabling elements. The structure does not move unless the right people are in the right place at the right time. Those people need to be trained and have the right kinds of experiences for the entire organization to function well. Human resource management brings the organization to life. Figure 8.1 represents the metaphor of a human form as an organization, showing both the skeletal organization and the flesh and muscle needed for movement. Like humans, organizations need both structure and muscle to function. Thus, human resource management is closely related to organizing.

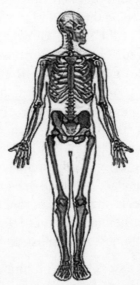

Figure 8.1: The skeleton of organizing with the muscle and skin of human resource management.

Human resource management (or HRM) is defined as the activities for attracting, retaining, and enhancing the performance of managers and workers in organizations. When someone mentions the term "human resources," they are typically referring to a unit or department in an organization. HRM is different and broader. All employees are involved in HRM, especially managers. There is a tendency to assume that human resource management is the job of the HR staff, but that is a false assumption. HRM should be viewed as a set of activities and programs, more than a separate department or unit. To be effective, all managers need to practice sound HRM.

The traditional goals of HRM are to attract, motivate, and retain good employees and managers. Line managers, HR staff, and employees work together to ensure that these goals are accomplished. Susan Jackson and Randall Shuler have termed this three-way partnership the HR triad.[1] Shuler quotes a saying from the pharmaceutical company Merck:

Human resources is too important to be left to the human resources department. Fully one-third of the performance evaluation of managers is related to people management.[2]

To illustrate this partnership, consider what happens when a manager has an employee leave to take another job. The manager typically contacts the HR department. An HR staff member visits the manager and reviews the requirements for the job. The job may have changed since the last hiring was done, so the job description is reviewed. The **job description** is the statement of tasks performed on the job and the conditions under which they are performed. Next a list of the skills, knowledge, and abilities needed to perform the job are reviewed. This list is termed the **job specifications** and is the basis for hiring. The manager and HR staff member collaborate to define these two components as part of a job analysis. The HR staff member takes this information and uses it to post and recruit for new hires. Generally the HR staff gathers applications or resumes and performs the preliminary screening to see if candidates have the ability to do the job. A short list of qualified candidates is then given to the manager to interview. A choice is made, sometimes by the manager but often in consultation with HR. The HR staff member may then check references before hiring the person the manager selected. At each step the manager and HR professional work closely. To get the right person on the job, each must do her or his part.

How do organizations assess how well human resource management is done? The same general criteria from chapter 1 can be applied. Efficiency represents the resources expended to complete a goal. Both line managers and HR staff must be concerned with efficiency. One measure of HR efficiency is how long it takes to fill a vacant position. Another measure of efficiency is the ratio of total employees to HR staff. A general benchmark for HR efficiency is 100:1, only one HR staff member for every one hundred employees. HR staff is facing increased pressure to become more efficient in the performance of their HRM tasks. Technology can improve efficiency. For example, applicant-tracking software can be used to track applicants through various stages in the hiring process, requiring less paper and staff time. Information technology such as an automated telephone application system can help hotel start-ups to process hundreds of job applicants in one day.

The other criterion for managers is effectiveness, or achieving the right goal. Likewise HR staff are challenged to shift their approach to HRM, from reacting to requests from line managers to being more proactive as a business partner by suggesting ways that HRM can help achieve business goals. Being more efficient at what HR used to do is not enough. New goals related to change and strategic alignment are now appropriate targets for HR. HR managers identify new goals and programs to help the business.

Human resource management has come a long way since the first personnel department was established at B.F. Goodrich in 1900.[3] Personnel departments began as a by-product of Taylor's scientific management. At that time managers needed help recording productivity data and time and motion results. Clerks were hired to keep track of standards and worker performance. This was the first staff department, created to reduce the burden on managers and provide support so they could spend more time managing workers. Over time other functions were added to the personnel department, such as dealing with the welfare of workers, often with the aim of reducing turnover. The world wars contributed greatly to the growth of personnel departments as large numbers of workers went off to war and needed to be quickly replaced with new workers. Hiring and training practices developed during these tumultuous periods. It was only fairly recently, in 1954, that the term *human resource management* was first used by Peter Drucker.[4] This new name was intended to distance this staff function from the clerkish roots of personnel, and connoted a more vital contribution to the organization.

HRM is now concerned with human capital. **Human capital** is defined as the economic value of the skills, abilities, and competencies of a company's work force. Human resources are frequently cited as a source of competitive advantage for firms, as their skills represent the core competencies of a firm that distinguishes it from others.[5] With the rise of the "knowledge worker" and the "learning organization," people and their *capabilities* are now viewed as vital assets for the long-term success of many organizations. Product features can be copied and similar information systems installed to match competitors. Having the people to make it all work right is more difficult to copy.

Another factor that has caused many firms to pay more attention to human resource issues is the balanced scorecard, as introduced in chapter 6. Kaplan and Norton (1996) developed the balanced scorecard to stress that corporate success is based on multiple factors, not just financial performance. They advocated that the key drivers of the firm should all be measured and managed. They identified financial, customer, internal business processes (quality and cycle time), and learning and growth (employee capabilities) as key performance drivers. The causal chain of these four categories begins with employee capabilities, which is a key aspect of HRM, as indicated in Figure 8.2.

Learning and Growth $\Longrightarrow$ Internal Business Processes $\Longrightarrow$ Customer $\Longrightarrow$ Financial

Figure 8.2: Key drivers of the balanced scorecard.

Besides being the foundation of the balanced scorecard, there are other reasons why HRM is important to an organization. Employee attitudes are important in satisfying customers. Negative attitudes from employees can be conveyed to customers, eventually impacting financial performance. Research has shown that human resource practices influence the levels of employee loyalty and commitment.[6] Sears department stores achieved a dramatic turnaround by developing an employee-customer satisfaction chain, built on the notion that satisfied employees lead to satisfied customers.[7] Thus, there are many positive reasons why HRM contributes to organizational performance.

LEGAL AND LEGISLATIVE ISSUES IN HRM

Another set of factors that have elevated the role of HRM in organizations involves the legal realm. Social activist legislation in the 1930s, 1960s, and later significantly impacted HRM. Table 8.1 lists some of the major legislation that continues to influence the practice of HRM. Many have to do with treating all employees fairly and eliminating discrimination in the workplace. Four major areas will be covered: discrimination, disabilities, workplace safety, and sexual harassment.

Table 8.1: Legal Issues in HRM

Legislative Act	Impact on HRM
National Labor Relations Act of 1935	Defined unfair labor practices, provided for secret ballots in union votes, and established the National Labor Relations Board.
Fair Labor Standards Act of 1938	Compensation issues such as minimum wage rates, over-time conditions, and child labor provisions.
Equal Pay Act of 1963	Guarantees equal pay for men and women doing equal work.
Civil Rights Act of 1964 (title VII), amended by the Equal Employment Opportunity Act of 1972 and the Civil Rights Act of 1991	Prohibits discrimination on the basis of race, religion, color, sex, and national origin.
Age Discrimination Act of 1967	Prohibits discrimination on the basis of age for anyone over 40 years of age (protected class).
Occupational Safety & Health Act of 1970	Established standards for a healthy workplace and created regulatory mechanisms to enforce violations of standards.
Pregnancy Discrimination Act of 1978	Protects pregnant workers from discrimination.
Americans with Disabilities Act of 1990	Protects qualified employees with disabilities from discrimination and requires employers to make reasonable accommodations.
Family and Medical Leave Act of 1993	Gives workers up to twelve weeks of unpaid leave for family or medical reasons each year in firms with over fifty employees.

Early Labor and Compensation Legislation. Legislation was passed during the latter part of the Great Depression that had a significant impact on HRM. Unions were vigorously and sometimes violently opposed by management.

Starting with the National Labor Relations Act of 1935, employees were given legislative protection to form unions. Unfair labor practices were defined and secret ballots were allowed in voting to determine if employees wanted a union. This act also established the National Labor Relations Board to oversee votes and labor-management practices. A few years later the Fair Labor Standards Act was passed in 1938. This act established a national minimum wage as well as provisions for when employees were given an overtime pay rate. These two historical acts continue to influence the practice of HRM today.

Discrimination. The piece of legislation with the greatest impact on HRM was the Civil Rights Act of 1964. This act prohibits discrimination on the basis of race, religion, color, sex, and national origin. Title VII of this act pertains to private employers. The act also created the Equal Employment Opportunity Commission, which was later given the power to file suits in federal court against employers who discriminate. The term **equal employment opportunity** (EEO) means that all employment practices are based on merit and not race, religion, color, sex, and national origin. A number of court cases have given power to these legislative acts and caused violators to pay substantial fines. Companies who have too few members of minority groups or women may be expected to engage in **affirmative action**, which involves making special efforts to recruit and hire members of these protected classes. Title VII also included a specific statement, termed the Tower Amendment, giving employers the right to use tests in hiring employees.

The Equal Pay Act of 1963 required that males and females performing the same jobs receive equal pay. This serves as the foundation for pay equity. The Age Discrimination Act of 1967 created a protected class of those over the age of forty. It is illegal to terminate those over forty years of age solely on the basis of age. Older employees are often targeted for layoffs because they frequently earn more money and may have less current skills. Performance-based terminations may occur, but not age-based. The courts have ruled that seniority is a legitimate basis for making employment decisions, typically with last hired being the first released.

Disabilities. A more recent piece of legislation with major impact was the Americans with Disabilities Act of 1990. This act requires employers to make **reasonable accommodations** for disabled employees who can perform the **essential functions** of the job. Through this legislation many more disabled citizens are able to work and lead productive lives with the help of HRM. Many companies have responded to this legislation by including essential functions in their job descriptions, so they can readily determine whether a disability would prevent someone from performing a job. Managers can also receive training on what constitutes reasonable accommodation.

As an example, this author received a request from a student to accommodate his back pain. The student gave a letter to each associate dean in the buildings where he took classes, requesting a special chair. Upon checking with the university's disability expert, the author found that giving him a pillow to sit on was reasonable accommodation, not necessitating the purchase of multiple chairs in the $300–$500 range.

There was a time in history when women were terminated when they became pregnant. With a high percentage of women now in the workforce, and fairness and equality cornerstones of employment law, it seems surprising that employers would continue to treat pregnant women unfairly. The Pregnancy Discrimination Act of 1978 prohibits discrimination against pregnant women, treating pregnancy instead as a disability. A more recent law, the Family and Medical Leave Act of 1993, gave employees the right to request unpaid medical leave for up to twelve weeks in the event of sickness, adoption, or to care for a family member. This act attempts to make the workplace more "family-friendly."

Workplace Safety. Work environments are now safer and healthier due to the passage of the Occupational Safety and Health Act of 1970. Standards were established on multiple workplace indicators to protect workers from harmful elements in their work environments. Workers are now protected from loud sounds, unhealthy air, hazardous equipment, and a variety of other contaminants. The Occupational Safety and Health Administration (OSHA) also inspects workplaces and can impose fines on organizations that do not comply with these standards.

Sexual Harassment. In addition to legislation, court cases can be important in interpreting laws and setting guidelines. Sexual harassment is another important legal issue for managers. The Civil Rights Act of 1964 prohibited discrimination based on sex, but court cases have extended and clarified the guidelines. If the repeated actions of a coworker or supervisor create a **hostile work environment**, where the employee cannot advance or work comfortably, then harassment has occurred. Managers need to be trained in what constitutes sexual harassment and what to do when it is reported. Failure to act when employees complain has been an important element in many court rulings against companies Some states, like Connecticut, Maine, and California, require all supervisors to undergo sexual harassment training. Sexual harassment is often a power issue with the supervisor harassing a subordinate who then feels her or his job may be in jeopardy if she or he complains; therefore, special procedures are sometimes created for reporting harassment. Someone in HR can be designated as the contact for reporting harassment and can advise the employee on how to proceed.

As business partners with line managers, HR staff need to be familiar with these laws and their impact, offering sound advice when asked. Managers may also need to have training in these legal areas so that they do not violate the laws and subject their companies to fines and costly lawsuits.

HRM PROGRAMS AND PRACTICES

Having shown the importance of HRM, our attention now shifts to human resource programs and practices. What does it take for effective HRM? The most widely used approach to HRM is based on a systems approach with inputs, throughputs, and outputs, sometimes called the flow approach. The flow approach also relies on other managerial functions, planning in particular. The typical programs and HR functions are presented in Table 8.2.

Table 8.2: HR Programs and Functions

HR Functions	Description
HR Planning	
• Job Analysis (micro)	Studying jobs to create job descriptions and job specifications
• HR Strategic Planning (macro)	Aligning HRM programs with business goals, determining future people needs
Recruitment	Attracting applicants
Selection	Selecting employees from applicants
Training and Development	Orienting new employees and enhancing skills related to present and future jobs
Performance Management	Measuring performance and providing feedback
Compensation and Benefits	Creating fair and equitable pay and benefit systems
Employee and Labor Relations	Communicating with employees and working with organized labor

HR Planning. For HRM to work well, planning is needed. There are two types of human resource planning. When illustrating the HR triad, the HR member and manager worked together to develop a job description and job specifications. Studying jobs to create these two components is part of **job analysis**, that is, planning at a local or micro level. In order to hire, both managers and HR staff need to know what tasks are performed and what skills are required. Job analysis is micro planning because it focuses on the relatively small components of a job.

A variety of methods can be used to perform job analyses. Interviews are most common. The manager or HR member can interview **job incumbents**, those currently performing the job. Sometimes group interviews are done with multiple incumbents. Each person may perform the job somewhat differently and the job description should reflect the way the job is most commonly performed, not how the rare "superstar" does it. Observation can be used for manual jobs, but with today's knowledge-based jobs, watching someone do his or her job does not provide much insight into the tasks performed and skills required. Some larger companies use questionnaires for job analysis, where job incumbents answer standard questions. The responses are computer-analyzed to determine common elements across jobs. The common elements are used to develop job families. Job families are helpful in guiding employees through different jobs as they develop over a career.

The other type of HR planning is macro HR strategic planning. This type of planning looks at business goals and directions. Given the business is planning an eight percent growth rate, what human resource needs does this growth require? How many more managers and sales representatives will need to be hired? This type of planning is based on economic notions of supply and demand. The future business needs determine the anticipated demand, or need, for employees with specific skill sets. For some jobs it may take years to develop skilled employees, so longer planning is needed to train and provide the experience needed for these jobs.

The demand is matched with the supply. The company has an internal supply of labor with current employees. A certain percentage of employees are promoted and some leave, leading to open positions. These open positions need to be filled along with those anticipated due to growth. To keep track of the internal HR supply, companies use human resource information systems (HRIS), which track the level, training, and skills that employees have. If a manager needs an employee with a specific skill set or certification, the HRIS can be queried. The HRIS may also contain a rating on how ready the employee is for promotion to the next level. The position below the open one may have an incumbent who needs more training and experience before advancing; the HRIS can also provide this type of information. For higher level positions, companies develop a **replacement chart**. For each critical position, three potential replacements are listed along with their readiness for moving up. Replacements charts are a type of contingency planning for the event that top employees leave or are unable to perform their jobs.

A second type of supply is in the external labor market. Companies track how available some skills or occupations are in the external environment. For example, how many engineers or computer programmers graduate from college each year? When planning, companies even choose to locate their businesses based on the external market labor supply in an area.

Next, the demand for human resources is compared with the available supplies to determine gaps. If demand exceeds supply, then programs are developed to hire and train new employees. If a surplus is anticipated, then plans need to be developed to reduce the supply with retirement programs or layoffs. In short, this comparison of demand with supply drives HR programs, as shown in Figure 8.3.

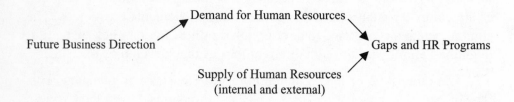

Figure 8.3: HR macro planning.

Recruitment. Continuing with the flow approach, the next HR function and set of programs involve recruitment. Assuming a shortfall in internal supply, programs are needed to attract employees for open positions. Most recruitment steps are typically performed by the HR staff, once the job has been reviewed. Likely sources for attracting applicants are examined. Walk-ins require little or no effort and are inexpensive. Prospective employees walk in and apply. This method may not generate many applicants who know about the openings. Employee referrals may be another low-cost source. Employee referrals tend to stay longer and perform better. Why? When an employee recommends a friend or relative, the employee knows something about the applicant and that prospective employee knows something about the job. An employee would not recommend a poor worker because it would impact his or her reputation; furthermore, the new worker is less likely to quit because they are familiar with the company and not as likely to be surprised or disappointed by the job. Studies have also found that employee referrals stay on the job and have lower quit rates than other recruitment sources for the same reasons. Companies often pay employees a bonus for referrals who remain with the company for at least a year. Hospitals, for example, pay bonuses to nurses who refer friends and acquaintances.

Recruits can also be obtained through a variety of media sources. The media reach out and let people in the community know about openings. Employers have traditionally used newspaper advertisements as a recruitment source. Job seekers have often consulted the "want ads" to find jobs. Newer media sources are being used with greater frequency. Radio and cable TV advertisements are used to attract recruits. By selecting certain stations or channels, employers target the specific demographic groups that the company is trying to attract. The Internet is increasingly being used, first for technological positions, and now more broadly for professional positions. As media sources can be expensive, it is important for HR to evaluate these sources to see if they are generating a sufficient number of recruits who perform well and remain with the company. Recruitment evaluation helps assess both efficiency (cost) and effectiveness (job performance).

In the legal section earlier in this chapter, the importance of equal employment opportunity and affirmative action was noted. When companies have predominantly white employees but operate in a diverse community with minorities, it may appear that their hiring practices are discriminatory. To remedy this situation, companies practice affirmative action via recruiting. Walk-ins and employee referrals are fairly passive recruitment methods that tend to attract the same type of employees as are currently employed. Affirmative action involves concentrated efforts to get more minorities and women in the applicant pool, frequently by using media that minorities are more likely to view. By expanding the applicant pool, companies increase the likelihood that qualified minorities will be hired.

Another source of potential employees is schools and universities. Companies establish relationships with trade schools and universities to provide a source of skilled applicants. Some companies offer internships to students so they can assess their performance and fit with the company before hiring them permanently. Universities are a source of engineers, business analysts, accountants, HR, and staff marketing employees to name a few. Trade schools provide technical employees.

Applicants can also be obtained from employment agencies. To receive unemployment compensation, individuals must register at a state employment office. These offices operate as public agencies collecting information on those who need jobs and offering this information to potential employers.

Companies contact the agencies and are given lists of applicants without being charged fees. Public agencies supply applicants primarily for manual and lower level jobs and can be a good source of minority employees.

Private agencies provide applicants for a fee. There are two basic ways that private agencies are paid. Contingent fees are paid only when an applicant is hired. The agency meets with the company, determines the type of applicant needed for the job, and then uses its sources to find applicants. The agency does the preliminary screening of applicants and then delivers a short list of applicants for the company to interview. The agency may also review the candidates with the hiring manager to help them choose the best one. If a candidate is not hired, then the firm does not receive a fee. Agencies are also hired on a retainer basis. These agencies have a long-term relationship with the employer and work until the position is filled. Retainer agencies typically search for executive positions and their recruiters are often dubbed "headhunters."

Selection. Once an applicant pool is formed, the process begins to decide whom to hire. In order to make that decision additional information is gathered. HR employs a variety of selection tools. A series of selection activities gathers different types of information related to the applicant's ability to perform the job. The pool is largest at early stages, so cost and efficiency are considered in sequencing the tools used at different selection steps. A typical sequence of selection steps and activities is presented in Table 8.3.

Table 8.3: Selection Tools and Steps

Selection Tools
1. Application blank or resume

2. Test or work sample

3. Job interview

4. Reference or background check

Most commonly either an application blank or a resume is first required of applicants. The application blank asks for specific types of information in a structured format. The company receives the same type of information for all applicants. The resume is unstructured, allowing the applicant some latitude in what information to present and how to present this information. Resumes are typically required for professional positions while application blanks are used for lower-level positions. The information gathered in this first stage can then be explored in subsequent selection steps, such as the interview. Candidates may be easily eliminated at this stage if they do not have key requirements, such as experience, college degree, or certification.

For some positions a test is administered as the next stage. Tests are effective at assessing abilities required for the job. Tests of problem solving and reasoning can be used for some jobs. Before any test is used, a determination is made to see if the test is valid for the job. Validity means that the test scores are related to job performance. Where cognitive skills are important, tests can improve the ability to identify good performers. Sometimes personality tests are used. It is more difficult to prove the validity of personality tests, but for some jobs, like a prison guard, personality can be important. Prison guards need to tolerate verbal abuse, and personality tests can help identify candidates with this ability.

Job samples are similar to tests. One of the oldest is a typing test for clerical jobs. Job samples take a portion of the job and ask the applicant to perform it. Samples are usually highly related to job performance, especially when prior experience is required. Honesty tests are being used with increased frequency. Where theft and cheating have been problems, honesty tests have proved effective at identifying those who are likely to cause problems on the job.

Job interviews are very common in the selection process. Though frequently used, they can be problematic if not structured. Untrained interviewers ask poor or even illegal questions. A structured interview asks each employee the same set of questions. Ideally the questions may probe for more details on resume information and are related to the job. Some of the best questions ask the applicant to describe how they solved a problem in a prior job. Past behavior is a good predictor of future behavior. Job interviews are good for demonstrating interpersonal skills, motivation, and job knowledge. Interviews also give the applicant a chance to ask questions about the job and company. In settings where teamwork is important, an entire team may interview candidates for an opening.

With interviews filling in some of the gaps on the application blank, a small group of three to five finalists is usually defined. Now more careful checks are done on the applicants' background. Prior employers may be called to verify positions held, salary levels, and length of experience. Lawsuits have prompted companies to be careful in doing background checks. **Negligent hiring** suits are filed when the employer does not carefully review prior histories. If a sex offender is hired as a custodian with master keys to all rooms in an apartment complex, then problems are likely to ensue.

Assistant men's basketball coach Clyde Vaughn recently resigned from his $125,000 position at the University of Connecticut, the home of the 2004 NCAA basketball champions, following his arrest for soliciting a prostitute. Upon further investigation, it was found that he had several prior arrests for solicitation. Although no suit was filed, the incident was embarrassing to the university. His behavior was a poor role model for student athletes. The athletic department did not require an application blank nor did it do a background check on Coach Vaughn prior to hiring him.

Training and Development. Once the decision has been made as to whom to hire, then orientation and training are the next phases of HRM. At a minimum, new employees need to be oriented to the policies and procedures of the firm. Orientation programs help new employees to adapt to their new work setting so that they feel comfortable and are familiar with initial aspects of the job. Training provides additional skills to perform the job. HR staff and managers make a decision to either buy or make human resources. If the decision is to "buy," then the employee hired has the skills to do the job right away, reducing the need for training. If the decision is to "make," then the employee needs further training to build their skills. Training adds skills for immediate use on the job. In contrast, **development** provides skills for the future. Leadership development programs prepare middle level managers for executive positions.

With billions of dollars spent on training annually, it is important that training be effective in achieving its purposes. The way to ensure effective training is to begin with a **needs analysis**. Training units have had a reputation for putting together trendy programs that did not always deliver. Needs analysis looks at issues in the organization that could be improved with training. Performance issues may be identified. A survey can be conducted of employees and managers regarding the types of training that are desired.

Training can occur in a variety of locations. Some initial training is done on the job as a manager orients a new employee. They learn how to answer the phones, change printer cartridges, and perform other common procedures. Another common location for training is in a classroom setting. Larger corporations have training centers with multiple classrooms that have audio/video systems and other technology, such as video conferencing. Groups of trainees attend these sessions and often discuss various ways of handling situations, learning from each other. Training programs on customer satisfaction, sexual harassment, and quality improvement are examples of some classroom programs.

With the fast pace of business, it can be a challenge for companies to keep their employees trained in the latest approaches and product versions.

For maintenance staff, each new product may require different parts and repair procedures. For global companies, training employees around the world can take time. Computer-based training can help. Programs are designed to walk employees through the design of new products. This type of training is self-paced. If an employee needs to repeat a module, they can go back and repeat it. Some of these programs are distributed on CD-ROMs, but even these take time to create and distribute. To overcome this challenge, programs are now distributed through a company's computer system or intranet. Employees anywhere in the world can log onto a company website with adequate passwords and be trained anytime of the day. Although expensive to create, these programs reduce the need for on-site trainers and improve both the speed and efficiency of training.

Following training, HR evaluates the effectiveness of training. Those attending are often given an evaluation form to assess their reactions to the training session, location, trainer, and even the food served during breaks. Someone may like the training workshop but that does not mean that it is effective. Did learning occur? A test can be given to see if trainees learned the intended concepts, as evidenced by their responses to questions. An even better approach is to see if the training improves the performance on the job. Several months later the performance of those who attended training can be compared with those who did not to assess training effectiveness. Finally, does the training improve the performance of the business? Reactions, learning, behaviors, and business results are all indicators to assess the effectiveness of training.

Performance Management. After working on the job, employees need some feedback to tell them what they are doing correctly and what needs to be improved. Performance management is an important ongoing process to keep performance levels high.

Performance appraisal is often an annual review of performance, done either at the anniversary date of hiring or at the same time of the year for all employees. To start, there must be some measure of performance. Companies use a variety of methods to measure performance. Some have employees set objectives for the year and then evaluate whether or not they attained them. Many companies use rating scales for performance. Dimensions of performance are identified based on job analysis information, and then different rating categories are reviewed. Rating scales with adjectives like *dependable*, *efficient*, and *cooperative* are problematic because each manager may have a different standard for such a vague scale, leading to what is termed *rating error*. Although more difficult to develop, scales with job behaviors have proven to be more accurate measures of performance. A manager can also rank employees on overall performance or individual dimensions of the job. Some companies impose a forced distribution on performance: only a fixed percentage, say 15 percent, can be outstanding, the bulk are in the middle, and the 15 percent at the bottom are designated as unsatisfactory. At General Electric, the controversial corporate philosophy was to eliminate the bottom 15 percent to improve overall performance.

New approaches to performance management have developed in recent years. One new approach is termed **360° feedback**. Typically managers' performance is reviewed by their immediate supervisor. A manager could impress his boss but be despised by his subordinates. To remedy this blind spot, feedback is gathered from different perspectives; hence the reference to 360 degrees of feedback. Performance information is obtained from subordinates as well as peer managers, providing a richer picture of performance.

Another new development involves coaching. Managers have realized that talking about performance once a year has many limitations. **Coaching** is a process of providing feedback and offering suggestions for improvement more frequently. A manager sees an employee speak harshly to a member of another department. That employee is taken aside and informed that the way they handled the situation was not effective. They are coached on better approaches. These immediate and more frequent feedback sessions are more consistent with learning principles and thus have a more positive impact on performance.

Compensation and Benefits. Employees are very sensitive about the fairness of their pay. Virtually no one feels overpaid but many feel underpaid. Pay is a source of attraction in hiring new employees and in turnover, when employees leave for better pay elsewhere. Pay fairness often revolves around base pay. Is the salary or hourly wage adequate? HR administers the compensation plan. Using a process called **job evaluation**, all jobs are categorized or ranked on the level of responsibility, skill required, and amount of supervision given and received. A system of **internal equity** is set up based on these rankings or ratings. Jobs that require high skill and responsibility receive more pay. Once the internal ranking of jobs is done, then the prevailing pay rates in other companies are examined. This external comparison is termed **external equity**. Many companies volunteer information about their pay levels through a salary survey. In return they get summary information about what other companies are paying for certain jobs. This external comparison provides one objective standard of fairness. Companies may choose to set their pay levels at this external benchmark, above it (termed *market leader*), or slightly below (termed *market follower*).

In addition to base pay, many companies are developing incentive pay to encourage performance. Since Taylor's scientific management era, pay-for-performance is an important part of a compensation system. There are many types of incentive pay. Merit pay provides pay raises for exceeding objectives or performance standards. Those judged outstanding receive more merit pay. Some companies use group incentive pay. If a team exceeds the standard, then everyone gets a bonus. This builds commitment to the group and encourages cooperation. Profit sharing has become more widespread. Again, the idea is that all have a stake in the well-being of the company, so those with profit-sharing are motivated to do the things that increase profits. Employees receive a share of the overall company profits. Some companies use a system called **skill-pay** in which employees are paid more for each additional skill that they learn on the job. If employees have the skills to do more tasks in a team, then they are more valuable and can be assigned to perform more tasks, giving the manager more flexibility. Although innovative, skill-pay systems tend to drive up compensation costs.

Benefits represent another component of total compensation. Sometimes referred to as indirect compensation, benefits were first developed to reduce turnover. Employees were given time off and vacations. Today health benefits are an attractive benefit to employees, as health insurance is very expensive for individuals to purchase. Benefits can be a basis for attracting employees to an organization. Some employers try to offer "family friendly" benefits, such as company daycare, flex-time, and job sharing to make it easier for employees to meet their family responsibilities and work. Where creativity and problem solving are important, companies create a college campus-like environment and bring in services for employees like meals, dry cleaning, and even laundry. Benefits are expensive and need to be a part of both the business and human resource strategies of the firm. Employee benefits can create loyalty and reduce turnover. Benefit managers also need to be efficient and find ways to reduce benefit costs.

Employee and Labor Relations. Following the flow model, employees are recruited, hired, trained, evaluated, and paid. Employee relations deals with the maintenance of human capital. Employees at all levels like to be informed of company events. **Employee relations** serves the functions of communicating and working with non-union employees. **Labor relations** works with employees in organized labor unions. Employee relations issues newsletters to employees. They are also involved in orchestrating presentations by the chief executive officer. Some companies have monthly presentations by top management to inform employees of company performance, new senior officers, and potential future issues. In the absence of information, rumors can run wild. Information helps employees feel connected and calms them in times of crisis or uncertainty. Employee relations may also conduct employee surveys to see what issues are of concern to employees and then create programs to address them.

While the percentage of the U.S. workforce that is unionized has been declining, unionization is widespread in Europe. Many argue that good HR—employee relations in particular—can prevent a union from developing. Once a union is in place, it can constrain what managers can do. With an established union there is a union contract that must be followed or administered. Union officers or stewards work with managers to see that the contract is followed. If actions are taken that workers believe are in violation of the contract, workers file grievances. The contract defines a grievance procedure, which gives workers a chance to vent their concerns and appeal to higher authority. If grievances cannot be resolved internally, some contracts provide for arbitration by a neutral party. Having an appeals process can prevent strikes and allow venting of concerns.

Together, all of these HR functions both enhance the human capital of the organization and contribute to the overall performance of the organization. Employees' distinctive skills are a source of competitive advantage. Cooperation between managers, HR staff, and employees is a necessary part of the management of the organization.

Chapter 8 Endnotes

1. Susan E. Jackson & Randall S. Shuler, *Managing Human Resources Through Strategic Partnerships* (8th ed.) (Mason, OH: South-Western, 2003), 13.

2. Randall S. Schuler, "World Class HR Departments: Six Critical Issues," *Accounting and Business Review*, (January 1994, 43–72), in *Managing Human Resources* (6th ed.) (Cincinnati, OH: Southwestern Publishing, 1998), 8.

3. H. Eilbert, "The Development of Personnel Management in the United States," *Business History Review* 33, no. 3 (1958): 352.

4. V. M. Marciano, "The Origins and Development of Human Resource Management," in *Academy of Management Best Papers Proceedings* (Academy of Management, August 1995).

5. C.K. Prahalad & Gary Hamel, "The Core Competence of the Corporation," *Harvard Business Review* 68 (1990):79.

6. John R. Ogilvie, "The Role of Human Resource Practices in Predicting Organizational Commitment," *Group and Organization Studies* 11, no. 4 (1987): 349.

7. A. J. Rucci, S. P. Kirn, & R. T. Quinn, "The Employee-Customer-Profit Chain at Sears," *Harvard Business Review* (1998, January–February): 89.

CHAPTER 9

Budgeting and Control

Chapter 9

BUDGETING AND CONTROL

In the movie *Office Space*, Bill Lumbergh, the manager, keeps reminding Peter Gibbons, the protagonist, about a "TPS report." There are meetings and numerous memos about the form. A great deal of time and energy is spent dealing with the form, which never seems to be used for anything. The movie pokes fun at this example of corporate bureaucracy. Mindless bureaucracy is the negative side of the control function—control gone awry. The control function is often maligned. Many use the expression "control freak" to describe someone who is obsessed with control, seeking to order and influence all events in his or her life. Control is a necessary element in any management system; however, achieving the right balance is the key. This chapter will review types of controls as well as quality control and budgeting. It will provide a general overview of control and then the next chapter will describe some specific techniques under operational systems.

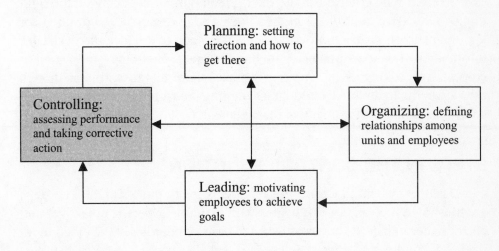

Figure 9.1: The control function.

As Figure 9.1 reflects, controlling closes the management loop with planning. Performance is reviewed and corrective action is taken. Were objectives reached? Was the organizing scheme appropriate? Did the leading activities motivate and direct employees to do the work properly? Without control, company programs and activities spend too much money and waste employees' time. Control has considerable impact on efficiency. A thermostat on a furnace is a valuable control device. When the temperature reaches the set level, the furnace is turned off. In an era of rising costs for increasingly scarce fuel, resources need to be conserved. Without the control of the thermostat, the furnace keeps running until the fuel is gone or it is manually turned off.

Control systems assure that organizational processes are doing what they were intended to do without excessive expenditure of resources. Systems tend to wear down (the systems principle of entropy as described in chapter 2). Variation is another natural tendency. People do things differently; parts are made with slight variations. However, one of the marvels of the industrial age is standardization. Parts need to be made so that they can be replaced with another part made years later. For this type of standardization, variations must be very small; uniformity and consistency are goals. Control systems counter the natural tendencies for variation and entropy to meet the high demand for standardization in today's global business.

The key with control is to do the right amount of checking on the right things. Obsessive control, as in the *Office Space* example, is not good for the organization or its employees. Managers need to balance the desire for information about performance with human issues. Hovering supervision or constantly checking up on employees makes them feel resentful, as though they are being treated like children. Designing the right types and amount of control is important for effective management.

STEPS IN THE CONTROL FUNCTION

The theory behind the control process is really quite simple. The steps are illustrated in Figure 9.2. It begins with planning. Specific objectives and performance standards are established. These standards serve as the guidelines that employees target to meet or exceed. The second step involves performance. The employees perform their tasks and management systems and processes are run. The work of the organization is performed.

Step 1: Establish standards for performance

Step 2: Run the processes, perform work

Step 3: Measure actual performance

Step 4: Compare actual performance with standard

Step 5: Take corrective action

Figure 9.2: Steps in the control process.

Measurement is the focus of step 3. The measurements are dictated by the standards. If specific objectives were set for the number of rejects or the time that it takes to process an application, then these elements are measured. Over the years we have learned how important it is to measure things.[1] People pay attention to what gets measured. It establishes priorities and places emphasis on the processes that are measured. Rewards are often tied to measured aspects, further emphasizing their importance.

In step 4 the measurements are compared with the pre-determined standards. As part of the first step, some criterion of acceptable performance is determined. For instance, a tolerance of +/– 0.005 inches is the only acceptable deviation for machining parts in some organizations. Anything beyond that tolerance is out of compliance. Some standards are imposed by regulatory agencies. For example, the pH level of tap water must be between 6.4 and 10^2 (the pH scale runs from 0 to 14). The standards serve as a reference point to determine what level is good enough or how much deviation can be allowed. Quality has become important for virtually all companies. For some, no acceptable level of error becomes the standard—zero defects. Although technically not possible, the mindset of removing deviation and error is a critical aspect of the corporate culture. The zero tolerance ideal creates values and beliefs related to continuously searching for ways to improve. All employees then strive to remove errors and defects.

When deviations are detected, action is needed to bring the process back into compliance with the standard. Experts review the process and make changes so that performance meets the standard. It may be necessary to reexamine the entire process and redesign multiple steps.

The feedback loop in Figure 9.2 notes that once corrections are made, the process begins again. The same standards may be used or they may also be revised. Then the process is run again and data is gathered and compared with the standard. Control and correction of deviations is an ongoing process.

TYPES OF CONTROLS

Closely following the steps in the control process, an organization often establishes three types of controls: feedforward, concurrent, and feedback controls. These controls actually correspond to timing or when in the process measurements are taken. **Feedforward** controls work at the beginning. The targets that are set guide actions throughout the process. Raw materials are sampled at the start of the production process to ensure that they meet quality expectations. Coffee beans are inspected as they arrive at the roasting plant. You can't have good coffee if the beans are inferior or contaminated. Feedforward controls also try to prevent or minimize problems from the start. Doing drug testing on applicants for a truck driver position is another way to prevent employee problems from the start. Sampling material inputs and testing employees is one approach, but others involve design. Humans are variable. Designing a process so that fewer routine steps are performed by humans and more by machines helps to prevent problems from the start.

Concurrent controls are employed during the process. Critical checkpoints are established for monitoring. In an effort to find balance, specific points in a process are established. The process is sampled at these points in time. Fermenting grape juice is checked at different points in time before it becomes wine. These intermediate checks are helpful in that they can detect a potential problem before the entire batch is ruined. A minor deviation can be corrected before it becomes a larger problem, ruining materials or damaging equipment. Most college courses in the United States test students at multiple points in time. Some courses employ quizzes between exams to give students an idea if their understanding of the material is meeting the instructor's standard. The British system has historically tested only at the end of the year with no concurrent controls. Most U.S. students would be uncomfortable with this departure from their experience. They have become accustomed to concurrent controls with ample feedback.

Feedback controls are employed at the end of a process or the production cycle. Did the completed product or service meet the standard? Many automobile dealerships survey their customers regarding how they find the purchase experience and then ask them about the service experience. These assessments determine how customers view the total process after it is completed. Some dealerships even pressure or encourage customers to give good ratings as they know that the manufacturer reviews these ratings.

THE EVOLUTION OF QUALITY

The adoption of quality standards in the United States came after the Japanese had gained competitive advantage through superior quality. U.S. business had the wrong approach and philosophy: quality was approached through concurrent controls or intermediate inspection. Inspectors reviewed production at various points and noted problems that were then corrected. You may ask, "What is wrong with this? They were applying control principles, weren't they?" The problem was that they were only applying one principle. Their approach was to obtain quality via inspection and to do so fairly late in the production process. The Japanese, on the other hand, took a strategic approach. Quality was their means of competitive advantage and it pervaded their organizations.

Although they were the first to implement high quality control systems, the Japanese did not invent quality principles; they imported the idea from the U.S. Three individuals were instrumental in developing many of our contemporary views on quality: Edward Deming, Joseph Juran, and Philip Crosby.

In the years following World War II, U.S. industry focused on quantity. The shortage of products during the war and the return of soldiers after the war ended, created a huge demand for goods. U.S. industry could not produce them fast enough. As demand leveled off, consumers sought not just products, but better products. The three quality pioneers all worked their way up through their respective organizations. Juran began working in inspection at the Hawthorne Works of Western Electric.[3] Crosby worked as a reliability engineer, eventually working his way up to become the first vice president of quality for ITT. Deming began by teaching statistical techniques to the U.S. Census Bureau. They all were discontent with current practices and searched for better ways of doing things.

Deming was the most philosophical.[4] He identified fourteen principles, including "adopt a new philosophy." That philosophy put quality at the center, a primary focus. Constancy of purpose was another principle, emphasizing that quality should permeate all that is done. Deming also urged ending a focus on mass inspection and on awarding contracts solely on the basis of price. Training, education, and continuous improvement were also key components of his philosophy. Deming also urged organizations to drive out the fear; he was trying to remove barriers to internal cooperation and other impediments to quality improvement. Even performance evaluations contribute to the fear, Deming believed. When workers have information about quality and share the vision, they will do the right thing.

Joseph Juran believed that three important principles should underlie quality programs.[5] The first is that the top people should be in charge. In terms of organizing, many early quality approaches delegated quality to inspectors or even a team of workers called a quality circle. "Fix yourself" was the approach of top management. Ownership of quality needs to run throughout the organization if it is to be effective. Second, like Deming, Juran urged extensive training. Workers need to know about statistical variation and how to use problem-solving tools. Juran's third point was that change should take place at a revolutionary pace. He infused a sense of urgency in the United States. Juran defined quality as fitness for use and believed that the customer should play an important role in determining fitness.

One of Philip Crosby's major contributions was the concept of zero defects. This concept, though illusive, was designed to overcome the common view that defects happen, that there is some reasonable level of poor quality. Crosby pushed for preventative measures and urged a total system approach. He anticipated that some managers would feel that quality costs too much. He explained that poor quality is expensive. Improving quality reduces rework and inspection. Quality actually increases profits, not just expenses.

To acknowledge and encourage quality in the U.S., President Ronald Reagan instituted the Malcolm Baldridge National Quality Award (MBNQA) in honor of the secretary of commerce who served from 1981 until his death in 1987. The award is currently designed to encourage and reward high quality in the categories of manufacturing, service, small business, education, and healthcare. The award is built upon a set of interrelated concepts that are presented in the left column of Table 9.1.[6] These organizational qualities represent the essence of sound management and are similar to many concepts reviewed in this book. Having agility, a systems perspective, innovation, and social responsibility are important principles of management. The right column of Table 9.1 contains the categories in which Baldridge companies report information about their performance. These likewise reflect key areas of management. Even pursuing the award helps to focus managers on the data and features that will improve the success of their organization. Winners take great pride in the award and believe that it has great public relations value.[7]

Table 9.1: Malcolm Baldridge National Quality Award

Core Values and Concepts	Organizational Profile Categories
Visionary leadership	1. Leadership
Customer-driven excellence	2. Strategic Planning
Organizational and personal learning	3. Customer and Market Focus
Valuing employees and partners	4. Information and Analysis
Agility	5. Human Resource Focus
Focus on the future	6. Process Management
Managing for innovation	7. Business Results
Management by fact	
Public responsibility and citizenship	
Focus on results and creating value	
Systems perspective	

Another approach that has pushed for high quality and zero defects is Six Sigma. The Greek letter Σ is spoken in English as "sigma." In statistics, sigma is a measure of deviation from the mean. Six sigma refers to six standard deviation units from the mean. It essentially translates into the fact that a product will fail very rarely. Six Sigma trains professionals in problem solving techniques and managing change so that their companies can produce products of very high quality. Motorola, GE, and Citibank all use Six Sigma.[8]

What conclusions about quality and control carry over to today? Quality has become a key component of most manufacturers' operations and, increasingly, service industries as well. Businesses simply cannot avoid focusing on quality. Even educational institutions are adopting quality measures and they have their own category in the Baldridge Award competition. The customer has become very important in all industries. As several experts have stated, quality means meeting customer expectations.

Another conclusion is that there is no simple fix for quality. The whole organization needs review and involvement. Senior management must be involved and improved as well. Jim Fairfield-Sonn has written a book that poses the question of how much quality is enough.[9] There can never be enough quality. Organizations need constancy of purpose to strive for zero defects. Fairfield-Sonn also stresses the role of corporate culture in quality improvement. The values and beliefs of all employees need to change to incorporate quality principles.

Thus, the evolution of quality involves a shift from a tactical, external approach to an internal, strategic approach. Early approaches to quality used concurrent controls and delegated the tasks to inspectors. After reviewing this section you should realize the shortcomings of this tactic. Quality is now everyone's task. The most effective organizations take a strategic approach, designing quality into all operations. Through training, all employees develop values and practices about quality work. Senior managers, as well as factory workers and customer service representatives, should apply quality principles.

CONTROL OF HUMAN BEHAVIOR

Thus far, the control of inanimate objects has been discussed. Control processes monitor and regulate products and services; however, employees also need regulation. In the Human Resource Management chapter, the importance of managing performance and coaching was discussed. The performance and behavior of employees also tends to vary over time. Managerial controls help to maintain order as well as a sense of fairness. Employees will complain when some do little and others work hard.

Control of human behavior is achieved using some elements of planning. Chapter 6 on planning described policies and procedures; these are often summarized in employee handbooks. This collection of rules describes intended behaviors and also the consequences for non-compliance with the rules. Nowadays these handbooks are available on company intranets for employees and managers to access quickly. At some point during the orientation process employees are asked to sign a piece of paper acknowledging that they have read the rules and guidelines.

Handbooks typically identify two types of violations. Major, or severe, violations are usually subject to immediate dismissal. Drinking or fighting on the job is usually grounds for immediate dismissal. Minor infractions are subject to disciplinary procedures. Most companies utilize some form of **progressive discipline** for these behavior problems. Tardiness, excessive absenteeism, and performance problems can lead to discipline. It is termed progressive because each step is successively more severe in its consequences. Typical steps include an oral warning, a written warning, suspension (with or without pay), and termination. It is important to document each step to avoid lawsuits and to provide the employee with suggestions for improvement. The review of performance problems should be a problem-solving session to mutually search for means of correcting the problems.

In a more positive approach, behavior can also be influenced through the shared values of the culture. William Ouchi[10] used the term *clan control* in describing Japanese control systems. Ouchi contrasted clan control with rules and procedures, what he termed *bureaucratic control*. Bureaucratic control is an external approach whereas clan is an internal approach to control. Like quality, a strong vision that is shared by members can lead to peer influence that helps control behavior to some degree. Discipline systems are still needed but clans avoid the external control, instead relying on the internal approach of shared values.

BUDGETING AND RESPONSIBILITY

Organizations have long used budgets as one tool for controlling expenses and the behavior of employees. An organization is typically divided into responsibility centers, often by units or departments. Budgets represent the allocation of dollars for the fiscal year. Each responsibility center is expected to monitor its costs and live within the constraints imposed by the budget. Sometime in advance of the new fiscal year, the budget is reviewed and a new allocation is made. The manager or director in charge of the responsibility center may seek additional funds. She or he has to justify the additional expenses, perhaps due to added employees or expanded responsibility for additional tasks. Responsibility centers can be set up to give accountability for different things.

One of the most common responsibility centers is an **expense center**, where responsibility is maintained for staying under expense targets. The progress on the annual expense budget is periodically reviewed so that there will be sufficient funds to cover expenses at the end of the fiscal year. Managers should not exhaust the expense budget in the first five months of the budgetary year. Most staff departments are set up as expense centers. Their expense budget covers office supplies, phones, staff training, equipment maintenance contracts, and so forth. This type of center does not usually collect revenue from customers; its primary accountability is internally focused on controlling its expenses.

Another type of responsibility center is focused more externally. It is termed a **revenue center**. Revenue centers establish, within the unit, a set responsibility for generating revenue targets. Sales units are commonly based on revenue budgets. They also have expense budgets but the focus is on generating specific revenue targets.

A third type of responsibility center combines the two prior centers into a **profit center**. Profit centers subtract expenses from revenue. How is this different from a revenue center with an expense budget? When a center is based on a profit center, it can break the expense budget as long as it brings in more revenue. This is an important difference. Profit is the ultimate goal. Budgets have sometimes been criticized because they focus on the wrong thing and limit profits. Sometimes spending more money can generate even more revenue, resulting in more profit. Thus a profit center is more focused on the ultimate goal of profits and gives the unit more flexibility with spending as long as it reaches the profit target.

To provide more accountability, some staff units are converted to a profit center. A training department, for example, formerly provided training and only had to not exceed its expense budget. As a profit center, the training department has to generate revenue. How can it do so? The training products need to be good enough so that other units of the company will pay for it. Internal customers purchase training from the department through an inter-departmental transfer. That transfer is revenue. This represents a higher level of accountability for the staff department. It may have a revenue budget or may combine revenue and expenses into a profit center.

Another type of center adds yet another type of expense. A capital budget is for large items that are atypical. A major renovation or expansion of a factory is not funded out of annual operating expenses. The cost would far exceed the expense budget. A capital budget funds these "big ticket" items. When the capital budget is added to a profit center, it becomes an **investment center**. Investment centers encourage the responsibility center to not spend too much on capital improvements. This type of center puts pressure on generating enough added revenue and profit to justify the capital expense.

Budgets can lead to unintended, negative behavior. Budgets may create the wrong focus. Meeting the budget becomes more important than the reason the budget was originally put in place. Budgets are intended as guides; when they become the goal, goal displacement has occurred. **Goal displacement** occurs when the budget becomes the ultimate goal, not profitability or doing more business. *Fortune* magazine ran an article entitled, "Why Budgets Are Bad for Business."[11] In this article the magazine explains why budgets often encourage negative things, such as spending wildly on items at the end of the budget year. Why does this occur? In many organizations if you don't spend your budget one year, it is reduced the next. To avoid a budget cut, managers buy unneeded items. There is little reward for saving money. On the other hand, breaking the budget can lead to proportionately greater gains and profitability.

How can budget problems be minimized? The *Fortune* article made some suggestions. The first is to focus on results. Budgets tend to focus on inputs. Profit is the key output measure. Planning should also drive budgets. Some companies have instituted zero-based budgeting; each year the process begins not with last year's budget but from scratch, or $0. This process can take more time, however. *Fortune* also suggests allowing for budget breaking or contingency plans. There are no rigid guides and some provision should be made for extra spending where extraordinary pay-offs are possible.

MORE EFFECTIVE CONTROL SYSTEMS

In the beginning of the chapter the dysfunctional consequences of control systems were illustrated through the movie *Office Space*. The need to balance control and the need to know with human reactions was discussed. Given that we need some type of control, what are the guidelines for creating more effective controls (See Table 9.2)?

One of the important lessons from the evolution of quality is that an external approach is inadequate. To the extent possible, internal approaches should be taken. Quality and control should be a part of the culture. All employees should own it and strive to produce and deliver the highest possible service and products. Control should also be selective and strategically focused. Everything cannot be measured. Decisions need to be made about key components to measure and track. Strategic control points need to be established.

Table 9.2: Guidelines for Effective Controls

Build an internal control orientation.

Be selective and strategic in designing.

Be flexible, allow budget busting, and have contingencies.

Be understandable and fair in appearance.

Focus on rewarding, not punishing.

Look at results.

From the discussion of budgets, effective control systems need some flexibility. Provisions for breaking the budget or procedures should be allowed where the potential for greater gain is possible. Rigid bureaucracy is not a good approach to control. Similarly the standards and process should be fairly simple and clear to employees. They should know what is being done and why. They should view the control process as fair and reasonable. Acceptance is an important prerequisite for self-control in the implementation of an internal approach.

Another aspect that encourages acceptance is rewards for positive achievements versus punishment for falling short. Some level of risk-taking should be encouraged and rewarded. If the control system is too punitive in nature, no one will take the risks to achieve the big payoffs. In a similar fashion, results are important. Concurrent controls are needed but it is the results that ultimately count. Be sure that the results, not the process, is the focus. You don't want to end up with a means-end inversion where the means (i.e., following the rules) becomes the focus at the expense of the results or the ultimate goal desired.

CONCLUSION

Control is a necessary function of management. The standards established provide measurements that allow managers to take corrective action and improve performance. Feedforward, concurrent, and feedback controls provide information at different points in the work process. A strategic, internal focus to control also contributes to improved performance. Effective control requires involvement of all organizational members and a reasonable, commonsense approach.

Chapter 9 Endnotes

1. Steven Kerr, "On the Folly of Rewarding A While Hoping for B," *Academy of Management Journal* 18, (1975): 769.

2. Arthur ONeill, Personal communication, (January 31, 2005).

3. Lloyd Dobyns & Clare Crawford-Mason, *Quality or Else* (Boston: Houghton-Mifflin, 1991), 70.

4. Ibid., 56.

5. Ibid., 70.

6. "Criteria for Performance Excellence" (2002). www.quality.nist.gov

7. www.quality.nist.gov

8. James W. Fairfield-Sonn, *Corporate Culture and the Quality Organization* (Westport, CT: Quorum Books, 2001), 180–181.

9. Ibid., 181.

10. William G. Ouchi, "A Conceptual Framework for the Design of Organizational Control Mechanisms," *Management Science* 25, no. 9 (1979): 834.

11. Thomas A. Stewart, "Why Budgets are Bad for Business," *Fortune* (1990, June 4): 179.

CHAPTER 10

Operations and Information Management

Chapter 10

OPERATIONS & INFORMATION MANAGEMENT

In chapter 9, basic concepts of control needed for any manager were introduced. Chapter 10 covers more specific issues related to management and control of the operations of a firm. Operations and information management are important in producing a product or delivering a service. Operations management is central in any organization, as that function delivers the service or produces a product. Control is important for operations and builds on those concepts from chapter 9. Management relies heavily on information to make decisions. **Information** is data made useful for management. The cost of storing and generating bits of data has fallen over the years. The lower cost has generated more data but not always information. Without good information, managers won't know how many units to produce, what activities are doing well, and what corrective actions need to be taken. The right amount of information needs to be available at the right time. Information is crucial to support operations and will thus be covered here also. This chapter will be divided into two sections: operations management and information management.

OPERATIONS MANAGEMENT

Operations management (OM) is the throughput process in the systems view of the organization, as discussed in chapter 2. Operations involve the transformation of inputs into outputs. Since Taylor's early twentieth century scientific management era, operations managers have been striving to find more efficient ways to make products and deliver services. Operational activities are closely linked to technology, which performs the transformation. **Technology** is the set of activities that transform inputs into outputs. Technology can be equipment, but it is also worker knowledge and know-how. Technology can be manual or involve sophisticated equipment like robotics.

Operations managers work to achieve effectiveness goals related to units produced, but efficiency has also always been important to them. Several different measures of efficiency are examined. Total productivity is determined by the ratio of outputs to all inputs. Inputs that are part of the denominator of the ratio include materials, labor, and capital. This measure reflects the efficiency of the entire system, or alternatively, the "value." Operations is also concerned with labor efficiency, or the ratio of outputs to labor. Managers can review the ratio of outputs to labor cost and total number of employees involved. These efficiency ratios can then be compared across companies to get an idea of how a firm is doing. Such a comparison of British and Japanese automobile manufacturers revealed that British automakers used twice as much labor as the Japanese.[1] Being aware of these comparative inefficiencies, British operations managers can then work to increase efficiencies and decrease costs.

In addition to efficiency, some of the other priorities for an operations manager, presented in Table 10.1, include cost, quality, time, and flexibility.[2]

Table 10.1: Priorities for Operations Managers

Priority	Explanation
Costs	Reducing labor, materials, and parts costs.
Quality	Producing products/services with as close to zero defects as possible.
Time	Meeting or exceeding customer demands for on-time delivery.
Flexibility	Having the capacity to adjust volumes and features of products produced.

Costs, a component of efficiency measures, are critical, whether they are labor or parts cost. Cost must be controlled and often reduced; customers demand it. The lower the cost of making products, the greater the potential profits are for a firm. **Quality** has become a pervasive concern in many different types of companies. Customers are demanding quality and firms need to deliver. Products and services must be consistently produced with minimal errors, to meet or exceed customers' expectations along a multitude of dimensions, many even implicit. The external customer is a dominant force and stakeholder for operations managers, directly influencing these priorities. **Time** is likewise a key issue for customers. Customers want products delivered on time to support rapid introduction of newer products, services, designs, and technologies. For many firms, time itself is the basis of competition. Federal Express was founded on the notion of overnight delivery. They can deliver it to you faster than the competition. Flexibility is another priority of operations related to customer concerns. **Flexibility** can involve changes in the volume of products made, based on shifting demand. Some industries and products have different cycles of demand to which operations must adjust. Another aspect of flexibility is customizing some product features. The ability to simply and easily change the product color or other features according to customer preferences is another concern for the operations function. Greater flexibility in operational systems means greater responsiveness to customer wishes for a unique product or service features.

Operations management often combines these concerns with outcomes to make decisions. In exploring new manufacturing technology, managers look for new tools that can improve delivery time and flexibility as well as productivity. They also look at cost. If costs are high, adding sophisticated technology may not add enough benefits to improve overall productivity.

OPERATIONS STRATEGY

Operations is not just about tactical issues like increasing worker efficiency, but is increasingly tied to the strategy of the firm. The Japanese gained competitive advantage in the 1980s through advances in operational effectiveness. They made electronics and automobiles better and at lower costs than almost any other company in the world. Operational effectiveness can be a source of competitive advantage. Noted Harvard strategist Michael E. Porter said:

> *Operational effectiveness (OE) means performing similar activities better than rivals perform them. Operational effectiveness includes but is not limited to efficiency. It refers to any number of practices that allow a company to utilize its inputs, for example, reducing defects in products or producing better products faster.*[3]

In his view of strategy, Porter also noted that OE was necessary, but not sufficient, for corporate success. To gain real competitive advantage OE must be linked to strategy. Companies do not just perform operational activities better than others but perform different activities or in different ways. Operations strategy is the means by which the operations area implements the firm's corporate strategy. Flowing from the firm's corporate strategy, its operations strategy must highlight the combination of cost, quality, time, and flexibility its customers want, and tailor the company's processes to focus on those priorities. However, corporate strategy drives the operations strategy, not vice versa.

Consider the following example of Southwest Airlines. Southwest Airlines has been very successful for over thirty years, winning five consecutive annual Triple Crowns for 1992 through 1996. The Triple Crown refers to Best On-time Record, Best Baggage Handling, and Fewest Customer Complaints, key outcome measures for airlines. Southwest's growth and success stemmed from a clear and distinct business strategy. The airline found a niche in short haul air travel between cities not served by larger airlines. They focused on lower costs. By flying shorter flights, they used mid-sized, fuel-efficient aircraft and they did not need to provide full meals. They improved turnaround by servicing their planes quickly and getting them back in the air faster than competitors. Turnaround is a measure of operations efficiency for airlines. They delivered their product in a fun, as well as efficient, way. In short, their business strategy was well matched with functional strategies, particularly their operations and human resource strategies. Their continued success is due to a distinct strategic idea, well executed by different functions within the company.

Within the operations area there are several service and manufacturing strategies that are available to support business strategies. Manufacturing strategies provide options for making products. Service strategies provide options for delivering a less tangible product. Service organizations include law firms, medical organizations, educational institutions, and investment firms. These service options are presented in Table 10.2.

Service strategies include standardized services, assemble-to-order services, and customized services. **Standardized services** are produced in large volumes. The focus is on consistent quality, low cost, and timely delivery. There is nothing fancy, nor any tailoring to specific customer needs. Retail banking offers a fairly standard package of services to all customers, as does the U.S. Postal Service. The focus is on providing the same service reliably to all. The **assemble-to-order** strategy provides some limited degree of customization. From a set of options, service packages can be bundled in different ways to meet customer needs. Telephone companies offer to their customers sets of options with different plans available to choose from. **Customized services** are small volume and specific to customer needs. Marketing research companies and law firms utilize this strategy. Services are customized and routed in different ways to meet customer needs. Flexibility of operations is important here. The packaging of tasks can be shifted easily to meet specific customer needs.

Table 10.2: Categories of Service and Manufacturing Strategies[4]

Service Strategies	Explanation
Standardized	Large volume services performed consistently at low cost.
Assemble-to-Order	Some degree of customization to customer needs and focus on delivery time.
Customized Services	Highly specific design of services to meet unique customer needs.

Manufacturing Strategies	Explanation
Make-to-Stock	Large volumes produced and stored in inventory, available for delivery to customer.
Assemble-to-Order	Customized products assembled from few standard assemblies.
Make-to-Order	High levels of customization in small quantities.

Services cannot be stockpiled or stored. Manufacturing allows for storage of products in inventories. The **make-to-stock** strategy relies on inventory. With some predictable demand forecasted, large volumes can be produced and stored for later delivery to customers. The costs saved in volume production offset the added storage costs of inventory. **Assemble-to-order** strategies create more customized products from a limited number of options. The focus is on delivery time and customer needs. Given the number of options, storage is not as feasible. Furniture companies make sofas with different fabric and wood trim, for example. **Make-to-order** is the most highly customized strategy. Each product may have unique customer specifications and thus volumes are low. Medical equipment and customized homes would be examples of this strategy. The customer may be involved in the design here.

DIFFERENT OPERATIONS ACTIVITIES OR FUNCTIONS

With operations management, a number of different activities are coordinated. We have characterized OM as the throughput of the organization but OM can also be viewed as a system. Its inputs are the materials, parts, supplies, services, and labor used by the organization, and often times even customers themselves, particularly in service companies. The operations function then acts to change these inputs. The transformation involves multiple steps and activities. Once the product is made, it is stored to await shipping.

Today much of operations management is often subsumed under the broader heading of **supply chain management** (SCM), which implies the management of the entire value chain from suppliers through to customers. SCM is a set of processes for improving the way a company finds the raw components it needs to make a product or service, manufactures that product or service, and delivers it to the customers.[5] In looking at suppliers of parts and materials for a company, SCM encompasses purchasing or purchasing control, inventory management, plant layout, and logistics.

Purchasing is the operations function that establishes relationships with a few key suppliers from whom parts and raw materials are ordered. By keeping the number of suppliers small and having good relationships with them, the company has the ability to respond better to its customers' needs in terms of better quality, timeliness, customization, up-to-date designs, and technology. These strong supplier relationships can leverage price reductions and special features if needed. Large and more powerful companies have more leverage to ask for price reductions from smaller suppliers. Major companies are even asking for tuition discounts for their employees who attend local universities. Leveraging the power of purchasing is standard practice; however, it is increasingly being realized that the best performing companies are the ones that accommodate and align the interests of all supply chain parties.

Inventory management is maintaining supplies of raw materials and products and coordinating their movements through the value chain. There are three different types of materials. **Raw materials** are the components before any transformation by the company. Raw materials include steel, wire, and fabric. Most manufacturing companies perform work on raw materials, converting them to sub-components of the final product. The pieces that will be assembled into the final product are referred to as **work-in-progress**. The third type of inventory is called finished goods. **Finished goods** are the products that are packaged and ready to be shipped to customers. As part of supply chain management, these three types of inventory are tracked so the company knows how many units they own and where they are located. All three types of inventory represent costs to the company. By maintaining lean inventories, operations managers are able to run more efficient operations.

Inventory management has evolved greatly over the last fifty years. There was a time when the goal was to have fairly large quantities of parts ready for the next step in the process. The thinking was that the worker needed supplies to be ready so there was no downtime. Efficiency was viewed too narrowly. The determination of the optimal production batch size was often done with what is known as an economic order quantity (EOQ) method. This method spreads out the cost of a machine setup over an optimally sized production batch. Unfortunately, inventory holding costs were often underestimated relative to the costs of machine setup, so larger production batch sizes were favored to spread the setup costs.

The **kanban** system was developed by Toyota to solve a problem with defective parts. With large quantities of parts stored in warehouses, quality problems would not be discovered until many products were finished and shipped. An experiment began by putting small quantities of parts on carts, which had a card containing information about where the parts came from. When each cart was emptied, the card was sent to the parts department, signaling the need for more parts, and another cart was sent.

The system not only worked well for identifying quality problems with parts but demonstrated that maintaining lower inventories saved money. Lean or just-in-time inventory management systems were born. Having too many parts between operations took up space and cost extra money. Having just enough parts to keep employees working was most successful. Other versions of this can be seen in a variety of businesses. You may have noticed cards near the back of greeting card display racks in drugstores. Those cards signal to employees to re-order more cards. It is a simple system in concept but, just like quality principles, it requires commitment and cultural change to support.

A pragmatic student may ask about the kanban system, "How do you determine the number of parts to put in each bin to keep the system working at optimal levels?" That question was answered with the economic order quantity (EOQ) method described in previous paragraphs. Much of operations management is a combination of applied quantitative techniques and practical, hands-on approaches. In lean systems thinking, for example, the hidden costs of holding inventory are factored into the EOQ method. Meanwhile, the cost of a setup itself is treated as reducible. Thus batch sizes are kept to a minimum.

The kanban example illustrates another aspect of operations management: facilities planning and design. The different steps in producing a product or delivering a service are not only broken down into component steps, but the location and placement of the activities and people are determined. Just as Frederick Taylor did with coal shovelers, the most efficient set of movements is found. The process that requires the fewest movements and steps is best. These efficiency criteria are also balanced with human ones.

Workers need to interact and the work flow must take into account job design and motivational aspects as well.

Once the products are made, other operations activities take over. Finished goods are often sent to a warehouse or distribution center. **Logistics** is the process of getting finished products to customers. Logistics involves warehousing and transportation systems. Transportation systems include trucks, railroads, and airplanes. Logistics also involves systems for invoicing customers and receiving payments for products or services.

One of the final elements in supply chain management is a system for returning products that the customer has rejected as defective or inadequate in some way. The products are returned and the customers' accounts are credited. Based on a call from a customer, a return address label can be sent to the customer. The label tracks the returned product and provides feedback to various units regarding why the product was returned. The feedback allows for corrections and continuous improvement.

As companies develop their supply chain system, they often combine some of the internal operations into one department. Combining purchasing, inventory management, and distribution creates materials management. The integration of these different functions into one department brings added control and coordination, resulting in better overall performance.

IMPROVING THE MANAGEMENT OF OPERATIONS

A continuous improvement mentality permeates operations management. Employees and managers seek to improve all steps in the supply chain. Sharing data is one approach to improving the process. Manufacturers share data with suppliers and clients to provide better service and deliveries as part of SCM.

Another recent development is **business process reengineering**, which evaluates business activities or processes to eliminate unneeded steps. Industrial engineers since Frederick Taylor have studied jobs and tasks looking to find more efficient movements and steps. Reengineering is more than that. Over the years work became more specialized, broken down into smaller units with pieces done by different departments. Then, to counter the differentiation and specialization, more coordination and control was needed. The latter generated more management and added approvals in the process. In the end, many companies had processes that evolved into overly complex activities. Michael Hammer and James Champy[6] wrote a well-known book in 1993, which they sub-titled, "A Radical Manifesto for Business." Reengineering is intended to be a more radical departure from the typical process of improvement. Steps and layers in the structure are removed. Benchmarking, a topic introduced near the end of the planning chapter, may also be used in reengineering, as the following example shows.

One of the most famous cases of business process reengineering involves the accounts payable unit at Ford Motor Company. Ford was using over 500 people to process accounts payable. In an effort to cut costs, they looked at one of their joint venture partners, Mazda, to see how they performed the accounts payable function. Although a smaller company, benchmarking, or studying Mazda's accounts payable process revealed that they completed the operation with only five people. Reengineering questions assumptions about all steps in the process and looks for simple, but often very different ways, of doing the job—not just improving existing processes. Following reengineering, Ford used 125 people to perform its accounts payable function. Not all reengineering projects achieve such dramatic results, but the Ford example illustrates the potential for improvement by taking a more radical approach to change.

Since the early stages of the Industrial Revolution, managers have used technology to replace manual labor and hence improve efficiency. The **management of technology** is another part of operations management that continues to search for cost effective ways to improve productivity through new and improved technologies. The management of technology seeks to find technological enhancements to improve the quality and quantity of performance. Breakthrough technologies can alter the way an operation is performed and introduce new operations. The introduction of bar scanners in supermarkets not only helped improve the speed and efficiency of the checkout process but also enabled the stores to better track inventory and reduce labor costs.

Technology not only allows for improving the way things are currently done, but can also play a role in creating new products and services. The Internet has provided many businesses with a new outlet for distribution of information and sales of products and services. Robotics involves the use of sophisticated robots to do the tasks formerly performed by humans. Auto manufacturers increasingly use robotics for welding, painting, and other repetitive tasks. Humans are better at novel problem solving, but machines are more consistent at repetitive tasks. As discussed in chapter 3 on environment, companies need to monitor the environment for changes in technology that can enhance their operations.

Flexible manufacturing (FM) is a type of advanced technology that is growing in importance as a component of facilities planning. FM systems configure parts and manufacturing systems that allow for both low cost and high variety. More companies are relying on manufacturing processes that customize products to meet increasingly specific customer needs. Traditionally, low cost and customization were opposites that did not work together. Flexible manufacturing allows operations to more easily and quickly change production processes to accommodate customer requests for unique product features. Flexible manufacturing uses complex tools that have multiple purposes that are linked to computer systems, which determine customer preferences.[7] Inventory is fed to machines mechanically (i.e., without human intervention). For example, the Ford Mondeo is assembled using FM methods. Different accessories and trim can be added as cars come down the line. Cars are assembled to customer orders instead of make-to-stock strategy and stored on dealer lots until the customer buys it. The flexible methods more easily allow for changes in product features with less inventory and reduced change over costs.

The final topic in this section also introduces the next section, information management. With so many activities in the supply chain, managers at all levels struggle to understand the whole process. Frequently each component has its own information system and they usually do not communicate well with each other. **Enterprise resource planning** is a term that refers to the integrated information systems that support all business functions and their data storage needs. It contains information about suppliers, customers, and internal operations such as different product lines, healthcare benefit systems of employees, and performance from various geographical operations. The systems can take revenue and profits from European countries and convert the earnings to U.S. dollars. These are very large, complicated, and expensive systems. The planning phase requires companies to analyze their processes. Reengineering of business processes is often required. Having all of these diverse information sources combined means that more inefficiencies can be identified and costs further reduced.

INFORMATION MANAGEMENT

Many of the operations activities have been described as needing information to function well. Managing information within organizations so that various functions have timely and accurate information to meet customer demands for products and services is vital today. The costs of acquiring, generating, storing, and transmitting data have fallen sharply in the past twenty years because of advances in technology. **Information management** uses computer hardware and software programs to store and make information readily retrievable to managers, as they need it to make decisions.

Note in the opening paragraph of this chapter that a distinction was made between data and information. Data are made up of binary codes stored on computers. Data by itself is not useful. Information is data that have value and meaning to managers. Think of your first accounting class or the first time you saw a balance sheet. Those numbers did not mean anything to you. Managers often receive several hundred e-mails a day. Not all of these individual items have meaning or value. Computers receive data from cash registers (really computer terminals) as consumers buy groceries or clothing and they store data about consumer purchases when the consumer uses an ID card. All of this data is not meaningful. Data overload is common today because of the ease with which information is generated and stored.

A new field of data mining has emerged which analyzes buying data to identify trends and patterns. These consumer patterns have value to retailers in terms of what products to order and stock. The mining process transforms the data into information. **Management information systems** (MIS) is the hardware and software that provide managers with needed and timely information. MIS help managers make decisions.

IMPORTANT QUALITIES OF INFORMATION

What qualities should information possess so that it is meaningful and valuable? Quality, timeliness, completeness, and relevance[8] are important qualities of information systems. **Quality** information accurately portrays what is going on in the organization. If managers are to make decisions with the information, they must trust the accuracy and consistency of the information. Sales figures need to be entered into the system and updated regularly. If forecasts for production runs are based on partial data, then the wrong decisions will be made.

Information systems today are typically networks of computers connected to databases. The information is sent and stored in the database and then managers retrieve information when it is needed. The **timeliness** of the information is important. If the information is a day old, then it may be less useful. Some systems take orders and changes from different sources but do not update the database immediately. If the database is updated during the evening, the data may not be timely. A customer calls or goes on-line to find out if an item is in stock. The system says it is available, but someone ordered the rest of those items already; the information is now both inaccurate and not timely. **Real-time systems** update the database automatically, assuring greater timeliness and accuracy.

Another desired quality of information is **completeness**. In chapter 4, some conditions were described under which managers commonly make decisions. Managers frequently face uncertainty, or a lack of knowledge about events. A manager needs to access budget expenditures, but one component is missing from the system or is posted later. The manager has incomplete information and her or his decisions may be hampered. The more complete the information system, the better the potential for sound decisions.

Relevance is the final quality of information. **Relevance** refers to the information needed to make decisions. Information systems can hold vast amounts of data. Managers need certain critical pieces for those areas for which they control and are held accountable.

IMPROVING INFORMATION FOR DECISION-MAKING

We also noted in chapter 4 that managers often function in conditions of bounded rationality, that is, they do not use all of the information available to them. Keeping this limitation in mind, Rockhart advocated that top managers only identify seven key indicators of performance. He called these *critical success factors*.[9] By limiting the list to seven, Rockhart believed that there would be less bounded rationality and managers would be forced to prioritize and choose which measures were most critical for the success of her or his business.

Besides prioritizing the information given to managers, other tools are available for assisting managers in making better decisions. **Decision support systems** (DSS) are models that combine information based on historical relationships. DSS's can only work when the same types of decisions are made regularly. They cannot be established for novel or unprogrammed decisions. The pharmaceutical company Merck uses a DSS to make decisions about investing in research projects.[10] Some of the variables used include demand conditions, research and development (R & D) spending, manufacturing costs, and marketing costs. The DSS can combine information in more complex ways than humans can and does so more consistently. Human decision makers still evaluate the model estimates and apply their experience and discretion. Relying on the model with guesswork is still better than guess work alone.

An even more sophisticated information system to aid managers in making decisions is an expert system. **Expert systems** (ES) try to extract knowledge from humans and codify it into decision rules or trees. The extracted information is then programmed into a computer application. The idea with expert systems is to acquire the systematic knowledge that humans hold. In the event that key employees leave the organization, the information is retained. Another advantage is that expert systems are more consistent in using information than humans. Expert systems have been developed for evaluating complex loan applications in banks and even diagnosing medical problems in hospitals. In the process of developing an ES, decision makers may get insight into how they make decisions from the questions asked of them.

In addition, expert systems and DSS information technology has become more mobile and accessible. Claims adjusters can use cell phones and computers to enter claims right from the location. In places like Florida, where several hurricanes destroyed homes, this mobile technology speeds service and increases customer satisfaction. Wireless connections are being established in restaurants, airports, and other public places. These connections allow employees to connect to their email and databases, allowing them to be productive in many more locations than were previously possible.

With access and connectivity come problems as well. As more people can access information from diverse locations, the security of the information becomes a problem. Companies need to protect this information from hackers and criminals who wish to steal the identity of customers. Similarly with enterprise systems, data confidentiality and control are potential problems. ChoicePoint, one of a few companies that maintain credit information on consumers, recently gave information to criminals who were posing as a legitimate business. These criminals received personal information on thousands of consumers whose identity they hoped to steal. ChoicePoint was fooled into giving the criminals the information rather than having their databases breached or hacked. Nonetheless, the loss of confidential information caused their stock price to tumble.

PROJECT MANAGEMENT

In chapter 6 on planning, a project was described as a plan that is used once for a specific purpose. More specifically, a **project** is a onetime set of activities with a definite beginning and ending point.[11] Both operations and information management areas make frequent use of project management to develop and implement systems. Managers supervise a project using multiple employees, often from different units. The project manager is charged with completing the assignment on time and under budget, meeting full performance specifications. The project manager uses the functions of management discussed throughout this text. The project is planned, coordinated, and controlled. Each of these phases will be further explained and are shown in Table 10.3.

The important first step is to plan the project. Since a project is a one-time endeavor, the scope and objectives must be clearly defined. These components dictate the specifics of what the team does. The project manager also needs to be focused on his or her chief customer. The individual(s) who requested the project is an important stakeholder and needs to be kept informed. Once the objectives are set, the project team is formed, typically drawing members from different functional areas with the expertise that is needed to complete the project.

Table 10.3: Project Management Phases

1. Planning the project
   a. Identify tasks needed
   b. Determine duration of each task

2. Coordinating and communicating among team members

3. Controlling project costs

4. Closing out the project

Once the team is formed and presented with the project scope and objectives, further planning is done. A division of tasks among members follows. The total project is broken into component tasks and deadlines are set for each component. Costs and other budgetary items may also be established. Several tools are available to project managers and team members to help define and track tasks and deadlines. Computer software is available to construct planning charts. One type of chart is a Gantt chart, named after Henry Gantt as mentioned in chapter 2. The Gantt chart identifies the tasks involved in the project along with the time planned to complete each project task. Linkages among the individual tasks can also be shown with arrows. Some tasks can be worked on simultaneously while others need to be completed before the next can be started.

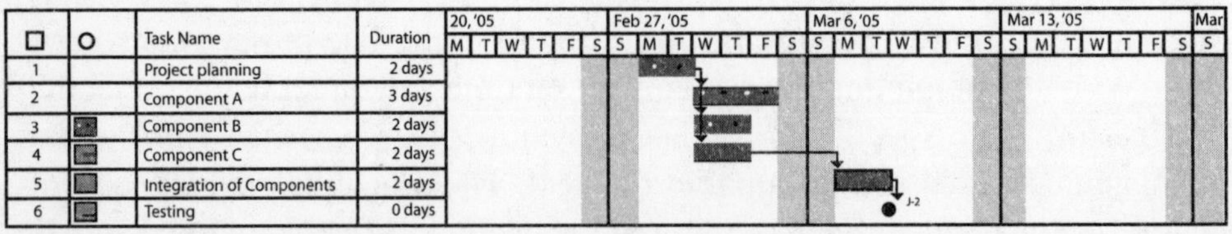

Figure 10.1: Gantt chart for project management.

Figure 10.1 illustrates a Gantt chart. The six tasks are defined on the left side of the figure. The bars also reflect the tasks, with the length of the bars indicating the planned time duration for each task. Task 5, integration of components, cannot begin until each of the three components is completed. The components cannot be started until the planning is finished. Notice the diamond-shaped figure. The "♦" indicates a critical milestone or checkpoint in the project.

Once the project has begun, the project manager uses a number of team skills. Since projects are usually a cross-functional team, member knowledge and skills must be harnessed and meetings run effectively. As members work on their component tasks, they need to share their problems and findings with others. Communication is an important aspect of project management.

Controlling the project is another feature. The manager needs to be aware of project progress and costs. Here project management software is also useful. Charts like the one in Figure 10.1 can also plot accomplishments against planned targets. In this way the team can see where they are falling behind. The software can also track time and resources spent by members on each task.

Once the steps are completed, the report is written and the presentations are made. The last step of closing the project is also in order. The project manager reflects on how this project progressed. What was learned? What could have been done differently? Should any recommendations be made regarding the project management process?

CONCLUSION

Operations and information management are key components of the transformation process for any organization. Managers need to have effective and efficient systems for transforming inputs into outputs. Technology plays an ever-increasing role in improving efficiencies and meeting customer demands. Better quality, faster delivery, and greater customizing of products and services are everyday concerns for managers in these two areas.

Chapter 10 Endnotes

1. J. Griffiths, "Europe's Manufacturing Quality and Productivity Still Lag Far Behind Japan's," *Financial Times* (November 4, 1994): 11.

2. Larry P. Ritzman & Lee J. Krajewski, *Foundations of Operations Management* (Upper Saddle River, NJ: Prentice-Hall, 2003), 15.

3. Michael E. Porter, "What is Strategy?" *Harvard Business Review* (November–December, 1996): 62.

4. Ritzman & Krajewski, 18–20.

5. http://www.cio.com/research/scm/edit/012202_scm.html

6. Michael Hammer and James Champy, *Reengineering the Corporation: A Manifesto for Business Revolution* (New York: Harper Business, 1993), 33.

7. http://www.brunel.ac.uk/~bustcfj/bola/operations/technol.html

8. Gareth R. Jones, Jennifer M. George, & Charles W. L. Hill, *Contemporary Management* (2nd ed.) (New York: Irwin, McGraw-Hill, 2000), 613–615.

9. John F. Rockhart, "Chief Executives Define Their Own Data Needs," *Harvard Business Review* 57, no. 2 (1979): 82.

10. Jones, George, & Hill, 627.

11. E. E. Adam, Jr. & R. J. Ebert, *Production and Operations Management* (5th ed.) (Upper Saddle River, NJ: Prentice-Hall, 1992), 33.

CHAPTER 11

Motivation in the Workplace

Chapter 11

MOTIVATION IN THE WORKPLACE

Motivation is a topic that has concerned managers for many years. Hundreds of books and articles have been written on the subject. As described in chapter 2, we know that over 100 years ago, early managers believed that the drive system would motivate workers; pushing, prodding, and manipulating workers was the best system, they thought. Later, McGregor pointed out that these Theory X attitudes of managers influenced worker behavior, creating the very behavior they were trying to avoid. Why did they use such an aggressive and, at times, offensive system? The drive system did achieve some results. More recently, a motivation expert acknowledged that a swift kick in the pants gets workers moving when more polite requests fail.[1]

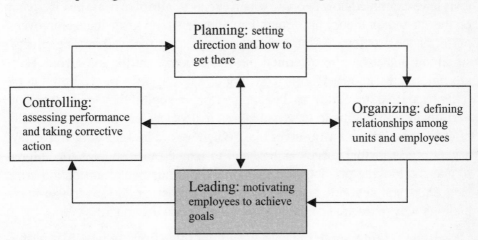

Figure 11.1: The leading function.

The leading function is of such concern to managers because they need workers to perform. With the competitiveness of the global marketplace, performance is more important today than ever. Managers' performance is dependent on their subordinates (remember Figure 1.1?). The leading function covers the last four chapters of this book. Motivation is the focus of this chapter, followed by teams and then leadership. Teams influence motivation and performance as does the leadership behavior of managers. The final component of leading is the subject of the last chapter, including conflict, change, and communication. Each plays a role, influencing employees to perform to achieve company goals.

First, workplace **motivation** is defined as the forces that drive people to behave in ways that energize, direct, and sustain their work behavior and performance.[2] It is one of the key areas of the leading function as represented in Figure 11.1. Motivation explains how much effort an employee is willing to put forth and toward what ends. All people are motivated to do things. Some choose to direct their efforts toward joking with coworkers or non-work tasks. Managers want employees to be motivated to perform job-related tasks at a high level of quality.

MOTIVATION AND PERFORMANCE

Productivity and performance are closely related to motivation, but motivation is not the only influence. In fact, managers tend to put too much emphasis on motivation as the determiner of worker performance. Managers have a tendency to view performance as caused by internal factors. Social psychologists have examined how people explain events or attribute causality. Research on the attribution theory has found that managers tend to attribute employees' performance problems to internal causes, primarily motivation. The effect is so strong that it has been termed the fundamental attribution error.[3] There are times when poor performance is not due to a lack of motivation. On the other hand, looking at it from the employees' viewpoint, they tend to attribute performance problems to external causes and successes to themselves. This effect is called the actor-observer bias. When we are looking at ourselves, we accept praise for the successes but tend to blame other sources for failures. Managers, looking at another person, use the fundamental attribution error. Hence a potential conflict can develop between worker and supervisor in explaining why performance did not meet the expected standard.

To help bring some balance, it is important to recognize that performance is influenced by a variety of factors, as shown in Table 11.1. Individual differences in worker characteristics influence performance. Workers cannot perform well unless their abilities fit the requirement of the job. In chapter 8, hiring workers with abilities was discussed. If the worker does not have ability or training, trying hard will not be sufficient to achieve performance expectations. Some workers have more work ethic or commitment and are willing to push harder. If the worker is well matched to the job requirements, then the next factor influencing performance is motivation. Workers need to be willing to exert effort to accomplish the goal and perform. Many theories and models have been developed to explain the willingness to exert effort. These approaches will be the focus of the rest of the chapter.

Table 11.1: Factors Influencing Performance

	Individual Differences	× Motivation ×	Work Environment	= Performance
Performance Equation:	Individual Differences	× Motivation ×	Work Environment	= Performance
Means of Improving:	Training, Skills matched with job	More challenges, Incentives	Clear assignments, Up-to-date equipment	Quantity and quality of work output

A third factor also influences performance, the work environment. A number of factors could influence performance in the work environment. If a worker is given deficient equipment, then it is more difficult to achieve the same performance standard than it is for someone who has the proper tools and equipment with which to work. Similarly, a sales agent could be assigned to a geographical region where he has to travel greater distances and has fewer companies on which to call to make sales. His potential to perform is limited by the environment. Supervisors are another component of the work environment. Some give clear assignments and check to see if workers have questions. If workers are not given proper direction, they may not perform the right task.

The "×" in Table 11.1 indicates that all three of these factors are multiplicatively related to performance. If any one is zero, the product is zero. Thus, in diagnosing performance problems, the managers should examine all factors: individual differences, motivation, and work conditions.

Because of the importance of motivation for managers, numerous models, theories, and approaches have been developed over the years. This chapter will describe eight of these. Some approaches to motivation focus on the content or what specific factors motivate employees. Another set are based on the processes by which individuals become motivated and are hence labeled process theories. Both of these approaches will be addressed.

CONTENT THEORIES OF MOTIVATION

Content approaches to motivation tend to specify categories of needs or drives. These approaches theorize that content issues cause individuals to become energized to exert effort. The theories or views of four different authors are covered in this section. Abraham Maslow theorized that human needs are ordered in a hierarchical fashion. Clayton Alderfer modified Maslow's approach saying that there are three categories of needs but they function somewhat differently than Maslow suggested. Frederick Herzberg proposed a two-factor theory of motivation that functions differently than both Maslow and Alderfer. Finally, Richard McClelland proposed three categories of learned needs. Prior to these theories, there were many other categories of needs or drives. Some were long lists. The contributions of these approaches were to establish more concise categories of needs ordered in different ways. They offer some direction to managers who wish to influence motivation in the desired direction.

MASLOW'S HIERARCHY OF NEEDS

Maslow wanted to develop a general model of motivation for human behavior. His focus was not specific to the workplace; however, it does serve as a foundation for later authors who were more interested in workplace motivation.

Maslow identified five categories of needs. When needs are unmet, humans strive to meet those needs. This is the energizing force that causes humans to act. Prior to Maslow, other authors had identified many different types of needs. The unique contribution of Maslow was the order or arrangement of the need categories relative to one another. The hierarchy of needs has become a pervasive motivational concept in many disciplines. It is shown in Figure 11.2.

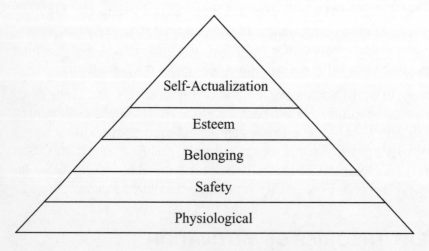

Figure 11.2: Maslow's hierarchy of needs.

Physiological needs are the most fundamental in the hierarchy. Physiological needs involve the body, including hunger, sleep, and sex. Maslow based the physiological needs category on research on the body's ability to maintain homeostasis, or steady state, and the tendency of the body to seek specific deficits.[4] When someone has an iron deficiency, they crave food high in iron content. If all needs are not met, then Maslow believed that physiological needs would dominate. Maslow stressed that unsatisfied needs motivate behavior. As physiological needs are satisfied, humans become motivated in more socially oriented ways. Gratification of lower order needs leads to the emergence of needs higher in the hierarchy.

The second category of needs in Maslow's scheme is safety needs. As with physiological needs, deficits in safety, by perceived threats or danger, can be powerful, motivating forces. Children and adults seek order and stability in their lives. Disruptions or threats to order can cause mobilization of energy and action. The threat of losing a job may cause individuals to search for alternative employment. Similarly, mergers or acquisitions are disruptive for employees. Normal tasks may be dropped as the perceived threat of a merger causes employees to convene at the water cooler to discuss potential impacts and consequences. The social actions calm and reduce the perceived threat, leading to the emergence of the next need category.

The third category in Maslow's hierarchy is love or belonging needs. Most people seek affectionate relationships with others. In a fast-moving society, relationships with family, friends, and coworkers satisfy important needs. Coworkers and work groups help satisfy this need. Valuing diversity seeks to make employees who are different feel comfortable and accepted, also satisfying this fundamental need.

One of the most important need categories is esteem needs. Many workers seek self-respect and high evaluation from others. Recognition, attention, reputation, and prestige are all factors that are important to workers. Satisfaction of esteem needs builds self-confidence and strength, enabling workers to challenge threats to their esteem later. Those whose esteem needs are chronically ungratified, perhaps through childhood abuse, feel weak and helpless. They will not accept challenging work assignments, or if given them, will not perform well.

As human esteem needs are met, the final category of needs emerges. Highly successful people often become restless. They seek something more. Self-actualization is the pinnacle of Maslow's hierarchy. It represents a desire for self-fulfillment. Self-actualization is "the desire to become more and more what one is, to become everything that one is capable of becoming."[5] Self-actualization accounts for high levels of creativity and innovation, a continued seeking of what one is capable of achieving.

Several principles underlie the functioning of the hierarchy. The lower the needs in the hierarchy, the stronger or more prepotent their impact is on motivation. Once the lower-order needs are satisfied, then those above start to emerge as motivational factors. This principle is termed **satisfaction-progression**. For managers, the application is to determine the need level at which employees are currently functioning. For new employees, showing them around and introducing them to coworkers helps to meet safety and belonging needs. These should be met so employees strive to accomplish more challenging tasks related to esteem needs. Managers need not be concerned with self-actualization in the workplace.

HERZBERG'S TWO-FACTOR THEORY

Although Maslow was trying to create a general theory of human motivation, Frederick Herzberg was more focused on motivation in the workplace. He began by doing interviews of workers and managers. He asked over 4,000 people what "turned them on" and what "turned them off." Some distinct patterns emerged in the responses. The things that excited workers were found in the *content* of the jobs they performed. These factors are called **satisfiers** and include responsibility, advancement, and personal growth. The things that turned them off were found in the *context* of work and are termed hygiene factors or **dissatisfiers**. Typical hygiene factors were pay, working conditions, and coworker and supervisor relations.

These two categories of motivation are related to each other in unique ways unlike Maslow's hierarchy. In terms of physical health, the lack of hygiene can lead to sickness. If not met, problems develop. In workplaces where hygiene factors are not satisfied, workers experience dissatisfaction, such as a sick attitude. Unions have organized to address problems with hygiene factors. Adding more of these does not lead to positive motivation, though it does lead to less "pain" in the work environment. Satisfaction of dissatisfying factors means that workers are not unhappy, or neutral. Herzberg hypothesized that hygiene factors were based on a drive to avoid things that cause pain, whereas motivators were directed toward growth. For workers to become motivated, a very different set of factors needs to be addressed. Satisfiers change the nature of the work performed, giving workers more responsibility and opportunities to perform more challenging tasks. These opportunities for growth build more positive strivings to perform.

Herzberg's approach was very significant in that it led to a focus on redesigning jobs and work to improve motivation. His model helps explain why the human relations approach was not very effective. Being nice to people only improved hygiene factors. The human resource approach was linked more to satisfiers and McGregor's Theory Y. People seek challenges and want to perform meaningful tasks. Those factors lead to positive, energizing motivation.

ALDERFER'S ERG THEORY

Maslow first described his theory in the 1940s. Herzberg developed the two-factor model in the 1950s and 1960s. Clayton Alderfer began to modify Maslow's approach in the 1960s and 1970s. Sometimes a simpler approach works better. Three categories of needs may be a better explanation of motivation than five.

Alderfer's existence needs are much like Maslow's physiological and safety combined. These are lower-order needs that are fundamental to our survival. When survival is threatened, the motivation can be powerful. The second category was relatedness. Relatedness needs are very similar to Maslow's belonging category. Humans need interactions with family, acquaintances, and coworkers. Connecting with others in the workplace is important in preventing turnover.

Growth needs, much like Maslow's esteem needs and Herzberg's satisfiers, move people to seek challenge and responsibility from the tasks performed at work. These are often termed higher-order needs. They relate to reaching beyond the basics or lower order needs (i.e., existence). Alderfer did not propose anything comparable to self-actualization. Maslow's concept of being-all-that-you-can-be is very difficult to measure and operationalize. It is also not as relevant to the workplace. Hence Alderfer's stripped down and more efficient model actually works better at capturing workplace motivation.

In addition, he added another feature missing from the hierarchy of needs. Both Alderfer and Maslow believed that motivation moved in a satisfaction-progression manner. As a lower need was satisfied, the person was motivated to seek the next level or step in the model. When existence and social needs are largely met, individuals begin to seek to satisfy esteem needs. Alderfer added a complementary principle, frustration-regression. He reasoned that people who are chronically frustrated in satisfying esteem needs eventually lose that drive. Have you ever had an arm or leg in a cast for an extended period of time? When the cast was removed, the muscles at that site have shrunk, or atrophied. This happens with needs too. Consider the clerical worker who regularly performs routine tasks but is not allowed to seek responsibility or challenge with more difficult tasks. That worker is apt to be fairly social. She or he is seeking need gratification with those factors that are available. After long periods without the opportunity for satisfying esteem, people may even resist responsibility, as they are comfortable at lower need levels.

McCLELLAND'S ACQUIRED NEED THEORY

The final content theory of motivation was developed by David McClelland. He believed that early childhood experiences developed a need or desire for certain types of goals. Many of the other content theorists assumed that needs are innate, although the level or category may be influenced by experiences. McClelland's approach has been frequently applied to the workplace.

One of the most important drives or needs for organizations is for achievement. High need for achievement pushes managers to seek success and higher performance levels. This category of need is similar to the esteem and growth needs of other content theorists. For McClelland, however, there is no necessary link to prior need levels. Need for achievement, or N_{ACH}, is developed at an early age. Parents who encourage self-reliance and independent action tend to raise children who become adults with high N_{ACH}.

Another need category is the need for affiliation, or N_{AFF}. Those with high needs for affiliation tend to conform to others' wishes and they have a strong desire for social approval. They are concerned with how others feel and react. This category is similar to social or relatedness needs. While N_{ACH} is important for managers, high levels of N_{AFF} may be harmful. If an individual frequently worries about how others think and feel, they may not be able to choose the actions that benefit the organization but may hurt one member of the group. These types of managers may also have difficulty in disciplining employees. Moderate levels of N_{AFF} may be useful, but not high levels.

McClelland's final category of needs is power, or N_{POW}. This type does not have a corresponding element in other content theories. Like N_{ACH}, the need to influence others is important for managers. Controlling the environment and influencing others are key parts of managers' jobs. Individuals in supervisory positions with high N_{POW} tend to be rated as high in leadership.[6] He also distinguished two different types of power, institutional and personal. A need for personal power is a need to dominate others. Institutional power is more desirable as it uses influence to accomplish results in the organization.

Thus McClelland's approach to motivation adds several elements that are missing from other content theories. He adds a power component and his approach is not linked to a progression, or hierarchy. As the need categories are learned, there is no necessary prerequisite need state. Given the learned aspect, he also sought to teach and develop N_{ACH}. Achievement motivation was encouraged by teaching individuals to think and act like a person with N_{ACH}. Individuals were also taught to set higher but still realistic goals for performance and were given feedback and knowledge about themselves.[7] Those with high personal power and low institutional power may be more prone to do unethical things that benefit them at the expense of the organization.

In describing each of the content approaches, some similarities were noted. Table 11.2 presents all four approaches, showing the similarities in need categories.

Table 11.2: Comparisons Across Content Theories of Motivation

Maslow's Hierarchy	Herzberg's Two-Factor	Alderfer's ERG	McClelland Acquired Needs
Self-Actualization	Satisfiers	Growth	Achievement, Power
Esteem			
Belonging	Dissatisfiers	Relatedness	Affiliation
Safety		Existence	
Physiological			

Do content theories really work? Does motivation correspond to Maslow's proposed hierarchy? Research has not provided strong support for these theories.[8] Need levels do not move or progress, as many of the theorists suggest. One area where need theories have proven more useful is in comparing higher and lower-order needs individuals. Those with higher-order needs tend to seek assignments with responsibility and challenge while those with lower order needs are more content with routine tasks that have social elements. Matching need level with job assignments is an important guideline for managers.

PROCESS THEORIES OF MOTIVATION

A second category of theories attempts to explain motivation by looking at the process by which people become motivated. They do not rely on needs or drives. The set of processes identifies steps or mechanisms by which motivation occurs. Expectancy theory, reinforcement theory, goal setting, and equity theory will be presented.

EXPECTANCY THEORY

Content theories rely on needs to explain motivation. No thoughts or cognitive processes are taken into consideration. Partly because content theories did not provide much explanation, experts began to consider how thought processes might influence motivation. Might someone choose not to do something even when a need or an attraction is present?

In expectancy theory, three components are important in influencing motivation, as shown in Table 11.3. Before someone does anything, they often examine the likelihood that making an attempt will lead to a reasonable performance level. A rational person does not attempt to run a 26-mile marathon without substantial training. He or she would never be able to finish and might do serious harm to his or her body. Similarly, in the workplace, people do not attempt to do things where there is little likelihood of accomplishment. Some may call this confidence, a belief that it can be accomplished. This component is termed **expectancy**. It can also be described or charted as "E → P" because it reflects the belief that effort will lead to performance.

Expectancy alone is not sufficient for motivation. The second component, **instrumentality**, is needed. It reflects the link between performing and the outcomes associated with good performance. An employee believes that he or she can perform well at a task and does, but then nothing happens. No one notices her performance; no rewards are given as a consequence. If nothing of value happens as a result of the performance, she may not be as motivated to try again in the future. This component of expectancy theory is referred to as "P → O" because it represents the performance-outcome link. It requires organizational systems that recognize and reward performance. This aspect also includes supervisors who recognize, promote, and assign bonuses.

Table 11.3: Components of Expectancy Theory

Expectancy Component	Symbol	Description	Example
Expectancy	E → P	Belief that it can be done	Confidence
Instrumentality	P → O	Likelihood of receiving outcomes with performance	Link to rewards or negative outcomes
Valence	O	Nature of outcomes received	Praise, promotion, bonus, teasing

The third component of expectancy theory is the **valence,** or value, of outcomes. This represents the "O." When performance occurs, the outcomes that the employee receives must be valued. Outcomes can have positive and negative values, and may have unique properties for each individual. A promotion may represent a valued outcome for one. For another employee a promotion may mean more time away from home and family, a negative outcome. Expectancy looks at each person's decision processes individually, not assuming that everyone seeks esteem or self-actualization.

These three components are also related in multiplicative fashion, as were the components that influenced performance in Table 11.1. Thus when any component is low, the force and direction of motivation is low. If someone lacks confidence, they do not attempt difficult tasks and may avoid responsibility. If someone feels that performance is not adequately rewarded, they may be less motivated to perform in the future. Also, if the outcomes associated with performance are not important, motivation is low. Test your understanding of expectancy theory by viewing the examples in Table 11.4.

Table 11.4: Applications of Expectancy Theory

Expectancy Theory Mini-cases	Motivated?
1. Terry has done well as a sales representative. He conscientiously calls on customers and has been a sales leader. He often spends three nights a week away from home. His wife wants him home more, especially with a young child. He knows he can continue to exceed the performance standard and get rewarded, but doesn't care as much about the money.	Is Terry motivated? Yes or No? Which component? $E \rightarrow P, P \rightarrow O$, and/or O
2. Gerald had been successfully performing his job for fifteen years, earning a good salary and bonuses. With a large family Gerald appreciated and needed the money. In an effort to cut costs, engineers added new computers and technology to his job. Now he struggles with the job and questions whether he can perform.	Is Gerald motivated? Yes or No? Which component? $E \rightarrow P, P \rightarrow O$, and/or O
3. Shanthi began working right after high school. She proved very capable and advanced, even while taking courses at a local college. She has received raises and promotions for her work. In her last performance review, she was told the company is seeking to bring in "new blood" from the outside for the next level job, making her prospects for promotion somewhat bleak.	Is Shanthi motivated? Yes or No? Which component? $E \rightarrow P, P \rightarrow O$, and/or O

In example 1, is Terry motivated? If not, which component explains the lack of performance? Terry has become less motivated, as the typical rewards are less meaningful and cause problems at home. In terms of expectancy theory, the valence of outcomes (O) is responsible for the decline. To motivate Terry, the manager must find other rewards or another job that provides reward that are meaningful to Terry. In case 2, is Gerald motivated? Changes in the work environment have caused him to question his ability to do the job. This case illustrates low expectancy (E ➔ P). Gerald needs confidence and training. The manager can encourage him and provide explanations on how to use the workplace tools. In case 3, is Shanthi motivated? Here her decline in motivation is tied to a change in policy. By hiring from the outside, the company has weakened the P ➔ O component. Changing the policy or providing other valued rewards that Shanthi can earn will help restore her motivation.

These examples illustrate some ways that managers diagnose and improve motivation using expectancy theory.

REINFORCEMENT THEORY

Another process approach to motivation is based on operant conditioning research. Psychologists have found that the consequences associated with behavioral acts influence future behavior. In a certain situation, if positive consequences follow an action, then a person is more likely to perform that same behavior again in a similar situation. This influence is so strong that it has been called the law of effect. It is somewhat like the valence of outcomes in expectancy theory, but reinforcement theory does not examine thought processes because they cannot be directly observed. Reinforcement theory only deals with observable events, sometimes termed the *black box*.

When someone does something, three things can happen: (1) a positive or rewarding outcome, (2) a negative or aversive outcome, or (3) no outcome. When a positive condition is presented following behavior, it is called **positive reinforcement**. The consequence of positive reinforcement is to increase the likelihood of that behavior again in the future, as described in Table 11.5. Managers use praise, promotions, and bonuses to reward behaviors that they want to see more often, such as productivity, quality improvements, and increased sales.

When something aversive or negative happens following a behavior, then it is called **punishment**. Managers use punishment or discipline to decrease unwanted behaviors like absenteeism, tardiness, rudeness to customers or coworkers, and insubordination. Many companies give employees a handbook that details rules and policies. One section covers employee acts that are subject to discipline or punishment. Major offenses, such as drunkenness on the job or insubordination, are usually subject to immediate dismissal. Another set of minor offenses, such as absenteeism, poor performance, or arguing with a coworker is subject to progressive discipline. **Progressive discipline** is a series of steps that get progressively more severe in their consequences for the employee. Typical steps include a verbal warning, a written warning, suspension, and dismissal. These steps represent punishment that is designed to reduce or eliminate undesired behaviors on the job.

Table 11.5: Reinforcement Theory Strategies and Outcomes

Label	Outcome	Impact
Positive Reinforcement	Positive outcome contingent on behavior	Increases likelihood of performance
Punishment	Negative outcome contingent on behavior	Decreases likelihood of that behavior again

Besides the nature of the consequences, another aspect of reinforcement theory is evident in the workplace. The schedule of reinforcement also impacts behavior. Reinforcement can be administered in two different ways. Reinforcement can be given based on time or based on the behaviors performed. A time-based schedule is called **interval** reinforcement. Most of us receive salary or wages on a fixed-interval schedule of every one or two weeks. A schedule of reinforcement based on behavior is called a **ratio** schedule, such as being rewarded for every ten assignments completed. The schedule can also administer the reinforcement on a constant or fixed schedule, such as every two weeks. A fixed-ratio schedule might be insurance salespeople who receive a bonus when the number of sales exceeds a million dollars worth for the year. Several types and examples are shown in Table 11.6

Another property of reinforcement is *when* the rewards are given. The closer in time the reward is to the behavior, the stronger the link between reward and performance, and the more likely the performance is to be repeated in the future.

Table 11.6: Different Types of Reinforcement Schedules

Name of Schedule	Explanation	Example
Fixed Interval	Rewards given at constant time periods	Paycheck
Variable Interval	Rewards given at varying time intervals	Praise after two days, then five, then one day
Fixed Ratio	Rewards given for fixed units of behavior	Commission
Variable Ratio	Rewards given for varying units of behavior	Praise for four reports completed, then two, then five

One of the problems with rewards administered on either a fixed time or behavior basis is that performance tends to decline following the receipt of rewards. "Blue Monday" is a term that refers to the Monday after Friday paydays. Absenteeism is higher on these days. College professors also observe a decline in attendance at the class after an exam. Variable schedules of reinforcement tend to be better at maintaining a more consistent level of performance. Verbal praise is best administered on a variable ratio schedule. Don't reward every incident and don't use consistent intervals. Behavior persists longer on variable schedules.

GOAL-SETTING THEORY

Somewhat like expectancy theory but in contrast to reinforcement theory, goal setting looks at the thought processes involved in motivation. Choices about goals drive action. Goal setting is based on a practical and thoroughly researched body of information.[9] Asking people to "do better" does not usually lead to change. When employees or students set specific, difficult goals, productivity and performance increases. In the planning chapter, SMART goals were described with specificity being an important characteristic. Specificity is important for motivation too.

Goals perform a number of functions in motivation. They *direct attention* and effort toward a specific end point. Goals also *energize* the employee and impact the amount of effort exerted. Similarly they affect *persistence,* or maintaining effort, in pursuit of an end point. Goals cause people to apply or *seek knowledge* related to the task. Thus they influence a search process to find better ways or strategies for performing.

How can managers apply goal-setting principles to improve motivation and performance? The first thing to do is encourage employees to set specific, challenging goals. This will focus their attention and energize them to persist in performing. Other goal-setting strategies are presented in Table 11.7. When goals are difficult, the level of commitment is an important factor. Involvement and participation in goal setting leads to more commitment as well. A public choice to pursue a goal also leads to greater perceived importance and commitment. Leadership (covered in the next chapter) can also inspire and develop commitment. Self-efficacy is task specific confidence. It is similar to E ➔ P in expectancy theory. Edwin Locke and Gary Latham note that employees with higher self-efficacy set more difficult goals and strive to find better task strategies for completing them. Training and confidence-building communication can increase self-efficacy.[10] Employees also need feedback about their progress toward the goals that they set. Feedback corrects performance and can build confidence. A final recommendation borrows from the reinforcement theory by suggesting rewards for goal accomplishment. Rewards build self-efficacy for the future and can lead to more challenging goals and higher performance.

Table 11.7: Goal-Setting Strategies for Managers

1. Encourage employees to set specific and challenging goals.

2. Develop commitment to the goals.

3. Raise self-efficacy.

4. Deliver feedback on goal progress.

5. Provide rewards for goal attainment.

EQUITY THEORY

The final theory of motivation, equity theory, is somewhat narrower in scope. Equity theory examines perceptions of fairness by making comparisons with others in the workplace. Fairness involves social comparisons. What is fair and equitable for us depends on a comparison with what others receive.

More specifically, equity theory proposes that inequity is motivating. Employees compare their **outputs** to what others receive. Joe may think that a 5 percent salary increase was good until he found out that Ellisha received 7 percent. Besides output, equity theory also looks at **inputs**. The inputs to a work situation may include effort, education, skill, and training. Outputs can be many different things besides money. Some are extrinsic, like pay, promotions, bonuses, or recognition plaques. There are also intrinsic or internal outputs, like satisfaction and a sense of achievement. To determine if a situation is equitable, employees compare their ratio of outputs to inputs (O/I) with those of others, typically coworkers. If their O/I is similar to the comparison person's O/I, then it is equitable and nothing happens. If, when making the comparison, the employee feels that the coworker received the same output but exerted far less effort, then there is a sense of inequity. That perception creates tension, which is the motivating force.

How do employees resolve the tension of inequity? The motivating force can direct them in a number of ways. They can adjust either output or input depending on the situation. In the example above, Joe may realize that Ellisha worked harder than he did and so he increases his efforts in the hopes of receiving a similar raise. This reaction would be likely if there are performance incentives in the pay system, so that working harder and performing at higher levels yields greater outputs. If Joe feels that Ellisha received a greater raise because of personal favoritism, Joe may talk to his supervisor about how the raise was calculated. If he feels that he cannot get a fair chance at pay raises, he may look for another job. In inequitable situations, employees may reduce inputs or try to increase outputs.

Table 11.8 illustrates several examples of resolving inequity. The choice of comparison person could also change. Joe may realize that Ellisha is an exceptional person and not relevant for him in comparing his O/I ratio. If he compares himself to another, then the raise may not be inequitable. Finally, equity perceptions influence turnover. An employee may begin searching for new job options if she perceives her current situation as inequitable. If any employee comes to a manager with equity concerns, the manager should take those comments seriously. A thorough explanation may help resolve the feelings of inequity. The employee may not have been aware of some of the circumstances surrounding the output. Equity theory is not very precise regarding what actions an employee will take. Nonetheless, these feelings of inequity or injustice should be recognized and addressed where feasible.

Table 11.8: Actions Taken to Resolve Perceived Inequity

Increase efforts to receive more outputs.

Decrease inputs (effort) and receive the same outputs.

Change your comparison person.

Change the situation, that is, find another job.

CONCLUSION

Four need-based approaches to motivation and four cognitive perspectives were presented. Individually, each has strengths and shortcomings. Taken together, they offer guidance to managers. Employees have different needs of which managers should be aware. They also make choices about situations, such as the effort they will exert and how long they will persist in performance. Specific goals and associated rewards (both positive and negative) impact performance as well as the likelihood that those same choices will be made in the future. A component of the motivational choices employees make is also dependent on comparisons with others in the workplace.

Chapter 11 Endnotes

1. Frederick Herzberg, "One More Time: How Do You Motivate Employees?" *Harvard Business Review* 46, no. 1 (1968): 53.

2. Richard M. Steers & Lyman W. Porter, *Motivation and Work Behavior* (3rd ed.) (New York: McGraw-Hill, 1975), 3–4.

3. E. E. Jones & K. E. Davis, "From Acts to Dispositions: The Attribution Process in Person Perception," in *Advances in Experimental Psychology* 2, L. Berkowitz (Ed.) (New York: Academic Press, 1965), 232.

4. Abraham H. Maslow, "A Theory of Human Motivation," *Psychological Review* 50, in *Classic Readings in Organizational Behavior* (2nd ed.), J. Steven Ott (Ed.) (Belmont, CA: Wadsworth Publishing, 1943), 45–56.

5. Ibid., 50.

6. Richard M. Steers & D. M. Braunstein, "A Behaviorally Based Measure of Manifest Needs in Work Settings," *Journal of Vocational Behavior* 9 (1976): 262.

7. Richard M. Steers & Lyman W. Porter, *Motivation and Work Behavior* (3rd ed.) (New York: McGraw-Hill, 1975), 44.

8. John Rauschenberger, Neal Schmitt, & John E. Hunter, "A Test of the Need Hierarch Concept by a Markov Model of Change in Need Strength" *Administrative Science Quarterly* 225, no. 4 (1980): 667.

9. Edwin A. Locke & Gary P. Latham, "Building a Practically Useful Theory of Goal Setting and Task Motivation," *American Psychologist* 57, no. 9 (2002, September): 705–717.

10. Ibid., 708.

CHAPTER 12

Making Teams Work

Chapter 12

MAKING TEAMS WORK

Ben was nearing the end of his bachelor's degree program. He had done well but had avoided group-oriented courses because he was worried that other members would not work hard and lower his grade. He saw the job posting (Figure 12.1) in his college's placement center: "Wanted: team members, no loners need apply." He squirmed a bit after reading the sign. How would recruiters view him? Although not usually stated in such stark and exclusive terms, companies today are seeking to hire workers who can function effectively in a team environment. Companies have developed core competencies and job specifications that now include team skills. The era of the individual performer is past. The focus of this chapter is the effective operation of teams and the skills required to be a good team member.

> **Position Openings:**
>
> Team members wanted, no loners need apply. Seeking business majors with good team skills for project assignments. Must be able to meet targets and coordinate with member of cross-functional team.

Figure 12.1: Job posting.

The workplace has come to expect team skills from individuals; however, teams do not work automatically. Many individuals have suffered through awful team sessions and meetings. Teams are now commonplace, but effective teams are not common. The promise of team potential is great, but the realization of the potential happens less frequently.

Why all the fervor over teams? Since chapter 1, the omnipresent role of change in business has been discussed. Adapting to external changes requires internal adjustments and coordination. No one individual has all of the information or perspectives necessary for adaptation. In addition, work is increasingly done in task forces and temporary, even virtual teams. Besides speed, agility, and adaptation, teams have the potential to be more innovative and productive.

To organize the material on groups and teams, we will return to the open systems approach that we used in chapter 3 to examine how organizations adapt to their environment. At a different level, groups operate as systems too. They obtain inputs from their environment, process them, and have outputs. What are the inputs? The **inputs** of groups are the individual members and the knowledge and information that they possess. Without capable members who possess information about customers, products, and services, groups would not be very useful. All things being equal, the better the skills of individuals, the better the results that they can achieve. Table 12.1 details these system features. Size is another input. A large group has greater difficulty in obtaining member ideas and even allowing all to speak.

Table 12.1: Group Inputs, Processes, and Outputs

Inputs	Processes	Outputs
Member skills	Stages of development	Productivity: Quantity and quality of work, timely delivery of results
Member information	Member roles: Task and socio-emotional	Member satisfaction
Size	Cohesiveness	Enhanced capabilities of team
	Group norms	Growth and development of members
	Minimizing process loss	

At the end of the group's activities, certain **outputs** or results should occur. The group will generate results. A report or set of recommendations is often expected. This work should be of high quality and sufficient quantity and be delivered by the established deadline. Members should be satisfied with the experience but should also be altered in some way by the experience. Every time people get together in groups there is opportunity for learning and development. The group should be better able to work together in the future. Members should develop greater team skills and acquire additional knowledge about the company that can help them in the future.

In order to achieve those results, certain processes need to occur within the group. Members need to engage in roles that encourage sharing and the effective use of information. Developing cohesiveness and the right norms can also aid group outputs. These topics will be further delineated later in the chapter.

Avoiding or minimizing process loss is another throughput that contributes to effective group results. Before explaining process loss, synergy must be described. **Synergy** is a principle best described as "the whole is greater than the sum of the parts." When creative people get together, the positive sparks can start to fly. Ideas are linked and something greater emerges. The collective ideas can be greater than the individuals working alone. Thus this synergy factor goes beyond individual abilities. Given this potential, group performance still falls short at times. The source of this shortcoming is often **process loss**. Dynamics within the group limit or prevent synergy. One example of process loss could be a dominant member who does not allow others to speak or who harshly criticizes initial ideas, causing members to refrain from speaking. The brilliant ideas or critical information held only by those persons is not shared and performance falls short of potential.

TYPES OF GROUPS

Many types of groups operate in the typical organization. As described in chapter 8 on organizing, teams are becoming one of the basic building blocks in organizing. Individuals who are permanently assigned to a team to do their work are members of a formal or **functional** team. If that team includes a supervisor, it may be called a **vertical** team, as it includes several vertical layers in the chain of command. Another organizing principle is coordination or integration. As organizations grow more complex, information is widely distributed. Key pieces of information need to be brought together and shared for sound decision-making. **Task forces**, or temporary teams for a specific purpose (sometimes also referred to as ad hoc groups), are coordinating devices. These temporary teams are often called **cross-functional** groups, as they are comprised of people from different areas in the organization, each with a unique perspective and different information about the problem. A cross-functional group with a permanent role is a **committee**. It meets regularly to share information and make decisions. Some groups never meet but instead interact electronically. These are called **virtual** groups and have members that are geographically distributed, often around the globe.

GROUP ROLES

What does it take for any of these groups to function optimally? Although members bring certain skills and information to the group, an effective group needs certain types of roles to be effective. You may have been in a group where everyone socialized or everyone was so task focused that battles erupted regularly. Which roles are best? Is there some happy medium? Two broad categories of roles are needed. One is termed **task-oriented** roles. Task roles address the **content** issues that the group is working on. It addresses questions of what are we to do and why. In these roles, members take the initiative to set up an agenda, ask questions, get members to share information, keep the group on target (i.e., focus or monitor), summarize what has been accomplished, clarify what others have said, and ask if the group is ready to decide (i.e., testing for consensus). Task roles are essential if results are to be achieved. For effective decisions, the information from different sources must be shared, processed, or weighed, and a sound conclusion reached that is consistent with the business interests of the firm, not the personal interests of members. Some additional task roles are presented in Table 12.2.[1]

Table 12.2: Group Roles for Effective Performance

Task-oriented Roles	Socio-emotional Roles	Self-oriented Roles
Initiator	Encourager	Dominator
Information seeker and sharer	Harmonizer	Approval seeker
Clarifier and elaborator	Compromiser	Blocker
Summarizer	Follower	Avoider
Focus monitor	Tension reducer	Jokester
Consensus tester		

The other major category of roles is termed **socio-emotional,** or maintenance, roles. These roles help maintain good relationships among members so work can be accomplished. Socio-emotional roles address the **process,** or how the group is working on its tasks. It is very helpful to have someone encourage quieter members to participate. Once people see that their ideas are accepted, they are more open and willing to share their views. Conflicts are inevitable in groups. At times someone may need to point out that two opinions are not that different. Tensions arise but conflicts need to be resolved. A timely joke can also help reduce tension. Similarly there are times when someone has to partially concede or compromise. It is also helpful when members follow and support ideas proposed by others. Some organizations appoint a process observer for every meeting. At the end, the process observer comments on how the group worked together and what socio-emotional roles are still needed.

No group can function well without both roles. The skilled group member knows when to engage in different roles. Each group may be different. In some groups there may be many task-oriented people, and so more socio-emotional roles are needed. In a different team, members may be too friendly and social, needing someone to focus them on the task and get things moving. Being able to "read" what is required in that context and at that point in time is a critical team skill. The process observer provides feedback to the group on its process.

Working groups go through phases of process and content. Some groups begin with process issues of how they will work together and then spend time on task or content issues. At some point process issues may arise again. Someone may ask, "Is our approach working?" "Should we adopt different procedures?" These process issues provide mid-course corrections and help develop the members as a working team. A feedback session provides an opportunity to discuss behaviors and roles that impede the progress or process of the group. New, more effective approaches can then be discussed and implemented.

Those undesired behaviors or roles are termed *self-oriented*. **Self-oriented roles** are sets of behaviors that members engage in at the expense of the group. The underlying cause is an emotional issue, related to the role of that person in the group. For example, the person may be concerned with his identity in the group. He or she wants to be viewed as competent and influential. As a result, he may try to dominate and not allow others to speak. A different person may be concerned about acceptance and feeling liked. She or he seeks approval and agrees too easily with others, praising ideas that are not sound. Another person may feel that the group cannot meet his or her goals. He or she hangs onto issues or ideas that are important to him or her—even long after the group has reached a decision and moved on. Others simply fail to engage other members and avoid discussions, disagreements, and controversies. Some roles involve taking a good idea too far. Each group needs some humor as part of socio-emotional maintenance, but the jokesters keep making humorous comments. Rather than help, these frequent attempts at humor divert the group from task accomplishment.

These self-oriented issues are natural during early phases of a group or during crises. When they arise, they need to be resolved so the group can be productive. Most groups experience self-oriented roles at some point. As stated earlier, feedback or a frank discussion about group process can identify these roles and find ways to address them.

GROUP STAGES

Just as all groups need certain roles to be effective, all groups go through specific stages. To become effective, groups need to develop and mature. Knowledge of the stages is important because different problems arise at each stage. These stages are predictable and most groups tend to experience them to one degree or another. They are described in Table 12.3.

The first stage is **forming**.[2] When groups begin, questions arise about purpose and if members will be able to attain it. Individual members are concerned with their role in the group. One potential problem at this early stage is member reluctance to criticize or speak out; cautiousness is common. Members expect the leader to bear responsibilities. To become more effective, the group needs to progress beyond this stage. Frequent interaction is important. Ice-breaker activities are common so that members get to know each other better and can feel more open about expressing concerns.

As groups continue to interact, differences among members become more salient. The group has entered the **storming** stage. Members notice that others seem to have slightly different agendas or goals. Some people knew each other before the group formed and naturally become a sub-group. Sub-groups talk more with each other and less with the group as a whole. Conflicts readily emerge. Due to these differences there is a tendency for some members to withdraw. Failure to interact stalls the group at this stage. The group needs to focus on process, discussing their differences and how to improve the way they work. Feedback and discussion are needed to advance to the next level. Some groups keep cycling through this stage because they have not resolved the underlying differences.

Table 12.3: Stages of Group Development

Stage	Group Issue	Leader Role
Forming	Orientation and purpose, dependence on leader	Encourage interaction, clarify purpose
Storming	Conflicts among sub-groups, counter dependence	Surface differences, continue interactions, problem solve
Norming	Order and acceptance of differences	Clarify roles and group norms
Performing	Cooperation, problem solving, shifting and sharing roles	Task accomplishment
Adjourning	Task completion	Bring closure and celebrate accomplishments

With differences acknowledged, a new sense of order emerges. Members realize that all will contribute in different ways. This is the **norming** stage. Norms about how the group will work and deal with members become clearer. Norms are informal guidelines for behavior. They are seldom openly discussed but nonetheless influence behavior. Norms develop about starting on time, preparation for meetings, and expectations about participation and leadership. Some norms are brought into the group from societal beliefs (i.e., like taking turns participating) or come from the corporate culture (e.g., quality is job number one). Others develop based on what members accept or question. Critical events and how they are handled also form the norms within the group. If members see undesirable behaviors at early stages, it is critical that these are challenged so the group can be more productive. Norming is the stage where things start to fall into place and task accomplishment becomes easier. It takes work to get to this stage, however.

The **performing** stage is a continuation and extension of some of the productive processes that develop in norming. In the norming stage some individuals assume fixed leadership or process roles. As the group matures, roles more readily shift and other members take on these roles as needed. Cooperation is easier as members do what is necessary to help the group, with less concern for self. The group, as it becomes comfortable with shifting roles, may also develop new and more productive ways of working on tasks. This stage represents the peak of performance and member satisfaction. New skills are also developed as roles are shared.

The final stage is **adjourning**. The work is completed but members need a sense of closure so they can comfortably move on to new assignments. The leader or senior management should praise accomplishments and explain how the work of the group will be used. A symbolic event such as a lunch or brief ceremony may be in order. A manager can never go wrong with sincere praise for good work.

COHESIVENESS AND GROUP NORMS

Another part of group process involves the development of cohesiveness and group norms. **Norms** are informal rules that guide behavior. Norms are most noticeable in novel situations. When we meet people for the first time, norms dictate how we act. In Western culture it is common to extend a hand for shaking and offer a greeting. If seated, business cards are often exchanged. These norms come from the society in which the group functions. Virtual groups that are global will be challenging because initial norms will come from different cultures, some potentially clashing. Explicit statements from leaders or members can also form norms. In global groups, the leader or team members may want to suggest some norms about meeting on-time or using emoticons (e.g., those computer faces made by keystrokes: (;-) —this one suggests a comment made in jest). Since virtual communication contains less information about context and emotions, emoticons add information that helps other members interpret what was typed. Norms also develop based on early events in the group's history. The first session sets the stage. If several members arrive late and unprepared and nothing happens, then norms may develop where timely arrival and preparation are not critical. Consequently it is important that members make conscious decisions about how they will respond to critical events. Responses to important events likewise influence the development of group norms.

Cohesiveness is a process factor that is not well understood by group members. It is often defined as the extent to which members are attracted and wish to remain with the group. Some might call it the glue or binding force in the group. Cohesiveness has been studied for many years in social psychology. Many assume that cohesiveness is a good thing—the more, the merrier. As an attraction force, cohesiveness influences group members. The more cohesiveness in a group, the greater is the impact of group pressures on members. Whether this force is positive or negative depends on the group's norms about performance. Some unions are very cohesive and influence members to keep production to a minimum (e.g., don't be a rate buster). The cohesiveness does not cause low productivity, but leads to pressure that results in more uniform productivity across members of the group. The level of performance is influenced by the norms. Some groups have high productivity norms. If they are also cohesive, then they will pressure members to also be productive. Groups with low levels of cohesiveness have more variable performance, as they are less likely to influence members regarding their norms for performance. The correlation between cohesiveness, norms, and group performance is illustrated in Table 12.4.

Table 12.4: Cohesiveness, Norms, and Group Performance

	Performance Norms	
Cohesiveness Level	Low Performance Norms	High Performance Norms
Low Cohesiveness	Low→Medium Performance	Moderate Performance
High Cohesiveness	Low Performance	High Performance

Knowing that group norms and cohesiveness influence productivity levels, should a manager want to increase cohesiveness? If she or he can influence productivity norms, then the answer is "Yes!" A manager then needs to know what influences cohesiveness. Based on research,[3] we know that the initial attraction of members to the group is influential. If the assignment to the group is viewed as prestigious or desirable, then members will have greater cohesiveness initially. Interactions also impact cohesiveness, as greater interactions lead to more positive feelings. As discussed under "stages," ice-breakers are designed to encourage interaction and build positive feelings. Groups where members have common values and attitudes are more likely to develop cohesiveness. Similarity leads to attraction. Groups that are diverse will have to work to develop common values. One aspect that can bring them together is a superordinate goal. Succeeding on the assignment may unite members, especially if the group was formed to address a crisis. A common enemy can also increase cohesiveness. Dictators, like former Iraqi leader Saddam Hussein, have used an external threat to unite a country. Finally, resolving member differences satisfactorily can also increase cohesiveness. Successful resolution of issues at the storming stage naturally leads to a more positive feeling about the group.

If a manager feels the group is too cohesive and has developed norms that restrict productivity, what can be done? The converse of cohesiveness-building steps represents possible tactics. More specifically, rearranging work so members have less opportunity to interact may decrease cohesiveness. Transferring members and introducing new, more diverse members may also lower cohesiveness. Failing at a task may also lower cohesiveness. In the process, the manager must avoid becoming the common enemy that unites the group against him or her.

REAL TEAMS OR PSEUDO-TEAMS?

The roles, stages, and application of cohesiveness information can have a positive impact on groups. Some groups of employees still never seem to develop into teams. Jon Katzenbach and Douglas Smith published a popular book in the 1990s that explored why some teams become great and others are only mediocre. In the *Wisdom of Teams*,[4] Katzenbach and Smith noted that although the potential for teams is high, few achieve the status of high-performing teams. Many groups of workers never become high performing teams. In studying a number of groups in a variety of organizations, they discovered that teams need several key components and must adhere to a series of principles to become successful.

The components of teams that they identified were similar to what we have termed group inputs. Teams need **skills**, **accountability**, and **commitment**. Members need to have technical, interpersonal, and problem solving skills to be effective. This recommendation is consistent with the prior knowledge of groups that we have discussed. Katzenbach and Smith suggest that many teams devote too much attention to skills; having the right mix and complement of skills is important.

Another key component is accountability. Members must hold each other accountable for a successful performance. The team must have the belief that "we" are a team. The boss or leader is not solely responsible. One principle that helps in developing accountability is keeping the size relatively small. Large groups make it easier to hide. Specific performance goals (i.e., similar to the objectives in chapter 6) also help to develop accountability among team members.

Commitment is the third component. Members must own or identify with the goals and intended results. Participation in the setting of specific performance goals helps build commitment. Some experts recommend developing a charter to build commitment. The charter identifies the purpose, inputs, targets, and milestones. Members commit to the charter and sign on. Members should also commit to a common method, or approach. The method should utilize member skills and address the targets. It should provide for interactions and updates over time. There should also be a commitment from senior management to support the group.

Collections of individuals can move along a performance curve from working group to pseudo-team to potential team to real team and finally to high-performance team, as described by Katzenbach and Smith. (see Table 12.5). One critical factor in progression is a significant need for incremental performance. The group needs a compelling reason to address and change performance targets. A working group lacks this quality. A pseudo-team has the need, but is not focused on collective performance or really trying to change. A potential team is trying, but is not clear about goals or approach. The distinction between real and high performing teams is subtle, much like that between the norming and performing stages of groups. Both are committed and accountable. The high performing teams seem to undergo a transformation whereby the team sets higher, stretch goals and members are more deeply committed to achieving them.

Table 12.5: Katzenbach and Smith's Categories of Groups and Teams

Type of Group/ Team	Need for Change?	Trying to Improve?	Focus on Team Performance?
Working Group	No	No	No
Pseudo-Team	Yes	No	No
Potential Team	Yes	Yes	No, needs greater clarity of goal and approach
Real Team	Yes	Yes	Yes
High Performing Team	Yes	Yes	Yes, more deeply committed

GROUPTHINK

While Katzenbach and Smith described some of the great successes of teams, another author described some great shortcomings of teams. In reviewing some major decisions, such as the Bay of Pigs Invasion and the Cuban Missile Crisis, Irving Janis[5] noticed that, in some instances, these presidential cabinet-level groups made very good decisions and in others, very poor ones. He termed the phenomena groupthink. Janis noted that groups who are very cohesive can reduce their ability to critically evaluate and use information. These failures lead to problems, among them NASA's decision to launch the *Challenger*, leading to loss of life and shuttlecraft.

Groups and teams should be aware of the symptoms of groupthink. When experiencing groupthink, groups have the **illusion of invulnerability**. They believe that they can do no wrong and are beyond criticism. They also tend to assume consensus prematurely with an **illusion of unanimity**. Others may have doubts but fail to raise them due to **self-censorship**. The group also believes in the **inherent morality** of the group; whatever the group does must be right. These symptoms tend to prevent critical information from being considered.

Another set of symptoms attack differing points of view when they are presented. Disconfirming data are **rationalized** away. Self-appointed **mindguards** emerge seeking to protect the group from dissenting viewpoints. If opposing views are presented, **direct pressure** is applied to these deviant positions. Those presenting alternative viewpoints may be **stereotyped** as evil, weak, or beneath the group (e.g., liberals, satanic foe, commie).

Teams and groups that make important, strategic decisions need to actively seek dissenting viewpoints. As President Bush began his second term in office, he appeared to have removed some dissenting voices from his cabinet. His team runs a greater risk of falling into the traps of groupthink.

To avoid the problems associated with groupthink, leaders can follow some suggestions. First, appoint a devil's advocate. Someone should take the other side and argue against the group's position. Outsiders to the group can also be brought in to review the positions. These steps will force consideration of alternate options. In presenting a proposal, the leader should do so impartially. President Kennedy was impartial when the Cuban Missile Crisis was presented; he took a clear stand in the Bay of Pigs Invasion. For key decisions, a second chance meeting can be scheduled several days later. After reflecting on a decision for a few days, doubts may surface that should be explored and reviewed.

Further recommendations for more effective teams are found in the decision-making chapter, under the heading of group decision-making. Brainstorming, nominal group techniques, and guidelines for meetings are useful topics to make groups more effective.

CONCLUSION

Groups are now pervasive in most organizations. Employees and managers need knowledge of group functioning to be effective. An open systems framework of inputs, throughputs, and outputs was presented. The focus of the chapter was on the throughput or group process issues. Groups need the proper balance of roles, cohesiveness, and norms. Knowledge of group stages is also helpful. The *Wisdom of Teams* showed that some process features are critical in getting groups to attain their peak performance. Finally, groupthink is a process loss that groups can avoid with the proper steps.

Chapter 12 Endnotes

1. K. D. Benne & P. Sheats, "Functional roles of group members," *Journal of Social Issues* 2 (1948): 45.

2. B. W. Tuckman & M. A. C. Jensen, "Stages of small-group development revisited," *Group & Organization Studies* 2, no. 4 (1977): 442.

3. B. Mullen & C. Cooper, "The relation between group cohesiveness and performance: An integration," *Psychological Bulletin* 115 (1994): 210–227.

4. Jon R. Katzenbach & Douglas K. Smith, *The Wisdom of Teams* (Boston, MA: Harvard Business Press, 1993), 92.

5. Irving L. Janis, *Groupthink: Psychological Studies of Policy Decisions and Disasters* (2nd ed.) (Boston: Houghton-Mifflin, 1982).

CHAPTER 13

Leadership

Chapter 13

LEADERSHIP

The concept of leadership is somewhat like quality; people know it when they see it but cannot always describe it. A list of leaders may include heads of state, successful athletic coaches, military officers, managers, and even teachers. Leaders are expected to inspire and motivate others. The bigger question is, Who can become leaders and how? This chapter will describe a number of different approaches to leadership. Much has been written on the topic, but real leadership is often missing in organizations. The concepts in this chapter will attempt to reduce the gap between the rhetoric and the results.

What is leadership? **Leadership** is a set of behaviors that inspire and direct employees in the performance of their tasks. Leaders are able to articulate a vision of where individuals and the organization should be heading. Leaders direct and encourage individual employees regarding how they are to reach those endpoints. These activities embody the leading function of management. Leaders also identify and remove impediments to task accomplishment, enabling employees to reach higher levels of performance. Leadership can be performed by any person, at any level. Senior management has greater responsibilities and potential rewards to be leaders, but even non-supervisory employees and team members can be leaders.

EARLY APPROACHES

Initial approaches to leadership believed that some individuals were predisposed to lead. They were born with the ability, not made. This became known as the "Great Man" theory, as most leaders at that time were men. Napoleon and Julius Caesar illustrate this perspective. However, no role was given to choice or development with this view of leadership. You either had it or you didn't. You were meant to be a leader at that point in time, also referred to as *Zeitgeist*, the German word meaning spirit of the times. The robber barons of the 19th century, John D. Rockefeller, J.P. Morgan, Cornelius Vanderbilt, and Andrew Carnegie, were viewed in this way, as were Franklin D. Roosevelt and Winston Churchill. It was presumed that the skills that these people possessed fit the times in which they ran organizations. Churchill demonstrated this best, as he possessed leader qualities that made him a great war-time leader, but less effective in peacetime.

TRAITS

A subsequent approach examined the qualities or traits of leaders. The sense was that if a list of traits could be identified, then persons with these traits could be found and put in leadership positions. The focus was on the qualities that leaders possessed or exhibited. Leaders obviously had cognitive abilities such as intelligence and creativity. Other traits found to be associated with leaders included decisiveness, self-confidence, independence, integrity, cooperativeness, and high energy. No universal set of traits was found in all leaders. Traits can be viewed as a precondition for leadership.[1] Having certain traits may predispose or give to individuals the qualities that will help them lead; it does not make them leaders. Kirkpatrick and Locke revisited the topic of leadership traits, finding that drive (e.g., ambition, energy initiative), leadership motivation (i.e., desire to lead), honesty and integrity, self-confidence, cognitive ability, and knowledge of the business remain important qualities.[2]

LEADER BEHAVIORS

Focusing on traits presents problems for trainers and teachers. Traits are difficult to teach and not always easy to identify. During the 1960s and 1970s the field of psychology was focused on behaviors. Behavioral psychology was also applied to organizational leadership. Researchers sought to identify the key behaviors that were involved in success so that these behaviors could then be taught to others.

The earliest research was conducted in Iowa by Kurt Lewin and his associates.[3] He examined autocratic, democratic, and laissez-faire leadership styles in groups. They found that groups performed well with autocratic leaders, but only when the leader was present. Democratic groups performed almost as well and the leader did not need to be present. Members liked democratic leaders better than autocratic ones. Laissez-faire leaders did very little; performance and satisfaction was lowest here. Thus, this early research suggested that specific behaviors, rather than just traits, could impact performance

At the University of Michigan, leader behavior in organizations was examined along a single dimension, from **job-centered** to **employee-centered** approaches. They examined effective and ineffective leaders. Managers who were rated as more effective were more likely to use employee-centered styles and behaviors, while less effective managers used job-centered behaviors. The job-centered focus on efficiency, meeting schedules, and task accomplishment proved less effective.

Ohio State University researchers approached leadership behavior in a slightly different way. They conceptualized leadership as two independent dimensions. Rather than being either job/task or employee/relations oriented, the leader could be high or low on each dimension independently. The task related portion was termed **initiation of structure**. Leaders set goals, defined reporting relationships, and told workers what to do to obtain those results. The second dimension was termed **consideration**. It involved listening to workers, being supportive, and encouraging them. These two dimensions still run through many approaches to leadership. The Ohio State University research found that high initiation of structure and high consideration yielded the best performance and highest subordinate satisfaction.

Robert Blake and Jane Mouton popularized and applied the work done at Ohio State University using what they termed a managerial grid[4] (see Figure 13.1). They arranged the two dimensions on a 9-point scale and plotted a number of styles in this grid. The impoverished leadership style is low on both production, or task, and concern for people. The leader does little to encourage work completion or to satisfy individual needs. The country club leadership style puts an emphasis on concern for people and creating an environment that satisfies worker needs. The task master leadership style sets clear direction for task completion, minimizing human aspects. The style that was high on both concerns for production and people was the team leadership style. They described another style as middle-of-the-road leadership (5,5), displaying a moderate amount of both task and people focus. Blake and Mouton offered leader training and workshops that emphasized the team style as best. Managers in these workshops had their styles assessed and practiced activities to become more team oriented.

		Concern for Production	
		Low	High
Concern for People	High	1,9: Country Club 5,5: Middle-of-the-Road	9,9: Team
	Low	1,1: Impoverished	9,1: Task Master

Figure 13.1: Managerial grid leadership.

SITUATIONAL APPROACHES TO LEADERSHIP

The drawback to both the trait and the managerial grid approaches was that the *situation* was ignored. Specific traits or behaviors were stressed as best, regardless of the situation. A situational approach to leadership assumes that one style or dimension is not universally successful across all conditions. A match between style, or behavior, and the characteristics of the situation determines optimal effectiveness. Several different models or theories of situational leadership will be covered. Each has two components. First, each specifies the style, or behaviors, that the leader should use. Second, each provides a set of guidelines for interpreting the situation to determine what style should be used in that situation. Three popular situational perspectives will be reviewed: Fiedler's contingency theory of leadership, Hersey-Blanchard's life cycle theory, and House's path-goal theory.

FIEDLER'S CONTINGENCY THEORY

Fiedler was the first to describe a situational, or contingency, approach. He began by asking subordinates to identify adjectives that described the qualities of their **least preferred coworker**, termed LPC. Some workers described their least preferred coworker as someone who was lazy and did not complete assignments. Others described their least preferred coworker in more positive terms that were related to human qualities, such as warmth and support. Over time Fiedler modified his approach to categorize the low LPC manager as task-motivated. He or she was motivated by task elements, such as work completion, attention to detail, and developing competence in subordinates. The high LPC manager was motivated by relationships. He or she focused on the people and building relationships, getting bored with task details. Thus his two categories are similar to the two dimensions of task and relationship.

The real contribution of Fiedler was to describe components of the situation that matched differences in leader style or motivation. He identified three situational components in decreasing order of importance: leader-follower relations, the amount of structure in the task, and the position power of the leader. With good **leader relations**, subordinates are willing to trust and follow the leader. The amount of **task structure** relates to whether the tasks performed by the group are defined and clear—the more options or uncertainty regarding how to complete the task, the less task structure in that situation. Finally, **position power** involves formal authority and the ability to reward, punish, and fire. Situations can be assessed on each of these three components and can be classified as high or low, yielding eight possible situations.

Overall these situations can be ranked in terms of favorability to the manager. Situations where the manager has good relations with the group, the task is structured, and she or he has strong position power are obviously very favorable. At the opposite end, poor relations, unstructured tasks, and weak power results in a very unfavorable situation. The full range of situation combinations are presented in Table 13.1. Those situational features in the middle of the figure (i.e., those that are shaded in gray) have medium or moderate favorability. In these moderate situations, a high LPC or relationships-motivated leadership style fits best. In situational combinations that yield very high or very low favorability, Fielder found that the low LPC or task-motivated style was best.

Table 13.1: Fiedler's Situations and Leadership Style Matches

Situational Dimensions	Situational Combinations and Leader Fit							
Leader-member relations	Good	Good	Good	Good	Poor	Poor	Poor	Poor
Task structure	High	High	Low	Low	High	High	Low	Low
Position power	Strong	Weak	Strong	Weak	Strong	Weak	Strong	Weak
Favorability	High	High	High	Medium	Medium	Medium	Low	Low
Leadership style	Task	Task	Task	Relations	Relations	Relations	Task	Task

Practically, these match-ups make sense. Where the leader gets along, has high power, and the task is fairly determined, a participative or very supportive style is not needed. Just get on with the work. Similarly in hostile situations, attempts to be supportive may be rebuffed or viewed as insincere. The leader needs to be more supportive in situations where the manager cannot command and yet needs some degree of subordinate involvement and cooperation.

There are several drawbacks to Fiedler's model. First, his LPC approach is really a trait-based approach to leadership. As a trait, the leader does not change from low LPC to high LPC. If the situation changes, a new leader must be assigned so the fit between style and situational favorability is good. This reassignment is not practical. Given the problems with Fiedler's trait-like approach to situational leadership, we turn to behavioral applications.

HERSEY-BLANCHARD'S LIFE CYCLE OR SITUATIONAL THEORY

Paul Hersey and Ken Blanchard were doctoral students at Ohio State University. They adapted OSU's dimensions and developed a situational component. They called their approach the life cycle model, as it takes employees through a cycle of development. Think about a new employee beginning to work for a supervisor; at first they do not know how to perform the tasks, they may not be able to set high standards of performance, and they may not be motivated to perform at high levels. Hence the manager cannot delegate in a very general way. Assignment must be direct and explicit. Sound familiar? This is a high-task or directive style.

They conceptualized the situation in terms of subordinate **readiness**. How ready is the subordinate for delegation? The manager's job is to develop the subordinate so tasks can be delegated in a simple and general way. Hersey and Blanchard identified three aspects of readiness:

- Education or experience level. Employees with extensive experience or formal education already know many features of the task and do not need specific direction.

- Confidence

- Motivation or willingness to assume responsibility

Subordinates with low levels of readiness need much more detailed direction. Hersey and Blanchard's first leader behavior was termed directing. Each style was also given a number. Directing is S_1 as it is the first step in the life cycle. The directing style is high in task but low in relationships behavior. It is matched with a low readiness level, or R_1. Hersey and Blanchard suggest that the readiness number should match the style number. The greater the difference between the style and readiness number, the less effective that style will be in that situation.

As the subordinate learns more about the job and gains some confidence, the manager can reduce the level of detail in task behavior to a degree. The manager also begins to use more relationship behaviors. Task is one-way communication, telling the subordinate how to perform the task. Relationship behaviors are more two-way in nature. The manager asks questions, encourages, and supports. This second style of task behaviors, selling (S_2), involves both high task and high relations. It matches a level two of readiness (R_2), moderately low. The arrow and dotted line in Figure 13.2 illustrates matching readiness and leadership style.

Leadership Style		Task Behaviors	
		Low	High
Relations Behaviors	High	S_3: Participating	S_2: Selling
	Low	S_4: Delegating	S_1: Directing
Readiness		R_4	R_3	R_2	R_1
		High Readiness	Medium High Readiness	Medium Low Readiness	Low Readiness
Level		Able, willing, confident	Able, but unwilling or insecure	Unable, but willing or confident	Unable, unwilling, insecure

Figure 13.2: Hersey-Blanchard's life cycle theory of leadership.

As subordinates continue to develop, they become willing to do more and set higher standards of performance. They know the job (are able), but still need encouragement to do the best possible job. The task level of leadership (S_3) has become low, not non-existent, and relations remain high. This third style (R_3) matches a moderately high level of readiness, able and moderately willing.

The mature employee has the knowledge, the confidence to set high, challenging goals, and the willingness to accept full responsibility. With level four readiness (R_3), the appropriate leadership style is delegating, or S_3. The delegating style is low in task and relationships. A mature employee does not need much task guidance or encouragement. Both dimensions are low, but not at a zero level. The manager can tell the employee what is needed and when it is due and further details are not needed.

Hersey and Blanchard put several qualifications on their theory. One is that readiness is specific to tasks; it is not universally applied. A subordinate can be ready for delegation on one task but not on another. The sales manager has a subordinate who is a great salesperson in terms of negotiating with customers. The manager can use an S_3 style for sales, but the salesperson is poor at documentation and follow-up with manufacturing. A lower level of readiness may dictate a selling style (S_2) on this task. Readiness and maturity are also dynamic or changing. A subordinate may have a spouse who died or is undergoing cancer treatments. He is preoccupied with these personal matters and not operating at as high a readiness level as usual. The manager may need to step down from the delegating style (S_3) to the participating style (S_3), providing more encouragement and support. Changes in the job can also reduce readiness levels. New technology may require a manager to return to an S_1 to tell the employee how to use the technology and what standards to set.

Of all of the situational leadership models, life cycle has been taught more in workshops. Managers are typically given questionnaires to assess their leadership style. Most have a dominant and back-up style. Usually these styles represent a row or column in Figure 13.2. For example, some managers use a participative style (high relationships, low task) as primary and selling (high task, high relationship) as back-up. This combination of styles is reflected in the top row. Then managers learn how to determine readiness and adjust her or his style. This model is easiest to understand how to match the style (S) and the situation (R). However, of all of the models, it has had the least research. Researchers have not proven that going from style S_1 to S_2 and on through the cycle to S_3 is best.

HOUSE'S PATH-GOAL THEORY

In contrast, Robert House's path-goal theory has been researched more extensively. Perhaps one reason for more research is that the path-goal theory is tied to another popular theory, the expectancy theory of motivation. Expectancy theory bases motivation on the confidence to exert effort (expectancy), followed by valued outcomes or rewards (instrumentality and valued outcomes). Satisfaction is linked to rewarded performance. Path-goal theory views the manager's job as helping the subordinate to perform, receive rewards, and be satisfied. The manager identifies the paths to performance and strives to see that good performance is rewarded.

Path-goal specifies four types of leader behavior. The **directive** style is much like the task styles of Fiedler and Hersey-Blanchard. The manager tells the subordinate how to perform, specifying steps with details on how to accomplish them. A **supportive** style is similarly related to relationships-motivated behavior. The manager asks questions and encourages the subordinate. House added two additional styles. **Achievement** behavior helps subordinates set higher, more challenging goals. It stretches or pushes them to do their best. You might comment that this is a type of task related behavior, but it has a very specific focus and therefore merits its own label. The fourth style is **participative**. This style involves subordinates in decision-making, asking for their input and involvement. It is similar to S_3 in the life cycle model.

There are two broad categories of issues that influence what style should be used in a particular situation. As with life cycle theory, **subordinate characteristics** are also important in the path-goal theory. The ability, skill levels, needs, and motivations impact the choice of leadership style. Lower skilled employees need more directive behaviors; employees whose performance is below expectations require achievement leadership style. The other category of situational factors is the **work environment**. This category is similar to Fiedler's task structure. The amount of structure in the task itself influences directive behaviors. One additional research finding is worth noting here. When the tasks are boring and repetitious, research has found that a supportive leadership style increases worker satisfaction (although not performance). The amount of formal authority is another component that is similar to Fiedler. A third aspect of the work environment is the work group. Relationships among members and their education level may allow a manager to use different styles. With good relationships and high education, a manager may not be as necessary.

Research has tended to support the path-goal theory in general. The weakness is that it does not provide precise match-ups of situations and styles as the life cycle theory does. Nonetheless, these three situational or contingency theories, taken together, provide managers with guidelines on how to adjust the styles of leadership that are used in different situations. Managers should have as many tools as possible to guide their actions. Find one that works for you or use multiple perspectives for guidance.

OTHER APPROACHES TO LEADERSHIP

Although the three contingency approaches to leadership that we just discussed are the mainstays in the field of management, a number of newer perspectives that have developed bear examination. Most of these perspectives focus on a more specific aspect of leadership.

DERAILED EXECUTIVES

Prior approaches specified activities and steps that managers perform to lead. Another approach is to examine problem areas. The Center for Creative

Leadership (CCL), one of the nation's leading institutions in the study, training, and coaching of leaders, has tracked a number of factors that cause executives to derail or experience career problems. Many of these managers were presumed to be potential stars but suddenly stalled in their careers. Why?

Researchers at the CCL identified four factors most commonly causing derailment.[5] One of the most commonly cited reasons was poor interpersonal relationships. Some managers were good strategic thinkers but were harsh and demanding of others. Two-thirds of derailed European managers had interpersonal problems. Being isolated, cold, arrogant, and aloof were other aspects of interpersonal skills cited for derailment.

Another problem area was failure to meet business objectives. Managers are expected to deliver. Like athletic coaches, if they don't meet performance expectations, they are demoted or forced out. Some managers brought the problem on themselves. They promised and over-promoted their success potential and then did not deliver.

A third cause of problems was the inability to build and lead a team. Some were strong individual performers whose assertiveness and personal initiative got them on the fast track. At some level, managers need to develop others and not do it all themselves. Building human capital and developing talent is important in today's knowledge work environment.

The fourth problem area was the inability to change and adapt to new conditions. Change drives the world of business and managers must become adept at adjusting to it. Furthermore they must be able to lead others in adjusting to new conditions. Being able to change and overcome set-backs is a key skill that today's managers need.

The Center for Creative Leadership offers recommendations for avoiding derailment. They include:[6]

- Identify those with whom you want to improve relationships. Develop an action plan for each person.

- Display empathy toward others. Take their feelings into account.

- Learn to listen. Ask questions to be sure that you understand. Repeat what was said to ensure comprehension.

- Collaborate with others. Share information and explain the reasons for decisions.

- Change and develop. Identify areas for personal change. Seek feedback from others and develop a plan to make it happen.

EMOTIONAL INTELLIGENCE AND LEADERSHIP

Research at the CCL pointed heavily at people issues as the main causes for career problems, rather than technical competencies. A similar notion is that a person's intelligence about emotional issues is likewise critical. Daniel Goleman popularized the concept of emotional intelligence. He also stressed that successful leaders also demonstrate emotional awareness.[7] The conventional type of cognitive intelligence was identified as a trait in early leadership research. Yet some people with this type of intelligence have difficulty successfully performing in organizations. At the same time, others with lower IQ scores can be quite successful in life. A different type of intelligence may account for these differences. Emotional intelligence (EIQ) is a type of social intelligence. It involves self-awareness and the ability to use emotions in influencing others. People with high EIQ are able to read situations well and act appropriately, being aware of their own emotions.

Goleman identified five areas where emotional intelligence is important for leaders. They need to know their own emotions first. Leaders have **self-awareness** and are in touch with their internal states. Moods are monitored. Beyond awareness, a second aspect of EIQ is leaders' **control or regulation of emotions**. They project a positive outlook and deal with negative emotions that arise. It is not that leaders never get angry. Sometimes an emotional outburst shows interest and compassion. Leaders with high EIQ do not get so angry that they say things that they regret. They do not humiliate subordinates.

Earlier, the drive of leaders was noted as an important trait. Their passion is an emotional quality that **motivates** them and others to achieve goals. As the CCL recommended, Goleman also stressed that leaders with high EIQ are also able to understand others. A fourth dimension of EIQ involves leaders' **empathy** for subordinates' problems and emotions. They realize that people are different and are able to respond according to their emotional needs. Finally, leaders use emotional skills to **influence others**. This fifth dimension of EIQ recognizes that leaders can be persuasive by using emotional arguments. They build trust and overcome the emotional barriers that undermine change. Being able to develop common ground requires an understanding of the other party's interests and needs. These social skills are also part of EIQ.

BASES OF POWER

Managers also need power to lead and influence. **Power** is the ability to get others to do things. Power can come from four different sources or bases. The traditional form of authority is derived from **legitimate** power. Subordinates believe that managers have the right to make certain requests of them. Back in chapter 2 Chester Barnard noted that this perception of legitimacy only applies to a certain zone of acceptance. The use of legitimate power must be viewed as appropriate to work. Managers have also historically used coercive power. **Coercive** power uses threats of punishment to get subordinates to do things. They can be threatened with firing or reassignment to less desirable position. Coercive power must be used sparingly. No one likes threats and it should only be a means of last resort. Another source of power for managers is expertise. **Expert** power is derived from knowledge and information. Managers have the skills and know-how acquired through years of experience. They may also have information from meetings. Subordinates accept influence from those with expert power because they believe that manager can help them with their job. A final source of power is called referent power. **Referent** power is effective because subordinates identify with managers and want to be like them. Some may also call those with referent power charismatic. Martin Luther King, Jr., and John F. Kennedy had charisma and used referent power to influence others.

A manager should try to develop as many bases of power as possible. They should have expertise because they know their job well. They should use coercive and legitimate power sources sparingly. Finally, it is good to develop liking and respect among subordinates so that referent power can also be used.

CHARISMATIC AND TRANSFORMATIONAL LEADERSHIP

A quality that is often used to describe some leaders is charisma. This is a special quality that attracts people to dynamic leaders. Martin Luther King, Jr., was a charismatic leader, as was John F. Kennedy. What specific thing made them charismatic? Can managers become charismatic?

One of the first things to understand is that charisma is not based on formal authority; it is derived from the personal qualities of the leader. Subordinates trust and believe in charismatic leaders. They are willing to give up personal interests for the greater good of the organization. An emotional bond is created that motivates subordinates to follow and perform. The next question is then, "How does one develop the trust?"

Charismatic leaders frequently have a different vision of the future.[8] Charismatic leaders are able to articulate some future state that is very appealing to followers. This future state is different from the present but still possible. Martin Luther King, Jr.'s "I have a dream" speech is one example. It is more than a goal; it is an inspiring goal that appeals to the needs and attitudes of subordinates. Charismatic leaders articulate emotionally appealing stretch goals. The vision causes subordinates to alter their view of the future and what is possible.

Bernard Bass termed this process transformational leadership.[9] The leader transforms subordinates into believing that they can attain the vision. This is a powerful motivational tool. Some argue that there is too much managing and too little visioning. Transformational leaders create an appealing end state and involve the employees in determining how best to get there. They do not describe steps or closely monitor progress. Transformational leadership is qualitatively different. Transactional leaders are more conventional. They use management principles to get things done but do not stretch employees to higher levels than they originally believed possible.

Transformational leaders utilize three sets of activities to bring about this change.[10] First they inspire with a vision. The vision creates an emotional bond. The vision must be articulated in an appealing way and other communication must support and sustain it. The transformational leader provides intellectual stimulation for followers. The status quo is challenged. Employees are prodded to be creative and find new solutions. Finally, the charismatic leader uses individual consideration. He or she makes people feel special; they are given attention and treated fairly. Emotional intelligence also underlies this style.

GENDER DIFFERENCES IN LEADERSHIP

In looking at diverse approaches to leadership, we have found that different styles can be effective. Men and women often have different outlooks. Do they use different leadership styles?

Stereotypes suggest that women are more nurturing and would therefore use more relationship-oriented styles, while men would be more concerned with task accomplishment. Although research is not complete, a review of many studies found that this stereotype did not hold up.[11] Women were not different from men in the use of interpersonal styles; however, women did tend to use more participative and democratic styles and less autocratic and directive styles than men. Given that women tend to focus more on empowering others, they may be better at transformational leadership too. More research needs to be done, but it is good to see that some stereotypes no longer persist.

CONCLUSION

Multiple perspectives and authors converge on the notion that leadership involves communication related to task accomplishment and toward establishing and maintaining relationships. The three contingency approaches of Fiedler, Hersey-Blanchard, and House all employ these dimensions. The best-fitting style is influenced by characteristics of the subordinate and characteristics of the tasks performed. Newer approaches find additional means of inspiring followers to reach for higher levels of performance. Some differences were found between female and male leaders, but the differences are not as great as the stereotypes imply. Leadership continues to be an important management process in all organizations.

Chapter 13 Endnotes

1. Shelley A. Kirkpatrick & Edwin A. Locke, "Leadership: Do Traits Really Matter?" *Academy of Management Executive* 5, no. 2, (1991): 48–60.

2. Ibid., 49.

3. Kurt R. Lewin, Ronald Lippit, & Robert K. White, "Patterns of aggressive behavior in experimentally created social climate," *Journal of Social Psychology* 10 (1939): 271–301.

4. Robert R. Blake & Jane L. Mouton, *The New Managerial Grid* (Houston, TX: Gulf, 1978), 11.

5. Ellen Van Velsor & Jean Brittain Leslie, "Why Executives Derail: Perspectives Across Time and Cultures," *Academy of Management Executive* 9, no. 4 (1995): 69.

6. Craig Chappleow & Jean Brittain Leslie, "Throwing the Right Switches: How to Keep Your Executive Career on Track," *Academy of Management Executive* 20, no. 6 (2001): 7.

7. Daniel Goleman, "What Makes a Leader?" *Harvard Business Review* (1998, November-December): 90–103.

8. Jay A. Conger & Rabindra N. Kanungo, "Toward a Behavior Theory of Charismatic Leadership in Organizational Settings," *Academy of Management Review* 12, no. 4 (1987): 640.

9. Bernard M. Bass, *Leadership and Performance Beyond Expectations* (New York: Free Press, 1985).

10. Afsaneh Nahavandi, *The Art and Science of Leadership* (2nd ed.) (Upper Saddle River, NJ: Prentice-Hall, 2000), 186.

11. Eagly, A. H. & Johnson, B. T., "Gender and Leadership style: A Meta-analysis," *Psychological Bulletin* 108, no. 2 (1990): 233.

CHAPTER 14

Conflict, Change, and Communication

Chapter 14

CONFLICT, CHANGE, AND COMMUNICATION

The final chapter covers several additional topics related to the leading function. Managers need to be proficient in these skills in order to accomplish goals. Perhaps these skills are most critical for senior management. In the leadership chapter, change and communication were both mentioned as management activities related to transformational leadership. This chapter will present additional concepts and applications related to these activities. Conflict is similarly important because differences and disagreements naturally occur. How differences are managed and disputes resolved influences effectiveness. Thus this chapter covers higher-level management skills from the leading function.

CONFLICT

DEFINITION

Authors have noted that early definitions of conflict were value-laden, implying that something went wrong when conflict emerged, such as March and Simon's "breakdown in standard mechanisms of decision making."[1] Contrast this early definition with Ken Thomas's "perception that someone has or is about to frustrate some concern of yours."[2] Thomas approaches conflict as something that happens without any implication of error or problem. It is a process without values.

There are several important elements of Thomas's definition. First it involves perception. It doesn't matter if someone is paranoid or if they are actually out to get you. You perceive and feel it the same. Conflict results either way. Managers need to accomplish goals. When those goals are blocked or frustrated, negative emotions are generated. The frustration can arise because another manager has attempted to lure a good employee from your unit. Not having that person in your unit means that you may not reach assigned targets. The frustration can also arise from a subordinate who goes to your superior with a problem without coming to you first. Violating the chain of command makes you look bad to your superior, again blocking attainment of future goals.

The contemporary perspective is that conflict happens as a natural by-product of human interaction. A survey of managers found that all levels average about 20 percent of the time in dealing with conflict, more at lower levels.[3] This finding supports the notion in the prior paragraph that conflict is not a symptom of something gone very wrong in a company, but something to be recognized and dealt with.

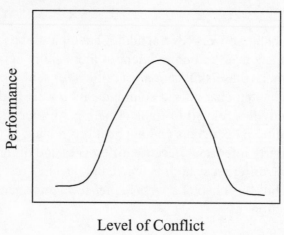

Figure 14.1: Relationship between conflict and performance.

You could then ask if conflict is good or bad for the organization. The relationship between conflict and performance is generally acknowledged to be a bell-shaped curve, as shown in Figure 14.1. Moderate levels of conflict are best in terms of the impact on performance. There should be some tension about goals and the best way to reach them. If there is too little conflict evident, then differences of opinion are likely being suppressed. Perhaps groupthink is operating or employees are fearful of the manager. Without dissent, bad ideas are implemented. At the other extreme, when conflict is very high, people are angry and often retaliate causing additional problems. In high conflict conditions, people withhold information and may act out to sabotage the other party. Their intense feelings consume them, limiting their productivity and often causing them to spend too much time saying negative things to others about that party. In short, high levels of conflict are costly in terms of dollars, productivity, and damaged relationships (i.e., the ability to work productively together in the future).

STAGES OF CONFLICT

Conflict often goes through several stages.[4] The first stage is labeled **latent** conflict. Something has happened but the employee has not yet perceived it. Unless the person finds out, there is no conflict for them, so it is termed *latent*. The second stage is **perceived** conflict. This stage represents a cognitive or "cooler" element of conflict. The person is aware that his or her goals are blocked or potentially blocked by someone's action. It could trigger an attempt to understand the other person's actions and explain why it happened. Did the person make a casual mistake or did they intentionally try to do something? Research has found that when conflicts result from intentional acts, people react more strongly. The next stage could be delayed or nearly simultaneous. **Felt** conflict is the "hot" or strong emotional response. Anger and hostility can result. Not all conflicts lead to strong emotions but they often do. The fourth stage is **manifest** conflict. With awareness and feelings, actions occur. The person experiencing the conflict takes some action and the other person often responds in kind. What follows is the conflict **aftermath**. With many conflicts the aftermath sows the seeds for future conflicts. This cycle of actions can cause the conflict to spiral upward, leading to more consequential and costly actions.

STYLES OF HANDLING CONFLICT

Recognizing conflict at earlier stages and preventing retaliation cycles can reduce some of the costs and negative consequences of conflict. The perceived definition that was related to blocked goals can also be interpreted as turf violations. Someone invades your turf, blocking your ability to accomplish goals. People respond differently in turf violation or conflict situations. Response tendencies can be primitive, going back a long way into our evolutionary past. For thousands of years people have either run away or confronted and fought the source of the conflict. This "fight or flight" response is thus deeply ingrained.

More recent approaches to conflict have suggested that the styles of responding to conflict vary along two dimensions,[5] much like leadership behavior. One dimension is concern for self, the vertical dimension in Figure 14.2. The aggressive response of fighting back is an attempt to seek resources of interest to you. This high concern for self has been termed a **competitor** style. Individuals act in their own self-interest without concern for the interests of the other party. An alternative response, the horizontal dimension in Figure 14.2, is to acquiesce to the other party or show concern for their interests without regard to one's own. This acquiescing style is termed **accommodator**. The person accommodates the interests of the other party without concern for self. Accommodation is not fleeing, however. A style that shows no concern for self or the other party's interests is called **avoidance**, low on both self- and other-interest seeking. Avoidance is closer to running away as accommodation has the effect of building social credits for the future.

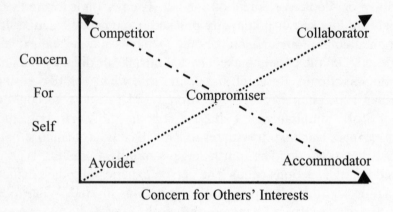

Figure 14.2: Styles for resolving conflict.

You may be tempted to argue that none of these three styles is good, but in fact they can all be effective in the right circumstances. Someone may accommodate another person's interests if the issue is of low importance to them and they seek to build good will in the relationship. Even avoidance can be suitable if you are cornered at a bad moment without facts. Avoidance is a temporary postponement of the discussion; rather than risk a bad outcome in the present, put it off.

Two additional styles remain. One is a **compromiser**. What happens when the two people in the conflict both use a competitor style? They either reach a stalemate or the stronger person wins. When parties of equal power are both competitive, they both may have to concede something in order to resolve the problem. The compromising style involves partial satisfaction of interests. At the same time, your concerns are partially satisfied and those of the other are partially met. Neither is content with the outcome, as each partially meets his or her concerns and partially meets those of the other party. This splitting of interests may be the only way to reach resolution.

Competitors tend to either win or compromise. They rely too exclusively on the competitive style. They have a difficult time recognizing the other party's interests. In negotiations this tendency is called a fixed-pie perception. They feel that they must attack first or be taken advantage of. They mistakenly see concession as weak and soft.

There is another, sometimes better, alternative. **Collaboration** is both high on self-interest and also meets the other party's interests. How is this possible? It is not always feasible, but could be used more often than it is. In disputes or conflicts people tend to express their differences as a position. It is hard to collaborate when individuals stick with positions that are often incompatible. Underlying those positions are interests. If the parties can build enough trust so that they share interests, then the conflict can be redefined in terms that may allow mutual satisfaction. Positions create obstacles or "boulders in the road,"[6] as one author calls it. To overcome the obstacle it is necessary to redefine the position in terms of interests. If parties stay focused on interests, then mutual agreement is possible. Once the problem is redefined, then both parties can brainstorm options and select the most mutually satisfying one.

In addition to these five styles, observe the two diagonals in Figure 14.2. The dotted line goes up and to the right. This line represents an integrative dimension. As the approach or style to resolving conflict goes up and to the right, both parties' interests are incorporated to a greater extent. An integrative approach takes both sides' interests into account. Compromising does this to a moderate degree and collaboration satisfies both parties' interest to a high degree. The dashed line that runs from top left to bottom right represents the distributive dimension. This line represents a splitting of the pie between the two parties. To a degree, the interests of one or the other are met. The competitive style satisfies the concerns of self and the accommodator style satisfies concerns of the other party. The distributive and integrative lines cross at the compromising style because that style is both partially integrative and partially distributive.

Managers should try to develop all five styles of dealing with conflict. Each has an appropriate place and time. Being too concerned with self or too concerned with the interests of others all of the time can lead to problems in the long run. Versatility and adaptability in using different styles is most desirable.

TYPES OR SOURCES OF CONFLICT

Another important skill in dealing with conflict is recognizing different sources and types of conflict. As suggested above, many conflicts can be viewed in terms of turf violations; however, greater specificity is needed in describing the types and sources of conflict. Conflict can occur at different levels. Some conflicts are **interpersonal,** or between two individuals. Other conflicts are **intragroup**, or among members of team or group. Some conflicts are **inter-group**, or between different units or groups.

As intragroup conflicts are common among teams, several sources of conflict will be described at this level. **Relationship conflict**[7] involves tension and friction between members of the group. Personal dislike can occur in the affective stage and lead to annoyance and irritation. This type of conflict is difficult to resolve. Differences can be confronted. If attempts to resolve fail, one or more members may need to be reassigned. **Task conflict** involves differences in opinion about the task facing the group. This conflict is more cognitive but can lead to excited discussions and exchanges. Differences in the priority and importance of components of the task may occur. Talking through these differences can lead to improvements in performance. The third type of intragroup conflict is **process**. This type of conflict involves differences in how group work is performed. It may involve questions about the distribution and fairness of assignments among members. This conflict can also relate to roles and who is responsible for which components. Here communication about process can lead to greater consensus about how to complete the work, resolving the differences.

Research[8] found that more successful teams had the highest levels of process conflict as the deadline approached. Better performing groups also had higher levels of task conflict in the middle of projects. These findings support the conclusion about the bell-shaped curve relationship between conflict and performance. Tension at some point leads to questioning the status quo and to problem solving for better approaches.

CONDITIONS THAT CREATE CONFLICT

Many people falsely assume that all conflicts are interpersonal—that someone has done or said something wrong to cause the conflict. As the relationship type of intragroup conflict suggests, some conflicts are about style differences. However, not all conflicts are of this type, as shown in Table 14.1. There is another broad category of sources of differences that are due to conditions or structural characteristics. Some conditions that lead to conflict are **role ambiguities**. When the duties and boundaries assigned to an individual are not clear, they are apt to stray into someone else's area of responsibility. In essence the problem becomes one of overlapping duties. A group member invades another's turf, generating conflict. It is not the employee's fault, but the supervisor's. **Resource scarcity** is another condition that leads to conflict. When the budget is very tight, one manager may be inclined to seek additional funds from his or her superior. The superior, who has little to offer, must take resources away from someone else. Turf is again invaded and conflict ensues.

Table 14.1: Structural Conditions that Foster Conflict

Conditions That Lead to Conflict
1. Role Ambiguities
2. Scarce Resources
3. Task Interdependencies
4. Competing Goals
5. Incompatible Evaluation or Reward Systems

When the tasks that are performed by units or individuals are highly **interdependent**, the potential for conflict is greater. Here the turf of both parties overlaps. Finished parts come from another area to be assembled. If the parts department does not finish the parts on time, assembly cannot do its work and conflict results. Today's organizations tend to run with lean resources and tight interdependencies. These conditions have the potential for more conflict, despite the best efforts of individuals.

In chapter 7 on organizing, the functional structure was described as creating a silo mentality. Within functional units different goal orientations develop; these can be sources of conflict. Airport operations wants to run a simple and efficient operation. If marketing proposes treating a category of customers differently, it complicates matters for operations. The functional goal of increasing sales with special treatment creates an added burden for another unit. Compounding the problem is the fifth condition, **incompatible reward systems**. The marketing manager gets rewarded for added sales. The operational manager gets rewarded for keeping costs down. Both their rewards and their goals are incompatible. Both are being good managers by trying to reach their goals and receive rewards. The conditions created the conflict, not the attitudes or styles of the managers.

METHODS TO RESOLVE CONFLICT

Thus far we have discussed the types, sources, and styles used in dealing with conflict. This section offers several specific steps to address and resolve conflict. In some situations more than one approach can be used.

The first method can be used in many conflicted situations. **Altering the issue** represents an attempt to focus on the issue, not the person. In the ground-breaking negotiation book, *Getting to Yes*,[9] Roger Fisher and William Ury advocate separating the person from the issue. Be tough on the issue but not on the person. All too often the conflict becomes "you are wrong and I am right." If the problem can be reframed in terms of issues, not people, then solutions are easier and less tainted with animosity. This and other methods are presented in Table 14.2.

Table 14.2: Methods for Resolving Conflicts

Method	Example
Alter the issue	Depersonalize; separate person and problem
Alter the relationship	Interact through a third person, buffering the two parties
Alter the context	Add more resources
Change the individuals	Train or fire

The second method is to **alter the relationship**. The relationship could be altered by a civil discussion to resolve the issues. If communication and open discussion does not resolve the differences, the individuals can be separated. Instead of directly interacting on interdependent assignments, the interaction can go through another party. Putting a buffer between individuals changes the relationship, limiting interactions and thereby altering the conditions that might lead to future conflicts.

Another method that changes underlying conditions is **altering the context**. This approach could utilize a structural change, providing additional resources. Once the conditions that lead to the conflict are identified, those components of the context are modified so that conflict is less likely to occur in the future. Another way to alter the context is for the manager to emphasize common or superordinate goals. These are high-level goals that serve to unite individuals in pursuit of broader company interests, giving less emphasis to the personal issues that may have lead to conflict.

Finally, the **individuals are altered**. There are two primary means of achieving this goal. The first is training. If someone is causing conflicts because of poor interpersonal skills, they can receive training and coaching to develop better interaction skills. In some instances training is not effective. If individuals do not respond to training, then replacement is necessary. They may have to be reassigned to a position with less contact. The most severe step is to terminate someone who frequently causes conflicts and does not respond to other means of improving the situation. In the long run, terminations help the unit and may cause the fired person to confront his problems and change.

MANAGING CHANGE

Conflict is about recognizing issues and making changes. In this section of the chapter, further issues related to change are discussed. Throughout the book the changing environment of business has been noted. Companies and managers eventually react to these changes out of necessity. A reactive approach may lead to incorrect responses or actions that come too late. Skills for more proactively managing change are critical in today's environment. The field of organizational development emerged to help with planned change.

Organizational development and management in general has been built on the many ideas of Kurt Lewin. Lewin[10] believed that the status quo, or present condition, was a product of forces for and against change. Termed *force field analysis*, Lewin's approach can be applied to personal and organizational change. To bring about change, managers often think that they need to encourage, if not push for, the change. Lewin suggested that careful analysis might reveal that change could be achieved by reducing the forces against change as well. Lewin believed that the group was a key unit in linking the individual to the rest of the organization.[11] Thus many change efforts in organizational development activities are group-based. They often address restraining the forces that are resisting change.

Today planned changed efforts often focus on overcoming resistance to change and allowing natural homeostatic forces to move in the right direction once resistance is addressed. Lewin also suggests that groups have key gatekeepers that are the sources of resistance. Winning over opinion leaders can, likewise, help to make the change. Lewin developed a three-step model that guides many organization development models. The first stage is **unfreezing**. To make needed changes, ties to the old way must be loosened. Unfreezing often deals with overcoming resistance to change. For change to occur, individuals need to have felt the need or strong desire to change. This motivation allows them to give up elements of the past and seek something better. For some, data about declining performance creates the felt need. Once ties to the former are reduced, the second stage of **moving** comes in. Changes are made in work, people, structure, technology, and relationships as needed. This second stage involves the focused change of issues or content. Then Lewin noted that **refreezing** must occur. It is not enough to make the changes, but there has to a "firming up" of the new processes. Training and rewards need to be established that support the new status quo. If the refreezing stage is ignored, then there is a tendency to return to, or slip back into, the old ways. These notions have proved powerful in helping managers and consultants to make productive changes in organizations.

Given the importance of resistance in the change process, two aspects will be discussed further. Managers should be aware of the sources of resistance and then know some tactics for overcoming resistance. First, to diagnose sources of resistance see Table 14.3. [12]

Table 14.3: Sources of Resistance to Change

Low Tolerance for Change

Parochial Self-Interest

Misunderstanding and Lack of Trust

Different Assessment

In general, people do not like change or they have a **low tolerance for change**. Change brings uncertainty and discomfort. People are comfortable with the status quo. They have knowledge and skills in the present state and newness brings questions about being able to do the job. Despite positive reasons for change, this sense of uncertainty with the unknown can be overwhelming. Somewhat related to this issue is **parochial self-interest**. Some employees receive status and rewards from the current system. The new changes may reduce their status and influence. Although the changes benefit the organization, their narrow self-interest causes them to resist because they are losing something with the change.

Employees at lower levels in the organization may not trust the person making the changes. If there has been a history of tension, **lack of trust** is especially likely. Employees may fear that changes will eventually result in the loss of jobs, or changes that require them to work harder for less. Rumors often run wild during periods of organizational change. Employees question the motives for the change and doubt the viability of the changes.

There are times when different groups have **different assessments** of the benefits associated with the changes. The changes may not be plausible to them; they just can't see them working out. This is more than mistrust or fear of uncertainty; it is a legitimate disagreement with the nature of the proposed change.

Managers have tools at their disposal to overcome some of these sources of resistance. For different ways to deal with change, see Table 14.5. One of the most useful is **communication**. In the face of unknowns, employees become more distrusting and resistant. Frequent communication tends to reduce these concerns. When coupled with **education**, employees are more apt to see the reasons for change and will accept it. Long ago Lewin noted that **participation** and **involvement** in making the changes reduces resistance. Participation also helps with understanding the nature and rationale for change. **Facilitation** and **support** constitute another means available to managers to reduce resistance. Encouragement for, and explanation of, new tasks are useful tools. Similar to a supportive leadership style, managers can reduce resistance by listening and acknowledging employees' concerns. Rewards and recognition for mastering new tasks shows additional support.

Table 14.5: Dealing with Resistance to Change

Education and Communication

Participation and Involvement

Facilitation and Support

Negotiation and Agreement

Manipulation and Co-optation

Explicit and Implicit Coercion

While the first three methods of reducing resistance are generally encouraging in nature, other more aggressive means may be necessary. Managers may directly negotiate with other divisions whose cooperation is important in the change. They may agree to do certain things in exchange for cooperation. Employees may be given time off, bonuses, or other explicit rewards for supporting the change. These agreements may even be written into contractual language.

Sometimes managers resort to more covert activities to bring about positive change. John Kotter and Leonard Schlesinger[13] suggest that manipulation take place through the selective use of information and structuring of events. This can be risky, as employees may feel deceived if they learn that it was **manipulation**. **Co-optation** is less risky. Giving an opinion leader or resistor a prominent role is an example of co-optation. He or she is co-opted by becoming part of the leadership. As a leader, he or she is more likely to speak in favor of what he or she helped develop. This option is similar to Lewin's recommendation to involve gatekeepers in the process.

Another tool that is risky is **explicit** or **implicit coercion**. These last two means should only be used when absolutely necessary. Managers can tell employees that these changes are vital and they must accept them and become involved; failure to do so will result in sanctions and punishments. Sometimes new technology requires some forcing. One large pharmaceutical company sent its employees for training on a new computer system. When they returned to their computers the next day, they found that their old, familiar system was gone. They were forced, or coerced, to use the new. They could not fall back on the old; they had to adapt or fail.

COMMUNICATION

Communication sounds so simple. We all do it, right? Even giving task directions should be uncomplicated. Why then are there so many communication problems? **Communication** is the process of transmitting information to others. A basic understanding of communication and communication behavior is essential for successful management. This section of the chapter will discuss the communication process, the richness of various communication media, the directionality and flow of communication in organizations, and overcoming barriers to communication.

COMMUNICATION PROCESS

Let's begin with a manager who wants to communicate with a single subordinate. Sharon manages six people. She has just learned from marketing that a customer is running short of parts and would like the order delivered two days earlier than scheduled. Her employee needs to shift some responsibilities in order to meet the customer's request. How is this communicated? First Sharon develops the meaning of the message she wants to communicate. She begins by encoding the message in some language system; in the U.S. it would be English. What if she has a team of Spanish-speaking subordinates? Then the encoding would be in Spanish. The steps in transmitting a message are depicted in Figure 14.3.

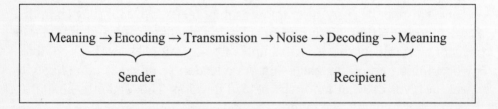

Meaning → Encoding → Transmission → Noise → Decoding → Meaning

Sender   Recipient

Figure 14.3: Communication steps in message transmission.

The sender next chooses a medium for transmitting the message. Will Sharon use the phone, e-mail, or walk to the subordinate's workstation and tell her face-to-face? Given the urgency of the message Sharon decides to communicate the message in person, or face-to-face. The message transmission process typically involves some type of noise. It is possible that a message can be distorted or altered by noise. In a face-to-face situation, noise can be distractions from ringing phones, production equipment, or other employees. Phone messages can have literal noise and even computer transmission can be garbled or altered. The point to make is that there are multiple opportunities for the meaning to be altered. The intended recipient then applies her language system for decoding the message and, following decoding, interprets the meaning. Will the intended meaning be the same as the received meaning? Not exactly. Often the subordinate communicates something back to the supervisor, going through the same cycle of encoding, transmitting, and decoding.

To illustrate how complicated the communication process can be, get a group of twenty people sitting in a circle. Whisper a message of several sentences to the first person and then have that person whisper to the next until it has passed through all twenty people sitting in the circle. Chances are the message changed through all of those transmission steps. Managers should not assume that sending even a short message is simple.

Means of improving accuracy will be discussed at the end of the chapter under the sub-heading overcoming barriers to communication.

COMMUNICATION MEDIA AND MEDIA RICHNESS

The communication medium does make a difference. Managers have at their disposal multiple media for communicating. Richard Daft has done research on the richness of media in managerial communication. **Richness** is the capacity of a medium for information. Face-to-face communication is the richest medium. What is communicated? The most obvious is the message content in the words chosen. In addition, the inflection in the voice makes a difference. What about the facial expressions? The nonverbal language of the speaker makes a difference too. A smile or wink usually connotes that the person is joking. Emoticons, those face like characters [(;-) for example], are designed to convey emotions. The emoticon in the example implies that the comment was made jokingly and is not to be taken literally or too seriously. Considerable emotional content is shared in face-to-face communication; as we've said, emoticons add some emotional content to e-mail communication but not as much as face-to-face communication. Telephone and video conferences have less richness than face-to-face, but more than written, as shown in Table 14.6.

Table 14.6: The Richness of Various Communication Media

Richness Level	Medium
High	Face-to-Face
	Video Conferencing
Medium	Telephone
	E-mail with emoticons
	Written, personal
Low	Written, formal

Research[14] has found that effective managers make better choices of media used to accomplish tasks. When tasks are complicated and somewhat ambiguous, more media richness is needed. You may have heard horror stories about managers who used e-mail to inform employees about layoffs. Some tasks require the full richness of face-to-face communication. Simple information sharing tasks can be done through low rich media, like memos and e-mail distributions.

In addition to the amount of information to be carried by the medium, two other conditions may influence a manager's choice of media. Since chapter 1, the importance of **efficiency** for managers has been stressed. Time is a valuable resource. Face-to-face communication takes more time. An e-mail may be a much quicker medium for sending routine information. The key is that the information should not be too complex or ambiguous. Another aspect of efficiency is how many employees need to be reached. Video presentations from senior managers can be sent through video conferencing equipment to reach thousands of employees simultaneously. The medium is less rich than face-to-face, but the executive saves time and travel expenses are reduced.

A second factor that influences the choice of communication media is the need for **documentation**. Managers communicate decisions and need to document the actions taken. There is no trace from oral communication. When disciplining an employee verbally, a memo is typically written to the file to provide documentation that the employee was informed of the problem. If progress is not made, then the memo documents the warning and the next step in progressive discipline is taken. Other actions may require a paper trail, as Max Weber suggested back in chapter 2.

DIRECTIONALITY OF COMMUNICATION

Most of the prior communication concepts focus on interpersonal communication. At the organizational and interpersonal levels, communication flows can also be examined. Messages move in a variety of directions. From chapter 7 on "organizing," it was noted that the hierarchy serves as a medium for coordination. Communicating information up and down the hierarchy is **vertical** communication. These messages are fairly formal in nature. **Top-down** communication often uses lower rich media, such as a memo or e-mail from senior management. These media are efficient but can cause ambiguity of meaning if not written clearly. Senior management informs employees regarding general company performance and business conditions. If employees are aware of the issues facing senior management, then they may be more accepting of changes. Revisions to the mission statement, news about possible mergers, and the amount of dividends paid to employee shareholders are examples of top-down communication. A richer message could be broadcast over video conferencing systems, where voice and facial expressions are communicated.

Vertical communication also occurs **bottom-up**, from employees up to management. Some of this communication is quite informal with face-to-face exchanges in the manager's office or in the workplace as managers walk about. In their book *In Search of Excellence*,[15] Tom Peters and Robert Waterman coined the term *management-by-walking around*. The manager takes time to visit various units to recognize good work and listen to concerns. This type of informal vertical communication improves morale and keeps the manager in touch with worker concerns. Suggestion boxes provide an opportunity for employees to comment, but they are often empty. A better way to find out about worker concerns is with employee surveys. Surveys measure worker attitudes and concerns. Focus groups or meetings that give small groups of employees a chance to speak their mind also provide upward communication from employees to higher levels of management.

Horizontal communication is a lateral exchange between individuals, often at the same level but not necessarily following the chain of command. This type of communication flow can be formal, following the chain of command, or more informal. Formal exchanges may occur to keep other departments informed of changes in one area that impact another. This accomplishes coordination. Managers may also communicate informally with peers to build networks (i.e., Mintzberg's liaison role). They can informally share approaches; the exchanges can help coach or mentor managers with less experience.

Diagonal communication is the exchange of information between individuals in different units and levels of the company. This type of information does not follow the chain of command and is often informal. Diagonal communication works because it does not follow prescribed channels of communication. Information is exchanged between individuals based on expertise and need. One employee goes to the expert on a particular topic impacting their project or assignment. W. L. Gore and Associates, maker of the fabric Gore-Tex® and other products, uses no official organizational chart and limits the size of units to less than 200 people. They believe that communication should be based on knowledge and expertise, not formal positions or the chain of command. By keeping each unit small, employees know who is good at which tasks and go right to the source. They get the best information they need to perform their jobs

BARRIERS AND OVERCOMING BARRIERS

Since communication problems are relatively common, it is useful to identify some of the barriers that can develop that lead to these problems. Some barriers are encountered during interpersonal communication and others are found in organizational communication, as shown in Table 14.7.

Table 14.7: Communication Barriers

Communication Barriers

Language

Conflicting Signals

Selective Perception & Defensiveness

Overload

Noise

When one individual is speaking Spanish and another English, it would be easy to understand why language could be a problem. Yet persons speaking the same language can also have language problems. Technical fields often rely on jargon and acronyms when communicating. Some individuals choose large and somewhat obscure words to demonstrate their knowledge and education. If the meaning of those words is not shared by both parities, meaning will not be transferred. Our language and dictionaries are changing with colloquial expressions. Abbreviated text messaging phrases, such as "C U" for the phrase "see you," are popular with those who use cell phones and e-mail. Those who do not know the codes do not understand. Even emoticons can be unclear to those unfamiliar with the meaning of the faces, like " :-/," which means that the person is skeptical of something previously written by the person with whom she is communicating.

Conflicting signals involve inconsistencies in the communication signals sent by individuals. If nonverbal signals are inconsistent with words, then usually the nonverbal message is followed. Similarly a manager may warn employees to keep their lunch hours to the prescribed sixty minutes and then he or she will take a ninety minute lunch. The inconsistencies are contradictory. Employees tend to follow actions rather than words in these instances.

Another common source of communication problems can be found with the tendencies of people to view events and communication in self-enhancing ways. Selective perception is seeing "what you want to see." People tend to observe events or hear messages consistent with their expectations. They may miss elements that are inconsistent with their self-image. Others, when confronted with conflicting information, deny it. Defensiveness prevents people from hearing messages that could damage their self-image.

Each day employees receive numerous e-mails, some of them spam and some real messages. E-mail makes it easy to send messages to lots of people. With high volumes, critical messages are easier to miss. When overloaded, people find ways to cut down on the amount of information. Some scan existing messages faster, others only look at messages from important people; either way, information can be lost. Phone mail messages can also be ignored. Employees struggle with prioritizing communication to try and receive, and then retain, what is important. Mistakes do happen.

OVERCOMING COMMUNICATION BARRIERS

How can a manager check for accuracy of the message received? **Feedback** is one way. Ask the subordinate to repeat the message. E-mail systems contain a mechanism where the receiver acknowledges getting the message. This feature acknowledges receipt of the message but does not confirm understanding the message. Feedback is not used as often as it could be because managers assume the message was received as sent or intended. **Redundancy** is also useful for important messages. Critical information can be sent through multiple channels or media.

CONCLUSION

This concluding chapter described additional leading skills related to conflict management, communication, and change management. Managers at all levels deal with conflict and need to be able to identify conflict sources and use appropriate styles to resolve them. Change management is a related activity that is essential for the company to adapt internally to external changes. Unfreezing, moving, and refreezing are important steps, as is overcoming resistance to change. Finally, communicating clearly and using the right communication media represents the final set of key behaviors for managers to master.

Chapter 14 Endnotes

1. Stuart M. Schmidt & Thomas A. Kochan, "Conflict: Toward Conceptual Clarity," *Administrative Science Quarterly* 17, no. 3 (1972): 359.

2. Kenneth Thomas, "Conflict and Conflict Management," in *Handbook of Industrial and Organizational Psychology*, Marvin D. Dunnette (Ed.) (Chicago: Rand McNally Publishing, 1976), 891.

3. Kenneth W. Thomas & William H. Schmidt, "A Survey of Managerial Interests with Respect to Conflict," *Academy of Management Journal* 19 (1976): 316.

4. Louis R. Pondy, "Organizational Conflict:Concepts and Models," *Administrative Science Quarterly* 12, no. 2 (1967): 300.

5. Thomas, 898.

6. Dan Dana, *Managing Differences: How to Build Better Relationships at Work and Home* (MTI Publications, 1989):30.

7. Karen A. Jehn & Elizabeth A. Mannix, "The Dynamic Nature of Conflict: A longitudinal study of intragroup conflict and group performance," *Academy of Management Journal* 44, no. 2 (2001): 238.

8. Jehn & Mannix, 247.

9. Roger Fisher & William Ury, *Getting to Yes* (Boston: Houghton Mifflin,1981), 21.

10. Marvin R. Weisbord, *Productive Workplaces: Organizing and Managing for Dignity, Meaning and Community* (San Francisco: Jossey-Bass Publishers, 1987), 88.

11. Ibid., 89.

12. John P. Kotter & Leonard A. Schlesinger, "Choosing Strategies for Change," *Harvard Business Review* 57, no. 2 (1979): 106–109.

13. Ibid., 110–113

14. Richard L. Daft, Robert H. Lengel, & Linda K. Treveino, "Message Equivocality, Media Selection, and Manager Performance: Implications for Information Systems," *MIS Quarterly* 11, no. 3 (1987): 355.

15. Thomas Peters and Robert Waterman, *In Search of Excellence* (New York: Harper & Row, 1981), 289.

▼
PRACTICE
TEST 1

This test is also on CD-ROM in our special interactive CLEP Principles of Management TEST*ware*®. It is highly recommended that you first take this exam on computer. You will then have the additional study features and benefits of enforced timed conditions, individual diagnostic analysis, and instant scoring. See page xiii for guidance on how to get the most out of our CLEP Principles of Management book and software.

CLEP PRINCIPLES OF MANAGEMENT

PRACTICE TEST 1

(Answer sheets appear in the back of this book.)

TIME: 90 Minutes
  100 Questions

DIRECTIONS: Each of the questions or incomplete statements below is followed by five possible answers or completions. Select the best choice in each case and fill in the corresponding oval on the answer sheet.

---

1. Which of the following is the best definition of effectiveness?

    (A) The best use of available resources in the process of accomplishing goals

    (B) Whether appropriate employees know what's expected of them

    (C) Doing the job right

    (D) Accomplishing appropriate goals and objectives

    (E) Be all that you can be

2. Which of the following options is a process that impacts the functioning of groups?

    (A) Member satisfaction

    (B) Member skills

    (C) Enhanced member capability

    (D) Member roles

    (E) Group size

3. Which of the following represents the best definition of the organizing term centralization?

    (A) The unbroken link of authority tying all individuals in the organization

    (B) The degree to which work is broken into small tasks and assigned to jobs

    (C) The location of authority or decision-making near the top of the hierarchy

    (D) The number of employees who report to a supervisor

    (E) The modification of jobs by adding several similar tasks

4. The tendency of managers to attribute the poor performance of subordinates to internal factors, primarily motivation, ignoring factors in the work environment has been termed

    (A) needs

    (B) fundamental attribution error

    (C) performance bias

    (D) actor-observer bias

    (E) ability ignorance

5. Which of the following categories of external forces has the most direct impact on a company?

    (A) General environment forces

    (B) Immediate environment forces

    (C) Corporate culture

    (D) Adaptation forces

    (E) Influencing forces

6. Which of the following actions is the first step in the control process?

(A) Measure actual performance

(B) Compare performance with standards

(C) Establish standards

(D) Take corrective action

(E) Run the process, perform the work

7. Which of the following statements best describes business ethics?

(A) Fundamental values that society imparts about right and wrong behaviors

(B) Minimal standards imposed by society for not harming others

(C) Beliefs about appropriate behaviors in the workplace

(D) Obligations that society expects of corporations

(E) Responses of corporations to pressures put on them by society

8. The current view of conflict in organizations is best described as which of the following?

(A) The result of poor decision making

(B) Happens because individuals made mistakes in interacting with people

(C) Occurs because of a perception that someone has frustrated a goal

(D) The result of poor organizational designs

(E) Happens rarely in well-managed organizations

9. Which of the following historical approaches to management emphasized keeping written records of decisions and hiring workers based on qualifications rather than personal ties?

(A) The humanistic perspective (Hawthorne studies)

(B) Mary Parker Follett of the administrative school

(C) Max Weber's bureaucracy

(D) Frederick Taylor's scientific management

(E) Henri Fayol of the administrative school

10. Which of the following statements is true of the classical approach to decision-making?

    (A) Decisions are based on consensus and negotiation, not an objective sense of right and wrong.

    (B) When making decisions people do not make full use of all information and their mental capacities.

    (C) Most managers make good decisions without extensive training in decision-making.

    (D) Decision makers are rational and make full use of information in reaching decisions.

    (E) Decisions are seldom purely right or wrong; the situation influences what works best.

11. Operations managers are concerned with measures such as productivity. Which of the following is the best measure of productivity?

    (A) total outputs – total inputs

    (B) total outputs/total inputs

    (C) (inputs + outputs)/inputs

    (D) total inputs – total outputs

    (E) total inputs + total outputs

12. Which of the following is the best definition of human capital?

    (A) The budgeted amount for training employees

    (B) The amount of compensation and benefits paid to all employees

    (C) The skills and capabilities of employees

    (D) The cost of facilities used by human resources staff in helping workers

    (E) The economic value of the competencies and skills of employees

13. Which of the following statements best defines the planning term, objectives?

    (A) Specific statements of intended outcomes

    (B) Set of activities chosen to reach goals

    (C) Procedures for responding to unexpected events or disasters

    (D) General statements of intended results

    (E) Evaluating the obtained results

14. Which early approach to leadership asserted that natural leaders emerge, fitting the times in which they lead?

    (A) Ohio State University's dimensional studies

    (B) Kurt Lewin's group studies

    (C) *Zeitgeist*

    (D) Trait approach

    (E) University of Michigan's studies

15. Which of the following statements best defines social responsibility?

    (A) Fundamental values that society imparts about right and wrong behaviors

    (B) Minimal standards imposed by society for not harming others

    (C) Beliefs about appropriate behaviors in the workplace

    (D) Obligations that society expects of corporations

    (E) Responses of corporations to pressures put on them by society

16. The local cable TV company offers a number of optional services to customers. Which service operations strategy does it employ?

    (A) Assemble-to-order

    (B) Customized services

    (C) Make-to-stock

    (D) Make-to-order

    (E) Standardized services

17. Which of the following categories of forces represents the set of beliefs held by organizational members about what is important and how work should be done?

    (A) General environment forces

    (B) Immediate environment forces

    (C) Corporate culture

    (D) Adaptation forces

    (E) Influencing forces

18. What is the term used to describe the many categories of people who have an interest in the performance of a firm or manager?

    (A) Efficiency

    (B) Multiple stakeholders

    (C) Human skills

    (D) Dependability

    (E) Effectiveness

19. Which of the following is an output of group functioning?

    (A) Member satisfaction

    (B) Member skills

    (C) Member knowledge

    (D) Member roles

    (E) Group norms

20. Jaron became aware of some puzzling events. He noticed that Barb has made several trips into his boss's office. Barb is a peer who heads another project team. Jaron began to wonder if Barb is requesting that one of his top performers join her team. She had casually asked Jaron about this team member last week. Jaron is suspicious but not angry. At this point, which stage best characterizes the conflict?

    (A) Latent

    (B) Perceived

    (C) Felt

    (D) Manifest

    (E) Aftermath

21. Which of the following options best describes the issues that can impact performance?

    (A) Ability and equipment used

    (B) Ability and motivation

    (C) Motivation and work conditions

    (D) Manager's attitude and motivation

    (E) Ability, motivation, and work conditions

22. Which of the following statements represents the current view regarding quality in organizations? Quality

    (A) is best achieved through inspection

    (B) involves frequent monitoring and some design

    (C) requires cultural transformation at all levels of the organization

    (D) is the exclusive focus of senior management

    (E) requires a specialized department to plan, organize, and inspect

23. Which of the following statements is true of the administrative approach to decision-making?

    (A) Decisions are based on consensus and negotiation, not an objective sense of right and wrong.

    (B) When making decisions people do not make full use of all information and their mental capacities.

    (C) Most managers make good decisions without extensive training in decision-making.

    (D) Decision makers are rational and make full use of information in reaching decisions.

    (E) Decisions are seldom purely right or wrong; the situation influences what works best.

24. Which of the following represents the best definition of the organizing term span of management, or control?

    (A) The unbroken link of authority tying all individuals in the organization

    (B) The degree to which work is broken into small tasks and assigned to jobs

    (C) The location of authority near the top of the hierarchy

    (D) The number of employees who report to a supervisor

    (E) The modification of jobs by adding several similar tasks

25. Which of the following objective statements most closely corresponds to the criteria defined as SMART?

    (A) Each unit should work extra hard for the next week.

    (B) Mary will get along well with Paul by the end of the quarter.

    (C) The team will complete the assigned project and submit the report two days before the December 1 deadline.

    (D) The corporation will perform better than any other company in its industry.

    (E) Bill, the operations manager, will run more effective meetings next year.

26. Which of the following historical approaches to management emphasized work layout movements and differential piece rates for higher performance?

    (A) The humanistic perspective (Hawthorne studies)

    (B) Mary Parker Follett of the administrative school

    (C) Max Weber's bureaucracy

    (D) Frederick Taylor's scientific management

    (E) Henri Fayol of the administrative school

27. Which early approach viewed leadership in terms of the two independent dimensions of initiation of structure and consideration?

    (A) Ohio State University's dimensional studies

    (B) Kurt Lewin's group studies

    (C) *Zeitgeist*

    (D) Trait approach

    (E) University of Michigan's studies

28. Which of the following legislative acts prohibits discrimination on the basis of race, religion, color, sex, and national origin?

    (A) The Civil Rights Act of 1964 and subsequent amendments

    (B) The Occupational Safety and Health Act of 1970

    (C) The Age Discrimination Act of 1967

    (D) The Americans with Disabilities Act of 1991

    (E) The Family and Medical Leave Act of 1993

Questions 29–30

Chris Talbott is the national sales manager for a medium-sized firm that designs and manufactures components for cellular phones. He reports to the vice president of marketing. Chris's current activities include assessing the expenditures of the regional sales managers to see if they have exceeded budgeted amounts and then taking any corrective action needed. He is also involved in developing the next year's marketing plan and awarding bonuses to the top performing regional sales managers who report to him. Chris reads several trade journals and newsletters to identify new industry trends and shares them with the sales force in a weekly meeting.

29. Which function of management is Chris engaged in when awarding bonuses to the top performers who report to him?

    (A) Planning

    (B) Organizing

    (C) Coordinating

    (D) Leading

    (E) Controlling

30. Which of Mintzberg's managerial roles most closely describes Chris's activities of reading trade journals?

    (A) Spokesperson

    (B) Negotiator

    (C) Resource allocator

    (D) Leader

    (E) Monitor

31. Which of the following conflict management styles is most appropriate when the issue is not important and you wish to gain social credits with the other party?

    (A) Accommodating

    (B) Avoiding

    (C) Collaborating

    (D) Compromising

    (E) Competing

32. Which term describes a decision situation where the options and the probabilities associated with them are known?

    (A) Risk

    (B) Politics

    (C) Vagueness

    (D) Certainty

    (E) Uncertainty

33. The term "hostile work environment" applies most closely to which legal area in HRM?

    (A) Discrimination against race and religion

    (B) Safety in the workplace

    (C) Sexual harassment

    (D) Pregnancy discrimination

    (E) Family medical leave

34. Which approach to leadership popularized early studies and offered training for managers to become team leaders?

    (A) Ohio State University's dimensional studies

    (B) Blake and Mouton's managerial grid

    (C) Lewin's group approach

    (D) Trait approach

    (E) University of Michigan's studies

35. Jacques is a wine exporter from France. Due to a political dispute with the U.S., a 10 percent tariff is imposed on French wines. The tariffs lead to higher prices, causing his U.S. customers to reduce their orders by 15 percent. Which sector of the general environment is impacting Jacques' business?

    (A) Economy

    (B) Technology

    (C) Legal-political

    (D) Socio-cultural

    (E) Human capital

36. Which functional activity within operations would most likely use a kanban system to maintain efficient levels of work-in-progress?

    (A) Purchasing

    (B) Logistics

    (C) Flexible manufacturing

    (D) Inventory management

    (E) Facilities planning and design

37. Which of the following statements represents the best definition of the organizing term work specialization?

    (A) The unbroken link of authority tying all individuals in the organization

    (B) The degree to which work is broken into small tasks and assigned to jobs

    (C) The location of authority near the top of the hierarchy

    (D) The number of employees who report to a supervisor

    (E) The modification of jobs by adding several similar tasks

38. Which of the following statements about ethics is NOT true?

    (A) Ethics represent internal standards that guide employee behavior.

    (B) Ethical failures have led to the passage of new legislation to enforce standards of behavior.

    (C) Ethics are important because laws cannot be written for every situation.

    (D) Ethical choices are often complex dilemmas.

    (E) Ethics violations do not really cost the firm any money.

39. Which of the following historical approaches to management emphasized that worker participation, shared goals, and empowerment are important for success?

    (A) The humanistic perspective (Hawthorne studies)

    (B) Mary Parker Follett of the administrative school

    (C) Max Weber's bureaucracy

    (D) Frederick Taylor's scientific management

    (E) Henri Fayol of the administrative school

40. Individuals from different parts of the organization who are assigned to a permanent team that regularly meets face-to-face to coordinate and make decisions are termed a

    (A) vertical team

    (B) virtual team

    (C) functional team

    (D) committee

    (E) task force

41. In Kaplan & Norton's Balanced Scorecard, which goal category is the starting point in the chain?

    (A) Financial

    (B) Internal business processes

    (C) Technology planning

    (D) Learning and growth

    (E) Customer

42. Which quality expert advocated zero defects, explaining that poor quality costs money?

    (A) Edward Deming

    (B) Philip Crosby

    (C) Malcolm Baldridge

    (D) James Fairfield-Sonn

    (E) Joseph Juran

43. Which of the following need-based approaches to motivation fostered the redesign of jobs to build in greater responsibility for work?

    (A) Herzberg's two-factor theory

    (B) Alderfer's ERG theory

    (C) Equity theory

    (D) Maslow's hierarchy of needs

    (E) McClelland's acquired needs theory

44. Saul runs a machine shop that supplies parts to companies in the aerospace industry. Saul reads that many aerospace companies are now using lighter composite materials instead of metal parts. Saul wants to expand his composite work but is having difficulties hiring designers who have knowledge in this area. Which of the following immediate environment forces is impacting his business?

    (A) Suppliers

    (B) Competitors

    (C) Community

    (D) Customers

    (E) Human capital

45. Job evaluations are done as part of which of the following human resources functions or programs?

    (A) Compensation

    (B) Recruitment

    (C) Performance management

    (D) Training

    (E) Selection

46. Which of the following group roles is task-oriented?

    (A) Harmonizer

    (B) Blocker

    (C) Initiator

    (D) Follower

    (E) Dominator

47. Which quality expert defined quality as fitness for use and advocated that transformation of the organization needed to occur at a revolutionary pace?

    (A) Edward Deming

    (B) Philip Crosby

    (C) Malcolm Baldridge

    (D) James Fairfield-Sonn

    (E) Joseph Juran

48. Which of the following is an integrated systems that contains data related to all of the functions of the business, including suppliers, internal operations, and customers?

    (A) Decision support systems (DSS)

    (B) Expert systems (ES)

    (C) Enterprise resource planning (ERP)

    (D) Management of technology

    (E) Project management

49. Which of the following historical influences advocated compensation related practices in the workplace?

    (A) Scientific management

    (B) Fayol's administrative principles

    (C) Weber's bureaucracy

    (D) Both Fayol and Weber

    (E) Scientific management, Fayol, and Weber

50. Goals in organizations vary by level. Which of the following categories is the highest level of goals in organizations?

    (A) Corporate goals

    (B) Individual goals

    (C) Unit goals

    (D) Strategic business unit (SBU) goals

    (E) Functional goals

51. Which of the following approaches to motivation asserted that self-actualization was the highest need that individuals seek to fulfill?

    (A) Herzberg's two-factor theory

    (B) Alderfer's ERG theory

    (C) Locke's goal-setting theory

    (D) Maslow's hierarchy of needs

    (E) McClelland's acquired needs theory

52. Which of the following is the first step in the decision-making process?

    (A) Formulation of the problem

    (B) Implementation of the problem

    (C) Awareness of the problem

    (D) Diagnosis and information gathering

    (E) Generation of alternatives

53. An inner-city hospital receives funding and free samples from the manufacturer of an infant formula product. Lower-income mothers are given samples. Activists complain that this practice is unethical because the new mothers are not given information about breast-feeding as a healthier, low cost option. Which ethical framework captures the objection of the activists?

    (A) Justice

    (B) Moral rights

    (C) Utilitarian

    (D) Universalism

    (E) Moralism

54. Conflicts that emerge when job boundaries and responsibilities are unclear relates to which of the following types or sources of conflict?

    (A) Competing goals

    (B) Role ambiguities

    (C) Scarce resources

    (D) Task interdependencies

    (E) Incompatible reward systems

55. Which of the items listed below represents the most visible manifestation of organizing?

    (A) Centralization

    (B) Task identity

    (C) Chain of command

    (D) Organizational chart

    (E) Corporate culture

56. Which of the following contingency approaches to leadership taught that managers should look at the readiness of subordinates in terms of ability, experience, and willingness?

    (A) Fiedler's contingency theory

    (B) Ohio State University's studies

    (C) University of Michigan's studies

    (D) Hersey-Blanchard's life cycle theory

    (E) House's path-goal theory

57. Which managerial skill provides managers with mental maps to see the organization as a whole and to understand the factors that impact it?

    (A) Technical

    (B) Human

    (C) Conceptual

    (D) Functional

    (E) Emotional intelligence

58. Maya has received complaints from both Ted and Sue. They just don't like each other and have different styles of working. Maya realizes that they need to share information but don't have to work closely together. She hopes to reduce the problem by having each interact with Adrienne, who gets along well with both. Which method of resolving conflict is Maya using?

    (A) Altering the issue

    (B) Altering the context

    (C) Altering the people

    (D) Altering the work

    (E) Altering the relationship

59. Organizations are often grouped into responsibility centers for control purposes. Which type of responsibility center incorporates capital expenditure as well as profit?

    (A) Investment center

    (B) Expense center

    (C) Revenue center

    (D) Building center

    (E) Profit center

60. The awareness that organizations interact with and are dependent upon their external environment was contributed by which historical school of thought?

    (A) Contingency approaches

    (B) Military organizations dating from the ancient times

    (C) Humanist perspective

    (D) Systems theory

    (E) Chester Barnard of the administrative school

61. Which of the following selection tools is most likely to be used as the first step in the selection process?

    (A) Background checks

    (B) Job interview

    (C) Ability test

    (D) Work-sample test

    (E) Resume

62. Which of the following contingency approaches characterizes leadership behavior in terms of the four dimensions of directive, supportive, participative, and achievement?

    (A) Fiedler's contingency theory

    (B) Ohio State University's studies

    (C) University of Michigan's studies

    (D) Hersey-Blanchard's life cycle theory

    (E) House's path-goal theory

63. Which of the following types of departmentalization is most common among businesses that have just begun?

    (A) Divisional

    (B) Functional

    (C) Matrix

    (D) Geographic

    (E) Customer

64. Which category of social responsibility is a restaurant following when it donates 5 percent of its dessert profits from one month in support of breast cancer treatment and research?

    (A) Legal

    (B) Caring

    (C) Economic

    (D) Discretionary

    (E) Ethical

65. Which of the following group roles is self-oriented?

    (A) Avoider

    (B) Consensus tester

    (C) Compromiser

    (D) Follower

    (E) Summarizer

66. All of the following are desired characteristics of information EXCEPT

    (A) timeliness

    (B) completeness

    (C) relevance

    (D) quantity

    (E) quality

67. A company agrees to allow two employees to spend ten hours of company time per week assisting a community development program one block from the company in building a database. This action addresses which of the following environmental issues?

    (A) Technological forces in the general environment

    (B) Ceremony as part of the internal culture

    (C) Lobbying as a way to influence the environment

    (D) Boundary spanning as an influence mechanism

    (E) Community forces in the immediate environment

68. Which of the following is the first step in the strategic planning process?

    (A) Implement strategy

    (B) Conduct SWOT analysis

    (C) Develop new mission and goals

    (D) Assess or define current mission

    (E) Formulate strategy

69. Which of the following Myers-Briggs types is most likely to demonstrate a decision-making style of attention to information detail and use of analytical reasoning?

    (A) Sensing-Feeling (SF)

    (B) Intuition-Feeling (NF)

    (C) Extroverted-Analytic (EA)

    (D) Sensing-Thinking (ST)

    (E) Intuition-Thinking (NT)

70. In expectancy theory which component is closest to what is termed confidence to perform a task?

    (A) Valence of outcomes

    (B) Output/input ratios

    (C) Expectancy (E → P)

    (D) Instrumentality (P → O)

    (E) Positive reinforcement

71. When a company hires a lobbyist to encourage legislation protecting its products from foreign competition with tariffs, it is doing which of the following in terms of its environment?

    (A) Adapting to general environment forces

    (B) Adapting to immediate environment forces

    (C) Modifying the internal culture

    (D) Increasing awareness of the environment within the company

    (E) Influencing factors in the environment important to it

72. Which of the following types of departmentalization has the advantage of full cross-functional authority at the first level of management?

    (A) Liaison

    (B) Product

    (C) Functional

    (D) Matrix

    (E) Job rotation

73. A prominent hotel chain creates a new division of luxury resorts. Instead of merely having high-end, luxury suites, the entire hotel is luxury-oriented. There is added security and limited access. The resorts are built in remote locations. The division intends to promote these resorts to wealthy, public personalities, such as movie stars and top managers. Which of Porter's competitive strategies are they using?

    (A) Differentiation

    (B) Cost leadership

    (C) Focus

    (D) Both differentiation and focus

    (E) Both differentiation and cost leadership

74. At which stage of development have norms become clear and group members accepted different roles?

    (A) Performing

    (B) Storming

    (C) Norming

    (D) Adjourning

    (E) Forming

75. Which of the following statements best describes the difference between brainstorming and nominal group technique (NGT) in reaching decisions?

    (A) Brainstorming uses different methods to evaluate ideas.

    (B) NGT assigns members a specific name to capture different perspectives.

    (C) NGT requires individuals to write down ideas before interacting with others.

    (D) NGT uses role names to assign responsibilities for follow-up.

    (E) Brainstorming requires greater cognitive skills.

76. The formal system of behavior control that imposes successively more severe sanctions on employees who violate the rules is called?

    (A) Quality control

    (B) Progressive discipline

    (C) Market control

    (D) Incremental discipline

    (E) Clan control

77. Which of the following managerial skills is used most often by lower-level managers?

    (A) Technical

    (B) Human

    (C) Conceptual

    (D) Functional

    (E) Expressive

78. Sam is charged with implementing new accounting software in a small division of a medium-sized company. Sam had sessions with employees where all phases were carefully explained. He feels that employees respect him; however, he is still getting resistance. The employees were very comfortable with their prior system, most have been using it for nearly twenty years. The workers do not want the new system. Which source of resistance seems to be operating?

(A) Parochial self-interest

(B) Different assessment

(C) Lack of trust

(D) Low tolerance for change

(E) Lack of understanding of the process

79. Which category of social responsibility is a company following when it installs electronic kiosks to process job applicants at the first stage of hiring so as to avoid bias?

(A) Legal

(B) Caring

(C) Economic

(D) Discretionary

(E) Ethical

80. The management theorist who expanded our understanding of worker motivation, noting that employees respond according to the attitudes held by their managers was

(A) Abraham Maslow

(B) Frederick Taylor

(C) Douglas McGregor

(D) Henri Fayol

(E) Max Weber

81. Which of the following statements is most true about the training component of human resources?

   (A) Managers generally know what type of training their employees need.

   (B) Computer-based training, especially via a company-based intranet, is needed to train global workers quickly and efficiently.

   (C) Assessing employee reactions following training is the best measure of training effectiveness.

   (D) On-the-job training is seldom done anymore.

   (E) Companies need more trainers than ever today and are hiring many.

82. When managers communicate with subordinates through formal written communication, what is the most likely direction of the communication flow?

   (A) Diagonal

   (B) Horizontal

   (C) Vertical, top-down

   (D) Circular

   (E) Vertical, bottom-up

83. Sonia, a supervisor of an accounts receivable unit, decides to change the way work flows through her unit and to switch several employees' positions in the process. Which function of management is she practicing?

   (A) Planning

   (B) Organizing

   (C) Coordinating

   (D) Leading

   (E) Controlling

84. A company operates in a rapidly changing environment. What structural features should go with this organizing contingency?

    (A) A functional structure

    (B) A tall organization structure

    (C) A structure that uses hierarchy, planning, and rules and procedures for integration

    (D) An organic structure that can readily adapt

    (E) A structure with a high level of centralization

85. The goal setting theory of motivation is closest to which of the following approaches to motivation?

    (A) Alderfer's ERG theory

    (B) Expectancy theory

    (C) Reinforcement theory

    (D) Herzberg's two-factor theory

    (E) Equity theory

86. Which of the following statements is true about charismatic, or transformational, leaders?

    (A) Their ability to articulate a vision that meets followers' needs creates an emotional bond with them.

    (B) Charismatic leaders are born with traits that cause subordinates to follow.

    (C) Physical attraction plays a major role in developing charisma.

    (D) Charismatic leaders use the right style in the right situation.

    (E) Leaders with charisma give additional pay to followers.

87. Tino listens intently as one of his subordinates complains about an unanticipated problem that he had with a vendor. Tino asks a few questions and then proposes a solution, which the subordinate accepts with minor modification. Both are happy with the decision. These activities represent which of Mintzberg's roles of management?

    (A) Monitor

    (B) Liaison

    (C) Entrepreneur

    (D) Disturbance handler

    (E) Resource allocator

88. Which of the following is the most important conclusion for a manager to know about the equity theory of motivation?

    (A) Over-rewarded employees always perform better.

    (B) Pay has little or no impact on motivation.

    (C) Only outputs are considered in the equity theory.

    (D) Employees may seek other employment if they feel that the rewards are inequitable.

    (E) Inputs are most important in the equity theory.

89. Which of the following is NOT a disadvantage of group decision-making?

    (A) Members tend to make riskier decisions.

    (B) Members tend to be less inhibited and insult others.

    (C) Some members engage in social loafing.

    (D) Group decisions take more time.

    (E) Some group members dominate, causing others to withdraw.

90. What is the planning activity called when a company sends a team to study specific processes in another company?

    (A) Strategy formulation

    (B) Policy

    (C) Contingency

    (D) Benchmarking

    (E) Project

91. Which of the following areas of HR would process grievances from unionized employees?

    (A) Compensation

    (B) Employee relations

    (C) Performance management

    (D) Training

    (E) Labor relations

92. Which theory of leadership used the favorability of the situation to match leaders with the situation?

    (A) Goleman's emotional intelligence leadership

    (B) Fiedler's contingency theory

    (C) Bass's transformational leadership

    (D) House's path-goal theory

    (E) Hersey-Blanchard's life cycle theory

93. Which of the following is NOT an integrating mechanism used in many types of organizations?

    (A) Liaison department

    (B) Rules and procedures

    (C) Task force

    (D) Planning

    (E) Hierarchy

94. A manager can use a number of strategies to bring about change and reduce resistance. Which of the following strategies is best in the initial phases of the change?

    (A) Co-optation

    (B) Explicit coercion

    (C) Negotiated agreement

    (D) Manipulation

    (E) Education and communication

95. Which of the following statements is true about corporate culture?

    (A) Most features of the culture are readily observable in an organization.

    (B) Much of the culture, except artifacts, is hidden from immediate view.

    (C) The culture is influenced entirely by internal company factors.

    (D) The culture of a company can be changed rapidly and easily.

    (E) Culture is based on the official policies of the company.

96. Which of the following options best describes the activities in project management?

    (A) Completing as many project tasks yourself as possible

    (B) Clarifying the scope and objectives of the project

    (C) Interviewing team members to decide who works on the project

    (D) Determining the pay level each member receives

    (E) Leaving the project team alone to do its work

97. The response of the American Council of Life Insurers to the selling of life insurance to marine recruits at Fort Benning was, "People who are mature enough to fight and die should be able to make decisions about life insurance." Their response represents which of the following categories of corporate social response?

    (A) Proaction

    (B) Reaction

    (C) Activation

    (D) Accommodation

    (E) Defense

98. Which of the following is NOT a desired quality of effective control systems?

   (A) Internal orientation of self-control

   (B) Measure frequently

   (C) Measure strategically

   (D) Flexibility, allowing for some deviation

   (E) Rewards for compliance and high performance

99. Shirelle has a subordinate who makes inappropriate comments to customers. Which of the following strategies of reinforcement would she be using if she reprimands him to decrease the behavior?

   (A) Positive reinforcement

   (B) Variable reinforcement

   (C) No reinforcement

   (D) Operant conditioning

   (E) Punishment

100. Which of the following is a correct statement about the principle of groupthink?

   (A) It is most common among groups that have experienced a recent failure.

   (B) It involves members doubting their ability to perform tasks well.

   (C) It occurs in cohesive groups as they have a sense of invulnerability and inherent morality.

   (D) It tends to happen only in high-level groups.

   (E) It helps teams to think better about the problems they are facing.

CLEP PRINCIPLES OF MANAGEMENT PRACTICE TEST 1

ANSWER KEY

1.	(D)	26.	(D)	51.	(D)	76.	(B)
2.	(D)	27.	(A)	52.	(C)	77.	(A)
3.	(C)	28.	(A)	53.	(B)	78.	(D)
4.	(B)	29.	(D)	54.	(B)	79.	(E)
5.	(B)	30.	(E)	55.	(D)	80.	(C)
6.	(C)	31.	(A)	56.	(D)	81.	(B)
7.	(C)	32.	(A)	57.	(C)	82.	(C)
8.	(C)	33.	(C)	58.	(E)	83.	(B)
9.	(C)	34.	(B)	59.	(A)	84.	(D)
10.	(D)	35.	(C)	60.	(D)	85.	(B)
11.	(B)	36.	(D)	61.	(E)	86.	(A)
12.	(E)	37.	(B)	62.	(E)	87.	(D)
13.	(A)	38.	(E)	63.	(B)	88.	(D)
14.	(C)	39.	(B)	64.	(D)	89.	(B)
15.	(D)	40.	(D)	65.	(A)	90.	(D)
16.	(A)	41.	(D)	66.	(D)	91.	(E)
17.	(C)	42.	(B)	67.	(E)	92.	(B)
18.	(B)	43.	(A)	68.	(D)	93.	(A)
19.	(A)	44.	(E)	69.	(D)	94.	(E)
20.	(B)	45.	(A)	70.	(C)	95.	(B)
21.	(E)	46.	(C)	71.	(E)	96.	(B)
22.	(C)	47.	(E)	72.	(B)	97.	(B)
23.	(B)	48.	(C)	73.	(D)	98.	(B)
24.	(D)	49.	(E)	74.	(C)	99.	(E)
25.	(C)	50.	(A)	75.	(C)	100.	(C)

DETAILED EXPLANATIONS
OF ANSWERS

PRACTICE TEST 1

1. **(D)** The correct response is (D), the precise definition offered in the chapter. Effectiveness is about reaching goals, the *right* goals. Option (A) is the definition of *efficiency*, a similar but distinct term related to the use of resources. Option (B) addresses employees' knowing what's expected of them. Although clear expectations are important for management, they do not relate directly to effectiveness. Option (C), "doing the job right" is Drucker's definition of efficiency. Effectiveness is "doing the right job." Option (E) relates to motivation on a personal level but does not deal with effectiveness.

2. **(D)** The correct response is (D), member roles. Task and socio-emotional roles are key aspects for group process. Option (A), member satisfaction, is an *output* of group activity, as is enhanced member capacity (C). Therefore neither (A) nor (C) is correct. Option (B), member skills, is an *input* to group activity, as is size (E), making (B) and (E) incorrect.

3. **(C)** The correct response is (C), the location of authority or decision-making near the top of the hierarchy. Centralization means that decisions are made at higher levels and the authority needed to implement them also resides at the top. Decentralization involves moving decision-making further down into lower levels. The unbroken link of authority tying all individuals together (A) is not correct because this response defines chain of command. Option (B) is not correct because the degree to which jobs are broken into smaller tasks and assigned to jobs is the definition of work simplification. The number of employees who report to a supervisor (D) is not correct because this phrase is a definition of span of control or management. Finally option (E) is not correct because adding similar tasks to a job is job enlargement.

4. **(B)** The correct response is (B), the fundamental attribution error. This error causes managers to put too much blame on motivation as a cause of poor performance. Needs (A) is not correct as needs are a component of motivation, not the reason for false attributions. Option (C), performance bias, is not correct as this phrase was not used in the chapter and is a contrived option. Actor-observer bias (D) is another type of attribution bias where the employee attributes success to self and failure to external sources. It is not correct for this question. Option (E), ability ignorance, is not correct as this term was contrived and not covered in the motivation chapter.

5. **(B)** The correct response is (B), immediate environmental forces. The word "immediate" provides a semantic clue. Immediate forces, such as customers and competitors, have direct and immediate impact on a company. The general environmental forces (A) is not correct. This category of forces is more indirect and general, such as the economy and technology. Option (C), corporate culture, is not correct as this is an internal aspect of environment and the question asks for an external set of forces. Adaptation forces (D) is not correct as this was not a specifically named set of forces, but instead is a means of responding to external forces. Similarly, influencing forces (E) is not correct either as this is another means for coping with external forces.

6. **(C)** The correct response is (C), establish standards. Figure 9.2 illustrated standards as the first step. You have to know what you are shooting for before you can check for quality. The standards establish expectations. Measuring actual performance (A) is not correct. Establishing the standard of measurement comes first. Comparing performance with standards was the fourth step in the model, making option (B) incorrect. Option (D) is not correct because taking corrective action comes last in the control process. Option (E) is not correct because performing the work is second, coming after establishing standards.

7. **(C)** The correct response is (C), beliefs about appropriate behaviors in the workplace. Option (A) is incorrect because fundamental values from society is the definition of morals. Option (B) is not correct as this definition applies to law. Obligations that society expects of corporations (D) is not correct as this is the definition of social responsibility. Finally option (E) is not correct because responses of corporations is also related to social responsibility and is not a definition of ethics.

8. **(C)**   The correct response is (C), perception that someone has frustrated a goal. Both the perceptual aspect and the frustration part are important. It does not matter if someone has done it or the person perceives she or he has. Either way, if a goal is blocked, frustration or anger may result. Option (A) is not correct as this response reflects older, somewhat archaic thinking that conflict is the result of mistakes. We now know that conflicts happen despite the best intentions of managers. Similarly option (B) is not correct because conflicts from underlying conditions happen regardless of how people interact. Even though poor organizational design can contribute to conflicts, they can occur with the correct design, making (D) an incorrect option. Finally, conflicts will happen in well-managed companies. Option (E) is not correct.

9. **(C)**   The correct response is (C). Max Weber advocated written documentation of decisions and any actions taken. He was also trying to overcome the patronage practice of giving positions to family members and friends. The Hawthorne studies and the humanistic perspective (A) is not correct. The importance of worker reactions and team dynamics was a conclusion of this school of thought. Similarly, Mary Parker Follett (B) advocated empowering workers and eliciting cooperation, not creating paper trails. Scientific management (D), which sought to study and time worker movements to improve efficiency, is not correct. Taylor and Weber were both concerned about training workers, but Weber is the more correct response for this question because of the record keeping aspect. Henri Fayol (E) identified a number of principles and functions for management but was more concerned with higher levels and broader organizational issues.

10. **(D)**   The correct response is (D), decision makers are rational and make full use of information. The classical approach relies on this assumption, based on traditional economic thinking. Option (A) is not correct because basing decisions on consensus and negotiation is characteristic of the political approach to decision-making. Not making full use of the information (B) is a characteristic of Simon's administrative model and is not correct. Option (C) is not correct because not all managers make good decisions; many can benefit from training. Option (E) is a feature of a contingency approach to management. It is incorrect when applied to the classical approach to decision-making.

11. **(B)**   The correct response is (B), total outputs divided by total inputs. Productivity is a measure of efficiency expressed as a ratio of outputs to inputs. The larger the number, the higher the efficiency level. Although Option

(A) contains outputs and inputs, it is written as the difference between the two, not the ratio, and thus is incorrect. Similarly Option (D) is incorrect as this is the same difference but in reverse order. Option (E) is incorrect because it adds the two terms. Option (C) does contain a ratio but is incorrect because it adds inputs and outputs before dividing by inputs.

12. **(E)** The correct option is (E), the economic value of employees' skills and competencies. This is the definition offered in the chapter. Capital has value so the skills must have value to be human capital. Option (C) involves skills and competencies but not the economic value aspect and is therefore incorrect. Budgeting for training (A) relates to enhancing skills but is not the definition of human capital. Option (B) is incorrect because compensation is not directly related to human capital. The facilities that house HR staff may be built with a capital budget but this does not make it human capital. Option (D) is incorrect.

13. **(A)** The correct response is (A) and is the definition offered in this chapter. Objectives must be specific. The acronym SMART can help you remember the qualities of good objectives. They are targets or outcomes that employees work to achieve. Option (B) is the definition for plans. Plans are the means to achieve goals and objectives. Option (C) is the definition of a contingency plan. It specifies steps to follow when disasters occur. Although these events may not be very likely, contingency plans allow organizations to move quickly during chaotic times. Objectives do not involve steps, only outcomes. Option (D) is the definition of a goal. Both goals and objectives deal with intended results. Objectives are the more *specific* statements; hence (A) is more correct among these four choices. Option (E) is actually part of the controlling function. It complements planning but is separate from that function and is therefore incorrect.

14. **(C)** The correct response is (C), *Zeitgeist*. This word means spirit of the times and was derived from the "Great Man" approach, which stated that leaders were born, not made. Option (A), the Ohio State University's studies, is incorrect because that was a behavioral study of leadership, which identified the behaviors of successful leaders. Behavioral research believes that leadership can be taught, not that leaders are born. Kurt Lewin's group studies of leadership was one early type of behavioral research, making option (B) incorrect. Option (D), trait approach, is not correct. The trait approach identified qualities of leaders, not just assuming that those people were born to lead. Option (E) is not correct because the University of Michigan's studies of job- versus employee-centered leadership was another example of behavioral research.

15. **(D)** The correct response is (D), obligations that society expects of corporations. Social responsibility tends to focus on corporations whereas ethics deals with individual employees. Option (A) is incorrect because it is the definition of morals. It is the foundation for doing good. Option (B) is not correct, as this definition applies to law; the law stresses not harming others. Option (C) is not correct as it is the definition of ethics; it focuses on both right and wrong behaviors in the workplace. Responses of corporations to pressure (E) is the complement to social responsibility but is not the same as those obligations or responsibilities.

16. **(A)** The correct response is assemble-to-order, option (A). Assemble-to-order is the service strategy that employs some customization from a limited range of options; so cable customers can order a basic package or premium channels and Internet service. Option (B) is not correct because customized services has the highest level of customization. Make-to-stock (C) is not correct because it is a manufacturing strategy based on volume production, not a service strategy. Option (D), make-to-order, is wrong because it is also a manufacturing strategy although it employs a moderate level of customization, making it somewhat comparable to assemble-to-order. Standardized services (E) is a basic service strategy with no options. It is wrong because cable companies offer customers some range of service options.

17. **(C)** The correct response is (C), corporate culture. Culture is internal and shared beliefs are a key part of the definition offered in the chapter. General environment forces (A) is not correct as this refers to the external environment. Similarly the immediate environmental forces (B) is another set of external forces and therefore incorrect. Option (D), adaptation forces, is not correct as this was not a specifically named set of forces, but instead is one means of responding to external forces. Similarly, influencing forces (E) is not correct either as this is another means for coping with external forces.

18. **(B)** The correct response is (B). *Multiple stakeholders* is the term used to describe the different groups who have an interest in the performance of a manager or firm. Option (A) is not correct because efficiency has to do with the use of resources to attain results. Human skills (C) focus on communication. Although stakeholders are groups of people, human skills do not apply to this question. Another term, *dependability* (D), does not apply either. Managers' performance is dependent on subordinates, one stakeholder group—but there are multiple stakeholders for managers and firms.

Finally, effectiveness (E) is not correct because it does not capture the multiple nature of groups with a vested interest in performance. Effectiveness is one type of performance.

19. **(A)** The correct response is (A), member satisfaction. Of those options presented, only satisfaction is an output. Member skills (B) and member knowledge (C) are inputs, making them incorrect. Options (D), member roles, and (E), group norms, are both process components and are therefore incorrect.

20. **(B)** The correct response is (B), perceived. Jaron is aware of something, so it cannot be latent (A), but he does not have an emotional response yet, so it cannot be felt (C). The manifest stage (D) comes even later, when action is taken, so (D) is not correct. Similarly, aftermath (E) is a late stage and not applicable here.

21. **(E)** The correct response is (E), ability, motivation, and work environment impact performance, so all three must be considered. Ability (A) is a factor, and equipment is part of the work environment, but motivation is missing. Similarly, motivation and ability represent a partial list, so (B) is incorrect. Motivation and work environment (C) are also incomplete. The most complete response must include all; even (D), combining ability and manager's attitude (part of the work environment), is not the most complete.

22. **(C)** The correct response is (C), requires cultural transformation at all levels of the organization. Quality cannot be isolated or relegated to a checking function; it must encompass all activities including the culture of the organization. Option (A) is not correct because inspection was a failed process of the past, as Deming criticized. Option (B) is not correct. Although some design with monitoring is an improvement over inspection, it does not go far enough in the transformation of the organization. Senior management plays an important role but quality is not their exclusive province, making (D) incorrect. Option (E) is incorrect because putting quality in a single department is like inspection and does not transform the organization enough.

23. **(B)** The correct response is (B). Herb Simon stated that people use bounded *rationality* when making decisions; they do not use full information as the classical approach presumed. Option (A) is not correct because basing decisions on consensus and negotiation is characteristic of the political approach to decision-making. Option (C) is not correct because not all

managers make good decisions; many can benefit from training. Decision makers making full use of information (D) is a feature of the classical approach, which the administrative approach contradicted. Therefore, (D) is incorrect. Option (E) is a feature of a contingency approach to management. It is incorrect when applied to the administrative approach to decision-making.

24. **(D)**   The correct response is (D), the number of employees who report to a supervisor. Span of management is a number—those employees who report to each supervisor. The span influences how flat or tall the organization structure is. The unbroken link of authority tying all individuals together (A) is not correct because this response defines chain of command. Option (B) is not correct because the degree to which jobs are comprised of a few tasks is the definition of work simplification. Option (C) addresses the location of authority, referring to centralization, not span of management, and is therefore incorrect. Finally, option (E) is not correct because adding similar tasks to a job is job enlargement.

25. **(C)**   The correct answer is (C). Completing the project with a written report is a specific outcome. Team members and managers will know if it done, thus making it measurable (although not quantitative). The statement has a time frame and it does appear to be feasible. It is clearly relevant to the team and the team's manager. In option (A), "extra hard" is not specific, nor measurable. Each manager and employee could have a different understanding of what this means. It is too vague. Although in option (B), "by the end of the quarter" specifies a time deadline, getting along well is not specific. It is hard to know what the manager means. The manager does not want to imply disagreements exist, because employees should be able to disagree about a real issue without fighting. Thus, it may not be feasible either. Option (D) is not correct because it is not clear what "will perform better" means. The company should have multiple goals of a specific nature. Should they do better on sales, profits, or cost containment? Specific targets that can be measured should be stated. It may also not be feasible to exceed all other companies in the industry. Option (E) is wrong because it is vague about running better meetings. Are they too long? Does he not allow others to speak or is the discussion dominated by a few people, shutting out others? A good goal statement should be specific about the intended results.

26. **(D)**   The correct option is (D), Frederic Taylor's scientific management. The scientific study of work entailed studying the motions and timing of work tasks. Taylor also urged training on these tasks and paying workers more for exceeding the standard—that is, a differential piece rate. The Haw-

thorne studies and the humanistic perspective (A) were a reaction to scientific management. Mary Parker Follett (B) was concerned about worker reactions to authority and other issues that grew out of scientific management but not work layouts. Weber's bureaucracy (C) was concerned with rules, documentation, and higher pay for higher positions in the hierarchy, but he did not advocate piece rates. Option (E) is not correct because Fayol was concerned with higher levels and broader organizational issues, not worker layouts and piece rates.

27. **(A)**   The correct response is (A), the Ohio State University's studies. They were most known for their two dimensions of leader behavior. Kurt Lewin's group studies of leadership was early behavioral research on democratic, autocratic, and laissez-faire styles, making option (B) incorrect. Option (C), *Zeitgeist*, is not correct because that approach assumed that leaders fit the times. Option (D), traits, is not correct. The trait approach identified qualities of leaders but did not focus on behaviors. The University of Michigan's studies (E) is not correct because it only viewed leadership on one dimension.

28. **(A)**   The correct response is (A)—the Civil Rights Act of 1964 prohibits discrimination on the basis of race, religion, color, sex, and national origin. It is the foundation of many HR legal practices. Option (B), the Occupational Safety and Health Act of 1970, has to do with safety, not discrimination. Option (C) focuses on a different type of discrimination, that based on age—not the categories listed in this question. Option (D) is not correct because the Americans with Disabilities Act of 1991 deals with accommodating disabilities, not these categories of discrimination. Finally, the Family Medical Leave Act (E) gives employees unpaid leave for family and health reasons and does not prohibiting discrimination. It is incorrect.

29. **(D)**   The correct option is (D), leading. The leading function provides the motivation for using plans structures. Awarding bonuses for performance motivates sales managers to strive for the goal. No planning (A) is evident in this option. If he was setting standards or objectives, then it would be planning. Option (B) is not correct, as he is not changing the reporting relationships or the design of work. Option (C), coordinating, is not one of the four contemporary functions of management. Although it is one of Fayol's original functions, it has been subsumed under organizing. Controlling (E) is not being practiced at the moment. Previously Chris may have compared the attained performance to the standard or goal as part of controlling; however, when he awards the bonuses, he is practicing leading.

30. **(E)** The correct option is (E), monitor. The monitor role is one of three information processing activities. It focuses on the gathering of information; reading trade journals informs a manager about new developments. Spokesperson (A) is another information processing role but it involves presenting information to those outside of the firm. Negotiator (B) is one of four decisional roles identified by Mintzberg. Nothing is being negotiated in this phase. Resource allocator (C) is another decisional role. Chris is not distributing resources here. Finally leader (D) is an interpersonal role focusing on directing and motivating subordinates. He is not leading while reading trade journals.

31. **(A)** The correct response is (A), accommodating. Allowing the other party to satisfy his or her concerns makes them feel good and can build trust and social credit. Especially when the issue is of minor importance to you, accommodating can be useful. Avoiding (B) does not satisfy your concerns or those of another, so social credits cannot be developed. Option (E) is not correct because competing also fails to satisfy any concern of another. Both collaboration (C) and compromising (D) involve both parties having some of their concerns met, but they also involve having some of your concerns met. These two options are less correct than (A), where the other party satisfies all of her or his concerns and none of yours are satisfied.

32. **(A)** The correct response is (A), risk. This question covers the definition of risk—known options with probabilities. Politics (B) is not correct. The political approach was one of the approaches to decision-making but does not apply to decision situations. Option (C) is not correct as vagueness was not a term discussed in the decision-making chapter. Option (D) is not correct because certainty is a situation with full information about options and outcomes. Uncertainty (E) involves incomplete knowledge of options. Here the options are known, making (E) incorrect.

33. **(C)** The correct response is (C). One of the key phrases in sexual harassment is "hostile work environment." A hostile work environment is created by repeated actions that limit the opportunities of employees based on their sex. Option (A) is not correct. Although sexual harassment is a type of discrimination, it is not against race or religion. Safety in the workplace (B) is not correct because it is part of the Occupational Safety and Health Act of 1970. Similarly options (D) and (E) are each part of different laws, neither of which are related to sexual harassment.

34. **(B)** The correct response is (B), Blake and Mouton's managerial grid. The team style was taught as most effective. The Ohio State University's studies (A) formed the basis of the grid with its two dimensions of leadership but the grid went further in application. Option (A) is not correct. Option (C), Lewin's group approach is not correct, as it examined democratic and autocratic styles. It did not have a grid, nor a category of team leadership. The traits approach (D) was not associated with team leadership and is therefore not correct. Option (E) is not correct because the University of Michigan used one dimension of leadership and the grid used two.

35. **(C)** The correct response is (C), legal-political. The establishment of a tariff is a political act. Although it has economic consequences, it is primarily a political change. Economy (A) is not correct because the problem was caused by the imposition of a tariff, not the general economy. There is no technological issue here, so option (B) is not correct. Option (D), socio-cultural, is not correct because there is not a demographic or consumer attitude issue here—e.g., consumers still want and like French wine. Option (E), human capital, is not correct because there is no evidence of a competency or skill shortage.

36. **(D)** The correct response is (D), inventory management. The kanban system strives to maintain lean amounts of inventory on the shop floor and in the warehouse. Option (A) is not correct because purchasing is the function that obtains the raw materials from suppliers that are then used in the manufacturing process. Logistics (B) is not correct because that function is concerned with the delivery of finished goods to warehouses and customers. Flexible manufacturing (C) is a system of producing that allows greater ease of customization. It may use a kanban approach but inventory management is more directly related. Similarly facilities planning and design (E) is a different function concerned with plant layouts and workflow. Again, kanban may become part of that plan but it is not as directly related as inventory management.

37 **(B)** The correct response is (B), the degree to which jobs are comprised of a few small tasks. Work simplification involves assigning relatively few, simple tasks to each employee so it is easier to train them and to improve efficiencies. The unbroken link of authority tying all individuals together (A) is not correct because this response defines chain of command. Option (C) addresses the location of authority, which refers to centralization, not work specialization, and is therefore incorrect. The number of employees who report to a supervisor (D) is not correct because this phrase

is a definition of span of control or management. Finally, option (E) is not correct because adding similar tasks to a job is job enlargement.

38. **(E)** The correct response is (E). As described in the chapter, ethical violations can lead to fines, legal costs, turnover, and morale problems. Option (A) is not correct because ethics are internal, individual standards. Option (B) is incorrect because ethical violations have led to the passage of laws, such as Sarbanes-Oxley. The statement in option (C) is not correct because laws cannot be written for everything. Ethical dilemmas are often complex choices, making option (D) incorrect.

39. **(B)** The correct option is (B), Mary Parker Follett of the administrative school. Writing late in that period, Follett was concerned with worker acceptance of authority. Empowerment was one means of accomplishing this end. The Hawthorne studies (A) is not correct because these began as scientific management experiments and ended with greater understanding of how workers and group dynamics impact performance. Option (C) is not correct because Weber's bureaucratic principles were concerned with rules, documentation, and higher pay for higher positions in the hierarchy. Scientific management (D) would not be correct because Taylor was more concerned with issues of work layout, training, and pay rather than worker acceptance of authority. Option (E) is not correct because Fayol described broad administrative principles, such as chain of command.

40. **(D)** The correct response is (D), committee. Both committees and task forces are cross-functional groups but only the committee is permanent. A task force (E) is ad hoc or temporary, making that option incorrect. Both vertical groups (A) and functional groups (C) are groups where work is done in teams. They are not coordinating bodies. Thus, these options are incorrect. Option (B), virtual team, is not correct because the group would be geographically distributed and not meet face-to-face.

41. **(D)** The correct response is (D), learning and growth. This is the first component in the Balanced Scorecard. The final step in the chain is financial performance (A), making that choice incorrect. The second step is internal business processes (B), so that choice is not right. Technology planning (C) was not one of the four areas of Kaplan and Norton's Balanced Scorecard. Finally, customer goals was the third step, so option (E) is wrong.

42. **(B)** The correct response is (B), Philip Crosby. Notions of zero defects and the cost-saving benefits of higher quality were his hallmarks. Op-

tion (A), Edward Deming, is not correct because he was associated with constancy of purpose and driving out the fear. Malcolm Baldridge is the former U.S. secretary of commerce for whom the Malcolm Baldridge National Quality Award was named, making (C) incorrect. James Fairfield-Sonn wrote about quality and culture, making option (D) incorrect. Joseph Juran defined quality as fitness for use, not constancy of purpose, and so (E) is not correct.

43. **(A)**   The correct response is (A), Herzberg's two-factor theory. Herzberg explained that only satisfiers could improve motivation. The fulfillment of dissatisfiers did not lead to motivation. Jobs had to be changed to meet the satisfier needs by assigning more responsibility and challenge. Alderfer's ERG (B) was a modification of Maslow's hierarchy and did not influence job redesign. Equity theory (C) is not a need-based theory and is therefore incorrect. Maslow's hierarchy (D) was a general approach to motivation that did not relate to job redesign. Option (E) is not correct, as McClelland's acquired needs theory was focused on training managers, not changing jobs.

44. **(E)**   The correct response is (E), human capital. Saul needs a critical skill that is not readily available in the labor market in which Saul's company operates. All of the other options represent other forces in the immediate environment. Suppliers (A) is a component of the immediate environment but there is no evidence that Saul cannot get parts, he just can't get employees who can work with the new materials. Competitors (B) is not correct because he is not losing employees to other competitors; they are not available for *any* company. Option (C), community, is not correct because community stakeholders are not seeking anything. There is no customer problem (D) either. The customer has new products but is not dissatisfied with Saul's work.

45. **(A)**   The correct response is (A), compensation. Job evaluation uses job information to rank jobs, forming an internally equitable system of pay or compensation. Recruitment (B) has nothing to do with job evaluation and is incorrect. Performance reviews are part of performance management (C), but job evaluation is different than performance reviews in that performance review provides a system to measure performance and provide feedback. Need analysis is part of training (D), but is not related to job evaluation. Option (E), selection, is not correct either because job evaluation is not used in that activity.

46. **(C)**   The correct response is (C), initiator. Of all the group roles presented, only initiator is task-oriented. Both harmonizer (A) and follower (D)

are socio-emotional roles and therefore not correct. Both blocker (B) and dominator (E) are self-oriented roles and therefore incorrect.

47. **(E)** The correct response is (E), Joseph Juran. Fitness for use and transforming the organization at a revolutionary pace exemplified his approach to quality. Option (A), Edward Deming, was the most philosophical with principles of constancy of purpose and ending mass inspection and is not correct. Option (B) is not correct because Philip Crosby was most associated with zero defects and lowering costs. Malcolm Baldridge is the former secretary of commerce for whom the Malcolm Baldridge National Quality Award was named, making (C) incorrect. James Fairfield-Sonn wrote about quality and culture. Option (D) is incorrect.

48. **(C)** The correct response is (C), enterprise resource planning (ERP). ERP integrates previously diverse and separate information systems. All business activities of the enterprise are contained in ERP. Option (A), decision support systems (DSS's), is not correct because DSS's take more limited pieces of information and combine them for a specific decision purpose. ERP is much broader. Expert systems (ES) (B) is also not correct as they capture human knowledge, again for a more limited decision task. Although ERP is a new and complex technology, option (D) is not correct because option (C) is a more direct and precise explanation for the question. Management of technology could involve the introduction of one sophisticated machine. ERP is broader and more comprehensive. Project management (E) is not correct because projects are focused, single time events. ERP continues to operate over time.

49. **(E)** The correct option is (E), scientific management, Fayol, and Weber. All of these perspectives addressed compensation in some way. Scientific management (A) addressed compensation through differential piece rates to raise productivity. Fayol's principles (B) addressed equity in compensation as well as bonuses and profit sharing. Weber (C) also addressed compensation by advocating greater pay for positions higher up the hierarchy. Option (A) is not correct because it ignores Fayol and Weber. Option (B) is not correct because it ignores scientific management and Weber. Similarly, option (C) is not correct because it omits Fayol and scientific management. Although option (D) includes both Fayol and Taylor, it neglects Weber.

50. **(A)** The correct response is (A), corporate goals. As depicted in Figure 6.2, corporate goals are the highest level, followed by strategic business unit goals (D). Next come functional goals (E), followed by unit goals (C),

and individual goals (B). Given this sequence, options (B) through (E) are all incorrect because corporate goals are the highest.

51. **(D)** The correct response is (D), Maslow's hierarchy of needs. Only Maslow talked about self-actualization. While distinctive, self-actualization is difficult to measure and has not worked well in tests of his theory. Herzberg's two-factor theory (A) does not have anything close to self-actualization and is not correct. Alderfer's ERG is close to Maslow's overall theory but did not have that highest category, making (B) incorrect. Locke's goal-setting theory (C) is not a need-based theory and is therefore incorrect. McClelland had needs for power and achievement, but not self-actualization; (E) is incorrect.

52. **(C)** The correct response is (C), awareness of the problem. Before doing anything the manager has to know that there is a decision to make or a problem to solve. Formulate the problem (A) is not correct because this is the second step, following awareness. Option (B), implementation, is not correct as this happens late in the process. Option (D) is not correct because diagnosis occurs in the middle, after awareness and formulation. Generating alternatives follows diagnosis, so (E) is not correct.

53. **(B)** The correct response is (B), moral rights. One component of the moral rights approach is to freely choose with full information. By pushing the formula without providing information on other options, the mothers' rights are violated. Option (A), justice, is not correct, as this option treats all mothers fairly, consistently, and impartially. All mothers are treated the same, so this option is ethical from a justice perspective and is incorrect. Utilitarian (C) advocates the choice that does the greatest good for the greatest number. Given that the hospital receives funding from the manufacturer, you could argue that the money received is used to help many others, thus making their actions ethical from the utilitarian perspective (and not correct for this question). Universalism treats all with dignity and respect, as the hospital does, making (D) incorrect. Moralism (E) was not a perspective covered in the text and is therefore incorrect.

54. **(B)** The correct response is (B), role ambiguities. When the boundaries for jobs are poorly defined it is easy for someone to wander into someone else's duties, causing a turf violation or conflict. There is no evidence of competing goals in this situation, so (A) is not correct. Similarly scarce resources is not an issue either, making (C) incorrect. Task interdependencies are also not evident, as there are no other tasks discussed; thus (D) is incorrect. Fi-

nally, option (E) refers to incompatible reward system, but rewards are not discussed. Option (E) is incorrect.

55. **(D)** The correct response is option (D), organizational chart. Most elements of organizing are intangible and abstract. The chart is visible and shows aspects of the chain of command. Centralization (A) is difficulty to see. It represents the location of power and authority, whether it is high or low in the hierarchy. Option (B) is not correct. Task identity is an individual perception of the job and is not visible. The chain of command (C) is not as visible as the chart and is not correct. Corporate culture (E) is not part of organizing and is therefore not correct.

56. **(D)** The correct response is (D), Hersey-Blanchard's life cycle theory. This approach viewed the situation in terms of the readiness of subordinates to assume responsibility and perform delegated tasks. Being able and willing to accept responsibility were key components of readiness. Option (A) is incorrect because, although Fiedler used leader-member relations to define the situation, he did not use readiness. Options (B), Ohio State University's studies, and (C), University of Michigan's studies, are not correct because they did not have situational features associated with them—just leader behaviors. House's path-goal theory (E) is another situational theory that looked at subordinate characteristics, but not specifically readiness.

57. **(C)** The correct option is (C), conceptual skills. Concepts provide guidelines or maps for understanding what cannot be seen firsthand. Option (A) is not correct because technical skills involve analyzing work problems that are tangible, not mental images. Option (B) is not correct because the question does not relate to communicating or dealing with others. Option (D) is not correct because functional was not a skill category mentioned in this chapter. Emotional intelligence (E) is related to human skills, not understanding the larger organization.

58. **(E)** The correct response is (E), altering the relationship. Ted and Sue don't work well together, nor do they like each other. By having the work flow through Adrienne, Maya is using a buffer and changing the nature of the relationship. Maya is not altering the issue (A), which would involve depersonalizing the conflict by focusing on the issue, not the people. Altering the context (B) would involve conditions, such as unclear boundaries or scarce resources. She is not trying to change these. Option (B) is incorrect. Option (C) is incorrect because she has neither sent them to training, nor reassigned either Ted or Sue, which would alter the people. Finally, Maya

has not changed the work done by either, just the interaction. Option (D) is incorrect.

59. **(A)** The correct response is (A), investment center. This type of responsibility center encompasses the most factors: expenses, revenue, and capital budgets. Expense centers only include expense budgets, not revenue or capital budgets, so (B) is not correct. Revenue centers only include revenue, so (C) is not correct as it does not involve capital budgets. Option (D) is not correct because building center is a fabricated term. Finally option (E) is not correct because profit centers include both expenses and revenue, but not capital budgets.

60. **(D)** The correct response is (D), systems theory. Open systems are dependent on the environment to survive. Contingency (A) is not correct. Although a contingency is a type of dependence, this option does not acknowledge the external environment. Option (B) is not correct, as ancient military did not articulate open systems. Napoleon was defeated in Russia as much by the winter (i.e., a larger, open systems issue) as by the Russian army. The humanist perspective (C) explained worker and group reactions, which expanded the system but not to the full extent that systems theory did. Chester Barnard (E) dealt with an issue of limited scope, worker cooperation, and not external factors. Systems theory is much broader.

61. **(E)** The correct response is (E), résumé. Either a résumé or application blank starts the selection process. Background checks (A) is not correct as that is usually one of the last steps. These take time and so checks are done for only the small set of finalists for each position. Option (B), job interview, occurs later with information from the resume used to form some interview questions. Ability test (C) is not correct either. Testing is also usually done after receipt of the resume. Similarly, option (D), work-sample test, is done subsequent to receiving a résumé or application.

62. **(E)** The correct response is (E), House's path-goal theory. Of all the contingency approaches only the path-goal used four types of leader behavior. Option (A) is not correct because Fiedler used least preferred co-worker. Options (B), Ohio State University's studies, and (C), University of Michigan's studies, used two types of leader behavior, not four. Also, Hersey-Blanchard used task and relationship behaviors, not four types, making option (D) incorrect.

63. **(B)**   The correct response is (B), functional. Most organizations begin with a simple functional structure. Option (A), divisional, is not correct because divisions duplicate functions within each division, requiring larger size and added resources. Small organizations do not use divisional structures. Likewise a matrix structure (C) is a form of organizing that fairly large organizations use in specialized conditions. Options (D) and (E) are both incorrect, as they are both a type of divisional structure used in larger organizations.

64. **(D)**   The correct response is (D), discretionary. Donating profits to breast cancer projects represents going beyond ethical activities and is purely discretionary. Option (A) is not correct because there is no legal requirement to donate profits to healthcare causes. Option (B) is not correct because caring is not a category of corporate social responsibility. Economic (C) is not correct because sharing profits does not support financial goals, it reduces them. Option (E) is not correct either, as donating profits goes beyond ethical actions.

65. **(A)**   The correct response is avoider, (A). An avoider fails to engage other members and avoids disagreements. These actions are self-oriented and harm the group. Both consensus tester (B) and summarizer (E) are task-oriented roles and are therefore incorrect options. Similarly, compromiser (C) and follower (D) are socio-emotional roles and are not correct responses for this question.

66. **(D)**   The correct response is (D), quantity. Timeliness (A), completeness (B), relevance (C), and quality (E) are all desired qualities of information. It is easy to generate large quantities of data, but excess data creates an overload with no value to management.

67. **(E)**   The correct response is option (E), community. By sharing employees on company time, the firm is providing a service to community agencies in the immediate environment. Although the employees are doing database work, which has a technological component, this is not a technological force in the general environment; thus (A) is incorrect. Such a general environmental issue would have to be new technology that was changing products and the way business is done, which is not the case here. Option (B) focuses on internal culture. Employees working on a database is not a ceremony and is not correct. Although working outside of the company, these employees are not lobbyists and option (C) is not correct. Option (D) is not correct because boundary spanning is not an influence activity but is

an adaptive strategy, moving in the reverse direction from the outward-oriented influencing.

68. **(D)** The correct response is (D), assess or define the current mission statement. The strategic planning process begins with the assessment of current performance and mission. You have to know where you are currently before plotting other goals and means. Option (A) is wrong because implementing the strategy is the last step, not the first. Conducting the SWOT analysis is the second step, so option (B) is not correct. Developing new mission and goals is the third step, so option (C) is wrong. The fourth step in the five-step model is formulate the strategy, so option (E) cannot be correct.

69. **(D)** The correct option is (D), sensing-thinking (ST). A focus on details is characteristic of a sensing approach to perception and the analytical reasoning is found among thinking types. Option (B) is not correct because an NF would look at longer term, big picture issues that focus on people and values. Option (C) is not correct because extroverted and analytic are not Myers-Briggs categories. An NT (E) would see patterns in the data, not details, and is therefore incorrect.

70. **(C)** The correct response is (C), expectancy or E → P. The belief that exerting effort will enable you to perform at a reasonable level is confidence. The two other components of expectancy theory are (A), the valence of outcomes, and (D), instrumentality. Option (A) is not correct because valence is the value that individuals place on those outcomes. Option (D) is not correct because instrumentality is the belief that when you perform, valued outcomes will follow. Neither of these relates to confidence. Option (B) is not correct because the ratio of outputs to inputs is part of equity theory, not expectancy. Similarly, option (E) is not correct because positive reinforcement is not part of expectancy.

71. **(E)** The correct response is (E), influencing factors in the environment. Lobbying is an active influence strategy, which in this case is intended to impact legal-political forces. Option (A) is not correct because lobbying is not adapting to the environment but attempting to influence it. Similarly option (B) also covers adapting to the immediate environment while lobbying influences it. This question does not relate to the internal culture, so option (C) is not correct. Lobbying is not done primarily to increase awareness of the environment (D), but to influence it. Option (D) is not correct.

72. **(B)** The correct response is (B), product. The product manager has responsibility for the product, with all functional areas for that product reporting directly to him or her. Liaison (A) is not correct as this is an integrating mechanism, not a type of departmentalization. Functional (C) is not correct, as this form has poor product responsibility or effort focus. In the matrix organization (D) the product manager has product responsibility but the functional manager does not, and thus this option is not correct. Job rotation (E) is not a type of departmentalization and does not relate to product responsibility. Option (E) is not correct.

73. **(D)** The correct response is (D), both differentiation and focus. The strategy utilized differentiation because the all-luxury resort with security strives to be different. It is also focus, or niche, because it appeals to a specific segment of the market. Since (D) is correct, neither option (A) nor (C) is correct. Option (B) is not correct because cost leadership competes on the basis of low price and this division will charge high prices. For that reason, option (E) is also wrong because it includes cost leadership as a component.

74. **(C)** The correct response is norming (C). Following the storming stage, the group settles down with clearer norms and acceptance of roles. Since norming follows storming, option (B) cannot be correct. Storming is also wrong because it is characterized by disagreements and conflicts. Option (A), performing, is not correct. Performing is close to norming in terms of development but performing is more advanced with shifting roles as needed. The statement in this question more closely approximates norming. Option (D) is not correct because adjourning is the final stage, related to closure when the group's tasks are finished. Finally, forming (E) is not correct because this stage involves cautiousness among members and an unwillingness to criticize.

75. **(C)** The correct option is (C). Individuals write down their ideas alone and then evaluate them later in a group. NGT uses a more structured approach to idea generation. Option (A) is incorrect because brainstorming and NGT use the same method to evaluate alternative ideas. Option (B) is incorrect, as no different names are used in NGT. "Nominal" refers to the fact that the first stage is really individual. Similarly option (D) is incorrect because names are not used in assigning responsibility either. Option (E) is incorrect because both brainstorming and NGT require cognitive skills.

76. **(B)** The correct response is (B), progressive discipline. The discipline is progressive because each infraction is met with progressively more severe discipline. Discipline is intended to suppress undesirable behavior. Quality control (A) is not correct because this type of system does not impose penalties on employees. Punishment is administered by supervisors. Market control (C) is an informal system that influences prices, not employees. It is incorrect. *Incremental discipline* (D) is a fabricated term that is similar to progressive discipline; however, it is not the correct term. Clan control (E) is an informal means of influencing employees with norms and values. Progressive discipline is a formal system. Option (E) is incorrect.

77. **(A)** The correct option is (A), technical skills. Technical skills account for the largest proportion at the lower level where managers frequently solve problems in the immediate work environment. Option (B) is not correct because human skills are equally important at all levels. Option (C) is not correct because conceptual skills are least used by lower-level managers. Option (D) is not correct because "functional" is not a relevant skill category. Expressive skills (E) are more closely related to human skills, which is not as important as technical at this level.

78. **(D)** The correct response is (D), low tolerance for change. Having done it the old way and being very comfortable, they appear to have low tolerance for change. They have received communications, so a lack of understanding (E) is not likely. It does not appear to be in their parochial self-interest to resist, so option (A) is not correct. Sam and the group do not have a different assessment of the situation, so option (B) is wrong. His employees respect Sam, so lack of trust is not the issue. Option (C) is not correct.

79. **(E)** The correct response is (E), ethical. Installing electronic kiosks is designed to be fair and unbiased with all applicants. This approach is characteristic of the ethical response. Option (A), legal, is not correct because there was no legal requirement to do so. Option (B) is not correct because caring is not a category of corporate social responsibility. Economic (C) is not correct because it is more costly to install kiosks, and thus economic interests are somewhat harmed. Installing kiosks would not be considered discretionary (D) as greater benefits would need to result for society.

80. **(C)** The correct response is (C). McGregor's Theory X and Theory Y asserted that managers held two different sets of attitudes about worker motivation. They communicated the attitude to the worker who, in turn, acted accordingly. Frederick Taylor (B) is not correct because Taylor only focused

on compensation issues in motivation. Abraham Maslow (C) was another mid-1950s motivation writer, but he is associated with the hierarchy of needs theory, not managerial attitudes. Henri Fayol (D) wrote about administrative principles related primarily to the organizing function, not managerial attitudes. Max Weber (E) is best known for his bureaucracy principles, which are also about organizing, and therefore (E) is not correct.

81. **(B)**   The correct response is (B). Company intranets are a rapidly growing means of training workers around the world, quickly and at their own pace. Option (A) is not correct, as managers may not be aware of employees' training needs. Training surveys can provide that information. Option (C) is not correct because reactions to training do not assess learning or changes in job performance, which are more meaningful measures of effectiveness. Option (D) is wrong because on-the-job training occurs everyday. Option (E) is not correct. Training is important but fewer trainers are now being used. Line managers, rather than professional trainers, now do more training.

82. **(C)**   The correct option is (C), vertical, top-down. Managers communicating to subordinates is vertical, and the specific direction is from top down to bottom. Diagonal communication (A) can be from higher to lower but also tends to be outside of the chain of command, making it incorrect. Option (B), horizontal communication, involves communication among peers at the same level. This does not apply to this example. Option (D) is not correct because circular communication was not one of the directionalities discussed in the chapter. Option (E) is also vertical but bottom-up would be a direction initiated by the subordinate, making it incorrect.

83. **(B)**   The correct option is (B), organizing. The function of organizing involves relationships among employees and the way the work is performed. Changing the work flow and moving people alters relationships, a key aspect of organizing. Planning (A) involves setting objectives. If Sonia were setting performance standards for the unit, it would be planning. Option (C) is not correct because coordinating is not one of the contemporary functions of management. Leading (D) is not correct because she is not communicating or motivating workers in this question. Option (E), controlling, refers to assessment and feedback. Sonia may have assessed prior to these organizing changes, but what is described in this question is more closely related to organizing.

84. **(D)** The correct response is (D), an organic structure that can adapt. In dynamic environments a flexible, or organic, structure allows for adaptation to environmental forces. In stable environments a vertical and efficient but less flexible structure is best. Option (A) is not correct because a functional structure is not very adaptive for a changing environment. Similarly a tall, or vertical, structure (B) is not correct because it is slow to adapt. Option (C) is not correct either because these three integration mechanisms are used by all organizations and would not provide enough integration for a dynamic environment. Option (E) addresses high levels of centralization which offers control but not adaptation. It is incorrect.

85. **(B)** The correct response is (B), expectancy theory, another process theory of motivation. Goal-setting addresses specific, challenging goals. With high self-efficacy, individuals try harder and perform better. Rewards also reinforce goals. These aspects are similar to expectancy and the valence of outcomes in expectancy theory. Option (A), Alderfer's ERG theory, is not correct as this is a content theory, quite different from the goal-setting. Reinforcement theory (C) is not correct as it did not consider cognitive issues, such as choices or goals, only observable behavior. Herzberg's two-factor theory (D) is not correct as this is a content theory, quite different from the goal-setting. Equity theory (E) looks at output/input ratios and does not have much in common with goal-setting.

86. **(A)** The correct option is (A). Charismatic leaders create a vision that meets followers' needs, articulate it well, and sustain it with other communication. Charismatic leaders are not born (B). Specific behaviors have been identified that are associated with transformational leaders. Option (C) is not correct because physical attraction has not been found to relate to transformational leadership. Someone who uses the right style in the right situation (D) may be a good transactional leader, but not a charismatic one. Option (D) is incorrect. Option (E) is not correct because pay has nothing to do with charisma.

87. **(D)** The correct answer is (D), disturbance handler, one of the four decisional roles of Mintzberg. Tino is responding to an unplanned event with the vendor problem. The questions and solution focus on a decision. Option (A), monitor, is not correct because Tino is making decisions to fix a problem. He is gathering information but the primary focus is a decision to address the vendor problem. Option (B) is not correct because the liaison role involves establishing contacts as part of an interpersonal role. Tino already has a relationship with this subordinate. The entrepreneur (C) role is

another decisional one but it would involve planned changes. This situation was unanticipated. Option (E) is not correct because Tino is not deciding how to distribute resources among subordinates.

88. **(D)**   The correct response is (D), employees seek other jobs in inequitable situations. If they feel that the tension of inequity cannot be restored in that environment, then they will seek another, more equitable job situation. Option (A) is not correct as over-rewarded people may reduce the effort to restore equity, which would not lead to better performance. Option (B) is not correct as equity theory shows that the level of pay does impact motivational choices. Option (C) is not correct because both inputs and outputs are used in equity theory. Similarly inputs are not most important (E) because outputs must be considered equally.

89. **(B)**   The correct response is (B). There is no evidence that group decision-making results in more insults. All of the other options, however, are disadvantages. Groups make riskier decisions, making (A) incorrect. Members may engage in social loafing, so (C) is incorrect. Option (D) is not correct, as groups take more time to make decisions. Finally domination (E) may occur, resulting in process loss, therefore option (E) is incorrect.

90. **(D)**   The correct response is (D), benchmarking. Companies search for best practices at other companies and send teams to study and copy them. Strategy formulation (A) is done within the company, so it is not correct here. A policy (B) provides general direction for how an activity is to be handled. Policies may be developed by sending teams to observe another company. A contingency plan provides a response to rare or unexpected events, but benchmarking seeks to understand how another firm performs a repetitive process. Option (C) is not correct here. Projects are single-use plans and benchmarking is for processes, so option (E) is wrong.

91. **(E)**   The correct response is (E), labor relations. Grievance procedures are part of the union contract which is administered by the labor relations unit of HR. Compensation (A) deals with salary administration, not union grievances. Employee relations (B) works to maintain good relations with non-unionized employees and therefore cannot be correct. Performance management (C) does not process union grievances and is not correct. Similarly training (D) has nothing to do with union grievances.

92. **(B)**   The correct response is (B), Fiedler's contingency theory. Fiedler proposed three dimensions comprising favorability: leader-member

relations, task structure, and position power. In moderate favorability, the relationship-motivated leader is best. In high and low favorability situations, the task-motivated leader is best. None of the other options or models involved favorability of the situation. Path-goal theory (D) and life cycle theory (E) were other situational theories but they do not employ favorability, making them wrong. Goleman's emotional intelligence (A) and Bass's transformational leadership (B) are not situational, nor do they include favorability.

93. **(A)** The correct option is (A), liaison department. This is an advanced form of integration that is not commonly used in many organizations. The most common ones are rules and procedures (B), planning (D), and hierarchy (E). Therefore, each of these options is incorrect. The next most common form of integration is task forces (C). Many organizations use task forces, making liaison department (A) the best choice here.

94. **(E)** The correct response is (E), education and communication. These steps help prepare employees for the change and build trust for the long haul. Of the choices presented, this is the most logical place to start. Coercion and manipulation represent tactics of last resort, making options (B) and (D) incorrect. Co-optation (A) is a process to win over resisters. It is not the best place to start, therefore, option (A) is wrong. Negotiated agreement (C) is also a change process that comes later, once resistance is encountered. Option (C) is incorrect.

95. **(B)** The correct option is (B). Much of the culture is hidden and not obvious, like an iceberg. Values and beliefs are not readily evident. It is only the artifacts that are visible. Therefore, option (A) is not correct because it states that culture is readily observable. Option (C) is not correct because the culture is influenced by how the company responds to external issues as well as internal ones. Option (D) is not correct because culture cannot be changed rapidly. Values and practices change fairly slowly. Option (E) is not correct because culture is based on informal practices. Official policies may be at odds with how things are really done.

96. **(B)** The correct response is option (B). A project manager needs to clarify the scope and objectives of the project (B) at the start. Option (A) is not correct because the project manager needs to delegate and rely on the skills of team members, not do the work alone. Usually the project manager does not interview members to be on the project (C), so that option is not correct. Option (D) is not correct because the project manager does not only

determine pay levels. Pay decisions are made within a compensation structure with input from human resources and higher management. Leaving the team alone to do its work (E) is not correct. The project manager needs to stay involved, assisting with problems and monitoring progress.

97. **(B)** The correct response is (B), reaction. The initial response of the American Council of Life Insurers was to fight the issue all the way. There was no attempt to question or investigate. It was a public relations statement without concern for ethics or corporate responsibility. Proaction (A) is not correct, as this response would require engaging in discretionary acts of social responsibility, which the council did not. Option (C), activation, is not correct as this is not a category of social responsiveness described in the chapter. An accommodation (D) response would require progressive actions going beyond the requirements, which did not happen. A defense (E) response is meeting requirements or expectations. The council fought any investigation without meeting expectations, so option (E) is incorrect.

98. **(B)** The correct response is (B), measure frequently. Although some control systems measure often, it is better to measure selectively and strategically. If people are overwhelmed with data, then they have a hard time making good decisions. Measuring frequently is not a major focus of effective control systems, making it the correct response. Option (A), an internal orientation of self-control, is not correct. Self-control is very important in control systems. External checking does not work as a sole approach. Similarly, measure strategically (C) is another key component of effective control systems, making it incorrect for this question. Option (D), flexibility, is also important. Provisions for breaking the rules should be allowed. Flexibility for measured risks can lead to greater gains. Rewarding compliance and high performance is also a desirable feature of effective systems, making option (E) incorrect.

99. **(E)** The correct response is (E), punishment. Shirelle wants to decrease an undesired behavior. To do so she presents an unpleasant consequence, the reprimand. This action follows the principles of punishment. Option (A), positive reinforcement, is not correct because that strategy involves a positive consequence following a behavior to encourage that behavior in the future. Option (B), variable reinforcement, is not correct as this involves the timing of reinforcement. Punishment is best administered on a fixed schedule. Option (C), no reinforcement, is not correct because a reprimand is not the absence of reinforcement. Finally, operant conditioning

(D) is not correct because that term refers in general to all of these strategies. It is too general for this question.

100. **(C)** The correct response is (C). Groupthink only occurs in cohesive groups where members value membership and are reluctant to criticize. Invulnerability and an inherent sense of morality are two symptoms of groupthink. Option (A) is not correct. Groupthink is more likely following success rather than failure. Option (B) is not correct. Members do not doubt their abilities. They tend to be over-confident with a sense of invulnerability and morality. High-level groups (D) are not the only ones who experience groupthink, making this option wrong. Groups at any level, who are cohesive, have the potential to succumb to groupthink and make poor decisions. Option (E) is not correct because groupthink causes groups to make worse decisions by limiting criticism and withholding doubts.

▼
PRACTICE
TEST 2

This test is also on CD-ROM in our special interactive CLEP Principles of Management TEST*ware*®. It is highly recommended that you first take this exam on computer. You will then have the additional study features and benefits of enforced timed conditions, individual diagnostic analysis, and instant scoring. See page xiii for guidance on how to get the most out of our CLEP Principles of Management book and software.

CLEP PRINCIPLES OF MANAGEMENT

PRACTICE TEST 2

(Answer sheets appear in the back of this book.)

TIME: 90 Minutes
100 Questions

DIRECTIONS: Each of the questions or incomplete statements below is followed by five possible answers or completions. Select the best choice in each case and fill in the corresponding oval on the answer sheet.

1. Which of the following is the best definition of efficiency?

    (A) The best use of available resources in the process of accomplishing goals

    (B) Whether appropriate employees know what's expected of them

    (C) Doing the right job

    (D) Accomplishing appropriate goals

    (E) Be all that you can be

2. Which of the following is an input that impacts the functioning of groups?

    (A) Member satisfaction

    (B) Member skills

    (C) Enhanced member capability

    (D) Member roles

    (E) Group norms

3.   Which of the following is the last step in the control process?

   (A) Measure actual performance

   (B) Compare performance with standard

   (C) Establish standard

   (D) Take corrective action

   (E) Run the process, perform the work

4.   Which of the following statements best defines the "rule of law"?

   (A) Fundamental values that society imparts about right and wrong behaviors

   (B) Minimal standards for not doing harm in society

   (C) Beliefs about appropriate behaviors in the workplace

   (D) Obligations that society expects of corporations

   (E) Responses of corporations to pressures put on them by society

5.   Human resource management is most closely associated with which of the following traditional functions of management?

   (A) Controlling

   (B) Planning

   (C) Organizing

   (D) Leading

   (E) Monitoring

6.   Which of the following historical approaches to management found that worker reactions and group dynamics also influence productivity?

   (A) The humanistic perspective (Hawthorne studies)

   (B) Mary Parker Follett of the administrative school

   (C) Max Weber's bureaucracy

   (D) Frederick Taylor's scientific management

   (E) Henri Fayol of the administrative school

7.   What is the relationship between conflict and performance?

   (A) The level of conflict is inversely related to performance—higher conflict, lower performance.

   (B) There is no consistent relationship between conflict and performance.

   (C) Conflict is only related to performance at very high levels of conflict.

   (D) Performance and conflict are positively related.

   (E) The relationship resembles a bell-shaped curve with high and low conflict adversely impacting performance.

8.   Which of the following represents the best definition of the organizing term "chain of command"?

   (A) The unbroken link of authority tying together all individuals in the organization

   (B) The degree to which work is broken into small tasks and assigned to jobs

   (C) The location of authority near the top of the hierarchy

   (D) The number of employees who report to a supervisor

   (E) The modification of jobs by adding several similar tasks

9.   Which of the following categories of external forces represents the broadest set of trends and forces impacting a company?

   (A) General environment forces

   (B) Immediate environment forces

   (C) Corporate culture

   (D) Adaptation forces

   (E) Influencing forces

10. Which of the following terms best describes the activities used to attain organizational goals?

    (A) Organizing

    (B) Plans

    (C) Objectives

    (D) SMART

    (E) Controlling

11. Which of the following statements is true of the political approach to decision-making?

    (A) Decisions are based on consensus and negotiation, not an objective sense of right and wrong.

    (B) When making decisions, people do not make full use of all information and their mental capacities.

    (C) Most managers make good decisions without extensive training in decision-making.

    (D) Decision makers are rational and make full use of information in reaching decisions.

    (E) Decisions are seldom purely right or wrong; the situation influences what works best.

12. Which of the following is NOT a concern for today's operation manager?

    (A) The cost of healthcare benefits paid to employees

    (B) The quality of work-in-progress

    (C) The cost of shipping products rejected and returned by customers

    (D) The length of time it takes to ship finished products to customers

    (E) The ability to make changes in the basic product to meet customer demands

13. Which early approach to leadership examined one dimension, ranging from job-centered to employee-centered?

   (A) Ohio State University's dimensional studies

   (B) Kurt Lewin's group studies

   (C) *Zeitgeist*

   (D) Trait approach

   (E) University of Michigan's studies

14. The tendency for employees to take credit for performance successes but blame failures on external causes has been termed which of the following?

   (A) Needs

   (B) Fundamental attribution error

   (C) Performance bias

   (D) Actor-observer bias

   (E) Ability ignorance

15. Which of the following legislative acts has influenced managers to make reasonable accommodations for those who can perform essential functions?

   (A) Civil Rights Act of 1964 and subsequent amendments

   (B) Occupational Safety and Health Act of 1970

   (C) Age Discrimination Act of 1967

   (D) Americans with Disabilities Act of 1991

   (E) Family and Medical Leave Act of 1993

16. Which of the following historical approaches to management emphasized the importance of working in a unified direction and having a clear chain of command?

   (A) The humanistic perspective (Hawthorne studies)

   (B) Mary Parker Follett of the administrative school

   (C) Max Weber's bureaucracy

   (D) Frederick Taylor's scientific management

   (E) Henri Fayol of the administrative school

17. Which of the following was NOT a trait identified with early studies of leadership?

   (A) Intelligence

   (B) Integrity

   (C) Happy and upbeat

   (D) Self-confidence

   (E) Decisiveness

18. Which of the following statements best defines morals?

   (A) Fundamental values that society imparts about right and wrong behaviors

   (B) Minimal standards imposed by society for not harming others

   (C) Beliefs about appropriate behaviors in the workplace

   (D) Obligations that society expects of corporations

   (E) Responses of corporations to pressures put on them by society

19. Which of the following need-based approaches to motivation views needs as learned in early childhood experiences?

   (A) Herzberg's two-factor theory

   (B) Alderfer's ERG theory

   (C) Locke's goal setting theory

   (D) Maslow's hierarchy of needs

   (E) McClelland's acquired needs theory

20. A Central American manufacturer is struggling. Inflation is 12 percent. As a result, workers keep demanding more money to feed their families and supplies get more expensive. These rising costs reduce the company's cash flow, so the firm buys fewer materials and produces less. What force in the general environment is affecting the business?

   (A) Economy

   (B) Technology

   (C) Legal-political

   (D) Socio-cultural

   (E) Human capital

Questions 21–22

Chris Talbott is the national sales manager for a medium-sized firm that designs and manufactures components for cellular phones. He reports to the vice president of marketing. Chris's current activities include assessing the expenditures of the regional sales managers to see if they have exceeded budgeted amounts and then taking any corrective action needed. He is also involved in developing the next year's marketing plan and awarding bonuses to the top-performing regional sales managers who report to him. Chris reads several trade journals and newsletters to identify new industry trends and shares them with the sales force in a weekly meeting.

21. Which function of management is Chris engaged in while assessing marketing expenditures and taking corrective action?

   (A) Planning

   (B) Organizing

   (C) Coordinating

   (D) Leading

   (E) Controlling

22. What level of management is Chris most likely to occupy?

   (A) Team leader (but not management)

   (B) Top

   (C) Diagonal

   (D) Lower

   (E) Middle

23. Large manufacturers, such as Procter & Gamble, manufacture tooth-paste in large quantities and store finished goods in warehouses for delivery to customers as needed. Which of the following manufacturing strategy do they use?

    (A) Assemble-to-order

    (B) Customized services

    (C) Make-to-stock

    (D) Make-to-order

    (E) Standardized services

24. Individuals permanently assigned to a group to do their work are described as which of the following?

    (A) Vertical team

    (B) Virtual team

    (C) Functional team

    (D) Committee

    (E) Task force

25. Which quality expert advocated constancy of purpose by driving out the fear and ending mass inspection?

    (A) Edward Deming

    (B) Philip Crosby

    (C) Malcolm Baldridge

    (D) James Fairfield-Sonn

    (E) Joseph Juran

26. Which of the following options best defines job enlargement?

    (A) The unbroken link of authority tying all individuals in the organization

    (B) The degree to which work is broken into small tasks and assigned to jobs

    (C) The location of authority near the top of the hierarchy

    (D) The number of employees who report to a supervisor

    (E) The modification of jobs by adding several similar tasks

27. Which of the following describes a decision situation in which the manager does not know the options or the probabilities associated with the options?

    (A) Risk

    (B) Politics

    (C) Vagueness

    (D) Certainty

    (E) Uncertainty

28. Which of the following descriptions would be classified as a single-use type of plan?

    (A) Policy on the use of drugs in the workplace

    (B) Procedure for reporting sexual harassment in the workplace

    (C) Five percent reduction in late orders

    (D) Seven percent increase in sales revenue in the next quarter

    (E) Strategy to achieve growth through a joint venture with an Asian partner firm

29. Antonio has just learned that Otto went to Antonio's supervisor to tell her that Antonio has been looking for other jobs. Both Otto and Antonio are being considered for promotion to a project leader position. Antonio is livid, as he believes that Otto gave his boss this information to damage his chances of getting the promotion. Which stage has this conflict reached?

    (A) Latent

    (B) Perceived

    (C) Felt

    (D) Manifest

    (E) Aftermath

30. Which description best characterizes the term supply chain management?

    (A) The management of companies who supply chains for various businesses

    (B) Managing the links among all of a firm's suppliers

    (C) Determining the best way to deliver finished products to customers

    (D) The processes for finding the raw materials to make a product, manufacturing that product, and delivering it to customers in the best way possible

    (E) The process of studying the layout of tasks in manufacturing in order to reduce unnecessary steps, improving efficiency and reducing costs

31. When a group of church members organized a boycott against Nestlé-products because they object to Nestlé's methods of marketing infant formula in third world countries, which component of the general environment was operating?

    (A) Economy

    (B) Technology

    (C) Legal-political

    (D) Socio-cultural

    (E) Human capital

32. Which of the following is the former U.S. Secretary of Commerce for whom a national quality award is named?

    (A) Edward Deming

    (B) Philip Crosby

    (C) Malcolm Baldridge

    (D) James Fairfield-Sonn

    (E) Joseph Juran

33. Which of the following legislative acts established standards and provided enforcement related to air quality in the workplace?

    (A) Civil Rights Act of 1964 and subsequent amendments

    (B) Occupational Safety and Health Act of 1970

    (C) Age Discrimination Act of 1967

    (D) Americans with Disabilities Act of 1991

    (E) Family and Medical Leave Act of 1993

34. Individuals assigned to a team to coordinate for a single, specific purpose form which of the following?

    (A) Vertical team

    (B) Virtual team

    (C) Functional team

    (D) Committee

    (E) Task force

35. Which of the following terms best reflects the modifications of jobs by adding more responsibilities and tasks that require more complex skill?

    (A) Job enlargement

    (B) Staff authority

    (C) Job rotation

    (D) Job simplification

    (E) Job enrichment

36. Which of the following is NOT one of Kaplan and Norton's goal categories in the balanced scorecard approach?

    (A) Financial

    (B) Internal business processes

    (C) Technology planning

    (D) Learning and growth

    (E) Customer

37. Which of the following styles for resolving conflict is most common in contract negotiations between parties of equal power, such as labor and management, who are only interested in their own gains?

    (A) Accommodating

    (B) Avoiding

    (C) Collaborating

    (D) Compromising

    (E) Competing

38. Many of the terms used in business today, such as "strategy," "penetration," and "send up a trial balloon," are derived from which of the following historical influences in management?

    (A) Contingency approaches

    (B) Military organizations dating from the ancient times

    (C) Humanist perspective

    (D) Systems theory

    (E) Chester Barnard of the administrative school

39. Which term describes the decision situation where the manager understands the goals, knows the options, and has full information about them?

    (A) Risk

    (B) Politics

    (C) Vagueness

    (D) Certainty

    (E) Uncertainty

40. Which of the following leadership approaches is closely linked to the expectancy theory of motivation?

    (A) Fiedler's contingency theory

    (B) Ohio State University's studies

    (C) University of Michigan's studies

    (D) Hersey-Blanchard's life cycle theory

    (E) House's path-goal theory

41. A company defends laying off employees as ethical because it saves the jobs of other workers who can still be employed. Which ethical framework are they using?

    (A) Justice

    (B) Moral rights

    (C) Utilitarian

    (D) Universalism

    (E) Moralism

42. Which of the following need-based approaches to motivation stated that chronically frustrated needs eventually regress to lower levels and cease to motivate workers?

    (A) Herzberg's two-factor theory

    (B) Alderfer's ERG theory

    (C) Locke's goal setting theory

    (D) Maslow's hierarchy of needs

    (E) McClelland's acquired needs theory

43. Which managerial skill enables a manager to respond to problems in his or her immediate work environment, applying knowledge gained through experience?

    (A) Technical

    (B) Human

    (C) Conceptual

    (D) Functional

    (E) Emotional intelligence

44. Replacement charts are associated with which of the following human resource programs?

    (A) Selection

    (B) Recruitment

    (C) Job analysis

    (D) HR macro planning

    (E) Labor relations

45. Which of the following is most true about the steps in the decision-making process?

    (A) It is best to quickly and efficiently identify the problem.

    (B) Decision makers should learn to make decisions on their own and not consult with others.

    (C) Making the decision is key; once made, implementation follows quickly.

    (D) All decisions should be treated as urgent and be quickly made and implemented.

    (E) Defining the context or boundaries of the problem is important in defining the problem.

46. Which of the following need-based approaches to motivation contained an institutional need for power that is important for managers?

    (A) Herzberg's two-factor theory

    (B) Alderfer's ERG theory

    (C) Equity theory

    (D) Maslow's hierarchy of needs

    (E) McClelland's acquired needs theory

47. Which of the following contingency approaches to leadership viewed leadership in terms of a trait-like variable called "least preferred co-worker"?

    (A) Fiedler's contingency theory

    (B) Ohio State University's studies

    (C) University of Michigan's studies

    (D) Hersey-Blanchard's life cycle theory

    (E) House's path-goal theory

48. Marsha works in the human resources department as a business consultant for first line supervisors. She answers their questions and provides suggestions for improving their operations. Her position in the organization would be classified as which of the following?

   (A) Having functional authority

   (B) Staff

   (C) Simplified

   (D) Line

   (E) Centralized

49. Jenny opens a store in the town where she attended college. She sells backpacks, raingear, and other outdoor wear for the college crowd. Another store opened in town. Jenny closely tracks the products in the other store and tries to price her products 10 percent less than theirs. Slowly her sales have been growing but her profits have declined slightly. Which force in the immediate environment is operating here?

   (A) Suppliers

   (B) Competitors

   (C) Community

   (D) Customers

   (E) Human capital

50. Your group needs some additional numbers to complete a report that is due tomorrow. Despite repeated calls and e-mails, the numbers have not arrived. Your group is anxious to complete the report on time but cannot without the numbers. This conflict is based on which of the following sources?

   (A) Competing goals

   (B) Role ambiguities

   (C) Scarce resources

   (D) Task interdependencies

   (E) Incompatible reward systems

51. Which of the following historical schools of management thought stressed that the effectiveness of a number of practices is based on factors in the situation?

    (A) Contingency approaches

    (B) Military organizations dating from the ancient times

    (C) Humanist perspective

    (D) Systems theory

    (E) Chester Barnard of the administrative school

52. Which the following options best defines business process reengineering?

    (A) Using robots to replace error prone humans in manufacturing

    (B) Reviewing processes to radically eliminate unnecessary steps and simplify the process

    (C) The process of evaluating how decisions are made in order to implement decision support systems to improve the process

    (D) Contacting suppliers to get better ideas for improving purchasing

    (E) Administering surveys to employees to get their ideas about the business

53. Which of the following ethical perspectives is most often used by human resource managers in developing ethical practices for a company?

    (A) Justice

    (B) Moral rights

    (C) Utilitarian

    (D) Universalism

    (E) Moralism

54. A small-business owner finds that she is receiving calls from customers asking about new products and lower prices. After questioning them, she finds that they have gotten information about competitors from the Internet. Which of Porter's competitive forces is operating for this business owner?

    (A) Rivalry among competitors

    (B) Power of buyers

    (C) Power of suppliers

    (D) Threat of substitutes

    (E) Potential new entrants

55. Which of the following statements is most true about the Malcolm Baldridge National Quality Award?

    (A) Awards are only given to manufacturing companies with the highest quality.

    (B) Criteria for the award are focused primarily on statistical precision in manufacturing.

    (C) President Clinton established the award.

    (D) Innovation, agility, and citizenship are values embodied in the award.

    (E) Workers' performance is more important than managers' in achieving this award.

56. Which of the following group roles falls into the socio-emotional category?

    (A) Avoider

    (B) Blocker

    (C) Initiator

    (D) Follower

    (E) Summarizer

57. Which of the following types of structures violates the unity of command principle by having two supervisors for a subordinate?

    (A) Divisional

    (B) Functional

    (C) Matrix

    (D) Geographic

    (E) Customer

58. A company is concerned that its product lines are becoming dated. It hires a consultant to conduct a study to determine what new developments might be relevant to its products and services. It is trying to cope with which of the following environmental issues?

    (A) Technological forces in the general environment

    (B) Ceremony as part of the internal culture

    (C) Lobbying as a way to influence the environment

    (D) Boundary spanning as an influence mechanism

    (E) Community forces in the immediate environment

59. In Hersey-Blanchard's life cycle theory of leadership, which of the following styles of leadership would be best in a situation in which the subordinate is unwilling and unable to do the assignment?

    (A) Delegating (S_4)

    (B) Telling (S_1)

    (C) Participating (S_3)

    (D) Abdicating (S_5)

    (E) selling (S_2)

60. Organizations are often grouped into responsibility centers for control purposes. Which type of responsibility center incorporates only revenue and expenses?

    (A) Investment center

    (B) Expense center

    (C) Revenue center

    (D) Building center

    (E) Profit center

61. The importance of the informal organization and the acceptance of authority were contributed by which historical school of thought?

    (A) Contingency approaches

    (B) Military organizations dating from the ancient times

    (C) Humanist perspective

    (D) Systems theory

    (E) Chester Barnard of the administrative school

62. A program called 360-degree feedback is part of which of the following HR functions or programs?

    (A) Compensation

    (B) Recruitment

    (C) Performance management

    (D) Training

    (E) Selection

63. Which of the following Myers-Briggs types is most likely to demonstrate a decision-making style of seeing the "big picture" and future relationships with customers and other stakeholders?

    (A) Sensing-Feeling (SF)

    (B) Intuition-Feeling (NF)

    (C) Extroverted-Analytic (EA)

    (D) Sensing-Thinking (ST)

    (E) Intuition-Thinking (NT)

64. At which stage of development are group members cautious and reluctant to criticize others when they disagree?

    (A) Performing

    (B) Storming

    (C) Norming

    (D) Adjourning

    (E) Forming

65. SWOT is a key component of strategic planning. What do the letters SWOT represent?

    (A) Strategy, Wins, Over, Tactics

    (B) Strengths, Weaknesses, Opportunities, Threats

    (C) Strategic, Wedge, Overcomes, Threats

    (D) Standardized, Workplace, Organizational, Talent

    (E) Stealth, War, Opposition, Team

66. Which category of social responsibility is a company following when it closes a plant that is unprofitable?

    (A) Legal

    (B) Caring

    (C) Economic

    (D) Discretionary

    (E) Ethical

67. Which skill is a manager using when she or he sees that a worker appears discouraged and asks, "How are you doing?"

    (A) Technical

    (B) Human

    (C) Conceptual

    (D) Functional

    (E) Analytical

68. Which of the following is a one-time activity with specific beginning and ending points?

    (A) Decision support systems (DSS)

    (B) Expert systems (ES)

    (C) Enterprise resource planning (ERP)

    (D) Management of technology

    (E) Project

69. Which of the following represents a very important first step in bringing about planned change in organizations?

    (A) Unfreezing or felt need to change

    (B) Having sufficient technical support ready if needed

    (C) Designing training programs to help employees cope with the change

    (D) Reward systems for sustaining the new changes

    (E) Clear communication about when the changes will occur

70. Jermaine has been transferred to a new division. He has the same position but procedures are handled differently here. He is unsure and has not been given any direction by his supervisor, who assumes he knows how to do the work. This division has performance-based incentives but he is unsure if he can reach the targets with the new procedures. He values the incentive pay, as he and his wife are saving money to buy their first house. In terms of expectancy theory, which component is contributing to his lack of motivation to perform?

    (A) Valence of outcomes

    (B) Output/input ratios

    (C) Expectancy (E → P)

    (D) Instrumentality (P → O)

    (E) Positive reinforcement

71. Which school of management thought emphasizes the importance of devoting resources to overcome the natural tendency of organizations to break down over time?

    (A) Contingency approaches

    (B) Military organizations dating from the ancient times

    (C) Humanist perspective

    (D) Systems theory

    (E) Chester Barnard of the administrative school

72. Which of the following statements best captures the distinction between information and data?

    (A) Data represent facts stored in computers. When people access the facts, data become information.

    (B) Information is data that has meaning and value to managers.

    (C) Data are customer characteristics; information is company characteristics.

    (D) Information represents product qualities; data represent employee qualities.

    (E) Data and information are really the same thing with different labels.

73. Which of the following is a common integrating mechanism used in many types of organizations?

    (A) Matrix design

    (B) Liaison role

    (C) Liaison department

    (D) Hierarchy

    (E) Functional design

74. The system of behavior control that is based on shared values and group norms is called?

    (A) Quality control

    (B) Progressive discipline

    (C) Market control

    (D) Incremental discipline

    (E) Clan control

75. When members of the marketing research unit present the results of focus interviews with customers regarding their preferences for two company product prototypes, the company is using which of the following strategies in terms of its environment?

    (A) Coping with technological forces

    (B) Responding to competitor forces in the immediate environment

    (C) Modifying its internal culture

    (D) Increasing awareness of the environment outside the company

    (E) Influencing factors in the environment that are important to them

76. A manager wants to use verbal praise as positive reinforcement to reward desirable behavior. Which schedule of reinforcement would be best for administering praise?

    (A) Variable ratio schedule

    (B) Fixed interval schedule

    (C) Continuous schedule

    (D) Spontaneous schedule

    (E) Fixed ratio schedule

77. Which of the following strategies for overcoming resistance to change did Lewin advocate in his early research on change?

    (A) Participation and involvement

    (B) Explicit coercion

    (C) Negotiated agreement

    (D) Manipulation

    (E) Education and communication

78. Which of the following is NOT an advantage of group decision-making?

    (A) Acceptance of decisions increases

    (B) Social loafing gives members a chance to rest

    (C) Group members all get a chance to participate

    (D) Synergy effects occur in groups

    (E) Members are more likely to understand the issues underlying the decision

79. What type of plan represents the steps to be taken in an emergency (i.e., a disaster plan)?

    (A) Strategy formulation

    (B) Policy

    (C) Contingency

    (D) Benchmarking

    (E) Project

80. Which of the following managerial skills is most important for top or senior levels of management?

    (A) Technical

    (B) Human

    (C) Conceptual

    (D) Functional

    (E) Expressive

81. The Center for Creative Leadership identified a number of reasons to explain why fast-tracked executives become derailed. Which of the following was NOT one of those reasons?

    (A) Not meeting business objectives

    (B) Poor interpersonal relationships

    (C) Inability to change

    (D) Weak financial skills

    (E) Failure to build a team

82. A company encourages its employees to tutor and mentor students at urban grammar schools and gives them one paid hour around their lunch break (11:30–1:30) to do so. They do not, however, share their profits with public organizations. Which stage of corporate responsiveness does this company appear to be practicing?

    (A) Proaction

    (B) Reaction

    (C) Activation

    (D) Accommodation

    (E) Defense

83. Wage surveys are designed to achieve which of the following HR objectives?

    (A) Internal equity

    (B) Valid selection

    (C) Affirmative action

    (D) External equity

    (E) Good labor relations

84. Which of the following communication media has the highest level of richness?

    (A) Formal, written communication

    (B) Telephone

    (C) E-mail

    (D) Face-to-face

    (E) Video conferencing

85. Brenda's secretary does not get work done in a timely manner. Brenda decides to set some specific objectives for her secretary on certain tasks. This setting of objectives represents which of the following functions of management?

    (A) Planning

    (B) Organizing

    (C) Coordinating

    (D) Leading

    (E) Controlling

86. Which of the following statements is most correct regarding contingencies of organizing?

    (A) Structure influences the choice of strategy.

    (B) Technologies adapt well to different structures.

    (C) The study of General Motors determined that size impacts structure.

    (D) Structure is not impacted by the environment.

    (E) Strategic choice influences the proper structure.

87. A manager is worried about the cohesiveness of her work group and seeks your advice. Which of the following statements is most true about how cohesiveness affects performance?

    (A) Cohesiveness always leads to greater group performance.

    (B) Group performance norms are important in assessing the impact of cohesiveness on performance.

    (C) High cohesiveness allows members the freedom to perform at their desired, optimal level.

    (D) Cohesiveness has no real impact on, or relationship to, group performance.

    (E) Cohesiveness always hurts performance.

88. Which of the following statements best defines the term "negligent hiring"?

    (A) Failing to adequately review an applicant's prior work record

    (B) Hiring a person who cannot adequately perform the job

    (C) Making a job offer to someone who does not accept it

    (D) Failing to make sure there is enough money in the budget to support the hiring of an applicant

    (E) A disastrous first day on the job

89. Which of the following statements is not a recommendation to managers based on the goal-setting theory?

    (A) Start with easy goals and work your way up to more difficult ones.

    (B) Challenging goals lead to a higher performance than easy ones.

    (C) High commitment to goals enhances performance.

    (D) Individuals with high self-efficacy set more difficult goals.

    (E) Rewarding goal attainment enhances performance.

90. All of the following are part of the culture of an organization EXCEPT

    (A) ceremonies

    (B) slogans

    (C) policies

    (D) rituals

    (E) jargon

91. Which of the following process theories of motivation focuses on perceptions of fairness when making comparisons with relevant co-workers in a company?

    (A) Goal setting

    (B) Expectancy

    (C) Equity

    (D) Reinforcement

    (E) McClelland's acquired need

92. Which of the following is NOT a desired quality of effective control systems?

    (A) Focused on results

    (B) Internal orientation of self-control

    (C) Measure strategically

    (D) Punishments for failure to meet the standard

    (E) Flexibility, allowing for some deviation

93. Which of the following is good advice for a manager in running a group meeting?

    (A) Use meetings to make decisions, not share routine information.

    (B) Be sure to make your views known on important matters.

    (C) Do not interfere with the discussion and allow full participation.

    (D) Wait until everyone has arrived before starting.

    (E) Surprising attendees with the agenda at the start gives you the advantage.

94. Marqus feels that the process for prioritizing projects in his department is not working. He thinks about improvements and discusses the changes with his team of subordinates. They recommend a few changes to make them easier to implement. These activities represent which of Mintzberg's roles of management?

    (A) Monitor

    (B) Liaison

    (C) Entrepreneur

    (D) Disturbance handler

    (E) Resource allocator

95. Which of the following statements is most true about the benefits component of HRM?

    (A) Employee benefits are not that important to most employees.

    (B) Healthcare is the most important issue in benefits today.

    (C) Benefits motivate workers but do not play a role in attracting them.

    (D) Turnover is related more to pay and the supervisor than to benefits.

    (E) No new benefits have been added for many years.

96. Which of the following is NOT a recommendation of steps that organizations take to improve the ethical climate?

    (A) Establish an ethical code of conduct

    (B) Create training programs that help managers make ethical decisions

    (C) Create a hotline for reporting ethical violations

    (D) Immediately fire anyone accused of an ethical violation

    (E) Publicize and communicate the ethical guidelines of the firm

97. Which of the statements below is most correct about organizing?

    (A) Decentralization tends to be the best way to make decisions.

    (B) Work specialization is not desirable as it leads to boring jobs.

    (C) Only higher-order need workers prefer enriched jobs.

    (D) Staff positions are usually more powerful than line positions.

    (E) All organizations should have a wide span of management.

98. Which of the following is NOT a barrier to communication in organizations?

    (A) Overload

    (B) Speaking too softly

    (C) Language

    (D) Selective perception

    (E) Noise

99. Which of the following statements is most true about group content and process?

    (A) Groups need to devote time to process in order to reach content goals.

    (B) Groups need to focus more on the task or content.

    (C) Group process is more important than content.

    (D) Group process will evolve over time and not need a manager's intervention.

    (E) Group process is unrelated to content goals.

100. Which of the following statements is true about leaders with high emotional intelligence (EQ)?

    (A) They are able to delegate the right tasks at the right time

    (B) They have a good sense of humor and tell jokes well

    (C) They feel good about themselves

    (D) They are aware of their own feelings and show empathy toward subordinates

    (E) They reward and praise subordinates often

CLEP PRINCIPLES OF MANAGEMENT
PRACTICE TEST 2

ANSWER KEY

1.	(A)	26.	(E)	51.	(A)	76.	(A)
2.	(B)	27.	(E)	52.	(B)	77.	(A)
3.	(D)	28.	(E)	53.	(A)	78.	(B)
4.	(B)	29.	(C)	54.	(B)	79.	(C)
5.	(C)	30.	(D)	55.	(D)	80.	(C)
6.	(A)	31.	(D)	56.	(D)	81.	(D)
7.	(E)	32.	(C)	57.	(C)	82.	(D)
8.	(A)	33.	(B)	58.	(A)	83.	(D)
9.	(A)	34.	(E)	59.	(B)	84.	(D)
10.	(B)	35.	(E)	60.	(E)	85.	(A)
11.	(A)	36.	(C)	61.	(E)	86.	(E)
12.	(A)	37.	(D)	62.	(C)	87.	(B)
13.	(E)	38.	(B)	63.	(B)	88.	(A)
14.	(D)	39.	(D)	64.	(E)	89.	(A)
15.	(D)	40.	(E)	65.	(B)	90.	(C)
16.	(E)	41.	(C)	66.	(C)	91.	(C)
17.	(C)	42.	(B)	67.	(B)	92.	(D)
18.	(A)	43.	(A)	68.	(E)	93.	(A)
19.	(E)	44.	(D)	69.	(A)	94.	(C)
20.	(A)	45.	(E)	70.	(C)	95.	(B)
21.	(E)	46.	(E)	71.	(D)	96.	(D)
22.	(E)	47.	(A)	72.	(B)	97.	(C)
23.	(C)	48.	(B)	73.	(D)	98.	(B)
24.	(C)	49.	(B)	74.	(E)	99.	(A)
25.	(A)	50.	(D)	75.	(D)	100.	(D)

DETAILED EXPLANATIONS OF ANSWERS

PRACTICE TEST 2

1. **(A)** The correct response is (A). Efficiency is about using resources well. Efficient activities use relatively few resources for the output attained. Option (B) addresses employees' knowing what's expected of them. Although clear expectations are important for management, they do not relate to efficiency. Option (C), doing the right job, is Drucker's definition of effectiveness. Efficiency is "doing the job right." Similarly for option (D), this is the definition of effectiveness offered in this chapter, a related but distinct term. Option (E) relates to motivation on a personal level but does not deal with efficiency.

2. **(B)** The correct response is (B), member skills. Of the options presented, only member skills is an input component. Option (A), member satisfaction, is incorrect because satisfaction is a component of group output, as is enhanced member capability (C). Member roles (D) and group norms (E) are part of group process, making these options incorrect.

3. **(D)** The correct response is (D), taking corrective action. Measuring actual performance (A) is not correct, as it comes prior to corrective action. Comparing performance with standards is the fourth step in the model, making option (B) incorrect. Establishing standards (C) is not correct because it is the first step. Option (E) is not correct because performing the work is second, coming after establishing standards.

4. **(B)** The correct response is (B), minimal standards for not doing harm in society. The focus is on not doing wrong. Option (A) is incorrect because it is the definition of morals. Option (C) is not correct, as it is the definition of ethics; it focuses on both right and wrong. Obligations that

society expects of corporations (D) is not correct, as this is the definition of social responsibility. Finally, (E) is not correct because corporate response is also related to social responsibility and is not a definition of ethics.

5. **(C)** The correct response is (C), organizing. Organizing is about formal relationships entered into for accomplishing specific goals. Human resource management (HRM) puts capable people into the structure. By hiring, training, compensating, and so forth, HRM brings the structure to life and helps accomplish goals. Controlling (A) is not the correct response. In order to be efficient, HR does evaluate and control its activities, but it is most closely tied to organizing. Similarly HRM does planning (B) but is more closely associated with organizing. Leading (C) is not correct because leading directs employees. HRM more closely supports organizing. Monitoring (E) is not correct because it is not a function of management.

6. **(A)** The correct response is (A), the humanistic perspective of the Hawthorne studies. By observing work groups, the Hawthorne studies found that workers react to management plans and orders. Groups can restrict production or help it. Mary Parker Follett (B) was concerned about worker reactions to authority but did not write about workgroup dynamics. Weber's bureaucracy (C) was concerned with rules and documentation, not worker reactions to them. Scientific management (D) preceded the Hawthorne studies and was not concerned with worker or team responses. Option (E) is not correct, either because Fayol was concerned with higher levels and broader organizational issues, not worker issues.

7. **(E)** The correct response is (E), the relationship between conflict and performance is best described as a bell-shaped curve. At very low and very high levels of conflict, performance suffers. Moderate amounts of conflict cause employees to re-evaluate procedures and problem-solve for improvements. Option (A) is not correct. Higher conflict and lower performance only works at high levels of conflict, not at moderate levels. Option (B) is wrong because the bell-shaped curve is the consistent shape of the relationship. Option (C) is not correct because there is a relationship at low and moderate levels too. Option (D) is wrong because although conflict is positively related to performance at low and moderate levels, it is inversely related to performance at high levels.

8. **(A)** The correct response is (A), the unbroken link of authority tying all members together. Fayol believed that employees should be linked together and that the chain of command was a vehicle for distributing author-

ity, decision-making, and communication. Option (B) is not correct because the degree to which jobs are comprised of a few tasks is the definition of *work simplification*. Option (C) addresses the location of authority which refers to centralization, not chain of command and is therefore incorrect. The number of employees who report to a supervisor (D) is not correct because this phrase is a definition of span of control or management. Finally option (E) is not correct because adding similar tasks to a job is job enlargement.

9. **(A)** The correct response is (A), general environmental forces. Legal-political and socio-cultural are general forces with broad, but less direct impact. The immediate environment (B) is not correct, as these forces are specific, such as human capital and suppliers. Option (C), corporate culture, is not correct as this is an internal aspect of environment and the question asks for an external set of forces. Option (D), adaptation forces, is not correct, as this was not a specifically named set of forces, but instead is one means of responding to external forces. Similarly, influencing forces (E) is not correct either, as this is another means for coping with external forces.

10. **(B)** Option (B) is the correct answer. Plans specify the activities that will attain the results identified in goals and objectives. They are the means to the ends. Organizing (A) is another function of management related to structuring relationships to attain goals. Option (A) is incorrect. Objectives (C) are specific statements of the intended outcomes, not activities to reach them. Associate SMART with objectives. They clarify what the target is. In setting plans, the steps are provided to reach objectives. SMART (D) stands for specific, measurable, achievable, relevant, and time-based. These are qualities of objectives, not plans. Controlling (E) is another function of management related to evaluating if goals are attained. It comes later and is not correct.

11. **(A)** The correct response is (A), decisions are based on consensus and negotiation. The political approach assumes no inherently right or wrong issue. The dominant coalition decides what is right. Not making full use of the information (B) is a characteristic of Simon's administrative model and is not correct. Option (C) is not correct because not all managers make good decisions; many can benefit from training. Decision makers making full use of information (D) is a feature of the classical approach, far from the political approach. Therefore (D) is incorrect. Option (E) is a feature of the contingency approach to management. It is incorrect when applied to the classical approach to decision-making.

12. **(A)** The correct response is (A), costs of healthcare benefits. Although healthcare benefits contribute to total labor costs, healthcare benefits are the concern of the human resource manager. Option (B) is incorrect because work-in-progress is one type of inventory that is the concern of operations managers (OM). When goods are viewed as defective by customers and sent back (C), these costs impact the operations managers, rendering this option incorrect. The time it takes to ship finished goods to customers is important. Delivery time is a primary concern for OM, making option (D) incorrect. The ability to make changes in product features based on customer demand (E) is flexibility, another concern for OM; thus option (E) is incorrect.

13. **(E)** The correct response is (E), University of Michigan's studies. They were the only behavioral approach to examine leadership on one dimension, from job-centered to employee-centered. Option (A) is not correct. Although Ohio State University's studies also took a behavioral approach to leadership, they used two dimensions, initiation of structure and consideration. Kurt Lewin's group studies of leadership was early behavioral research on democratic and autocratic style, making option (B) incorrect. Option (C), *Zeitgeist*, is not correct because this approach assumed that leaders fit the times. Option (D), trait approach, is not correct. The trait approach identified qualities of leaders and did not focus on behaviors.

14. **(D)** The correct response is (D), actor-observer bias. The key here is that employees are observing themselves, not a supervisor looking at a subordinate. In this situation employees take credit for success but blame failure on external causes. Needs (A) is not correct, as needs are a component of motivation, not the reason for false attributions. The fundamental attribution error (B) is close but refers to supervisors making incorrect attributions and is therefore incorrect. Option (C), performance bias, is not correct as this phrase is a contrived option. Option (E), ability ignorance, is not correct, as this term is irrelevant to motivation issues.

15. **(D)** The correct response is (D), the Americans with Disabilities Act of 1991. Two sets of terms are critical elements of this law. First, employees must be able to perform the "essential functions." If so, then the company must make "reasonable accommodations." Both phrases relate to this law. Option (A) is not correct because the Civil Rights Act is concerned with discrimination, not accommodating disabilities. The Occupational Safety and Health Act (B) is not correct because this law is focused on workplace health, not accommodating disabilities. The law in option (E) provides time

off for family or medical issues, not accommodations, and is incorrect. Option (C) is incorrect because it applies to age discrimination, not disabilities.

16. **(E)** The correct option is (E), Fayol of the administrative school. Unity of direction and chain of command were two of his fourteen principles. These are administrative issues related to the organizing function. The Hawthorne studies (A) are not correct because these began as scientific management experiments and ended with greater understanding of how workers and group dynamics impact performance. Although Mary Parker Follett (B) was also from the administrative school, she wrote more about worker reactions to the organization and scientific management. Option (C) is not correct because Weber's bureaucratic principles were concerned with rules, documentation, and higher pay for higher positions in the hierarchy. Scientific management (D) would not be correct because Taylor was more concerned with the smaller issues of work layout, training, and pay rather than broader administrative issues.

17. **(C)** The correct response is (C), happy and upbeat. This quality was not a trait identified in research. The remaining categories were all documented traits. Intelligence (A) and integrity (B) were traits of leaders, making them incorrect options. Similarly, self-confidence (D) and decisiveness (E) were additional traits found in leaders, making them incorrect here.

18. **(A)** The correct response is (A). The definition is "fundamental values that society imparts." Option (B) is not correct, as this definition applies to law; the law stresses not harming others. Option (C) is not correct, as this is the definition of ethics. Obligations that society expects of corporations (D) is not correct as this is the definition of social responsibility. Finally, option (E) is not correct because "responses of corporations..." is also related to social responsibility and is not a definition of ethics.

19. **(E)** The correct response is (E), McClelland's acquired need theory. McClelland believed that needs were learned from early childhood experiences while most of the other theorists viewed them as innate. Herberg's two-factor theory (A) is not correct as he believed that satisfiers and dissatisfiers were not learned. Alderfer in his ERG theory (B) believed that adult experiences could cause frustration to lower levels but did not give childhood experiences a role in motivation; it is incorrect. Locke's goal setting theory (C) is not a need-based theory and is therefore incorrect. Maslow's hierarchy of needs (D) is a general theory of motivation, but he believed

that all humans had the five categories without an impact of early childhood experiences, making it incorrect.

20. **(A)** The correct response is (A), the economy. Spiraling inflation, an economic factor, is reducing cash flow and the amount of materials purchased. Technology (B) is not correct because these issues are not influencing the manufacturer. Option (C), legal-political, is not correct because this set of forces relates to laws and regulations. There is no evidence of legal-political change here. Socio-cultural (D) involves consumer attitudes, which are not apparent here. Hence (D) is not correct. Finally human capital (E) is not correct because there is no evidence of a competency or skill shortage.

21. **(E)** The correct option is (E). Controlling involves measuring progress toward goals and taking corrective action if needed. "Assessing marketing expenditures" is a measure of how many resources marketing is using. This assessment and the subsequent corrections helps the manager to control resources and be more efficient. Option (A), planning, would be about setting goals; there is no planning in this phrase. Option (B), organizing, would entail work layout and the relationships among workers; again, not visible here. Option (C), coordinating, is not one of the four contemporary functions of management. Although it is one of Fayol's original functions, it has been subsumed under organizing. Option (D), leading, would be encouraging and rewarding his regional sales managers for staying under budget, but he is not doing that here.

22. **(E)** The correction option is (E), middle. A middle-level manager reports to top level managers and has managers reporting to her or him. Chris has regional sales managers reporting to him and he in turn reports to the vice president of marketing. Option (A), team leader, is not really a manager and would not have managers reporting to him or her. Chris is not likely a top manager (B) either. That title would be reserved for his superiors, the vice president of marketing and the president. Option (C) could not be correct as it was not one of the three levels of management discussed. Chris could not be a lower-level manager (D) because he has managers reporting to him.

23. **(C)** The correct response is (C), make-to-stock. This is the manufacturing strategy that relies on large volumes of consistent product at low cost. There is no tailoring of product to customer needs. Assemble-to-order (A) is a manufacturing strategy that customizes based on a limited number of options, so it is not correct for this question. Option (B) is not correct because

customized services is not a manufacturing strategy. Similarly, option (E) is also a service strategy. Standardized services is a service strategy comparable to the manufacturing strategy of make-to-stock in that no customization is involved. Option (D) is not correct because make-to-order involves the highest level of customization and flexibility in manufacturing. It would not be used in this Procter & Gamble example.

24. **(C)** The correct response is (C), functional team. Individuals assigned to a permanent team to perform their work assignments are in functional teams. Their work function is through the team. A vertical team (A) is close to a functional team, but is not correct because it would also include a supervisor. Option (B), virtual team, is not correct because the group would be geographically distributed and not meet face-to-face. A committee (D) is a cross-functional group that meets for coordination over time. Committee members have other tasks assigned and therefore this option is not correct. A task force (E) is a temporary group with cross-functional composition. This choice is not correct.

25. **(A)** The correct answer is (A), Edward Deming. Constancy of purpose and ending mass inspection were key components of his principles. Option (B) is not correct because Philip Crosby was most associated with zero defects and quality lowering costs. Malcolm Baldridge is the former secretary of commerce for whom the Malcolm Baldridge National Quality Award is named, making (C) incorrect. James Fairfield-Sonn wrote about quality and culture. He wrote about Deming but constancy of purpose was not his concept. Option (D) is incorrect. Joseph Juran defined quality as fitness for use, not constancy of purpose, and so (E) is not correct.

26. **(E)** The correct option is (E), modifying jobs by adding several similar tasks. This is the definition of job enlargement—adding more of the same. Job enrichment adds more complexity. The unbroken link of authority tying all individuals together (A) is not correct because this response defines chain of command. Option (B) is not correct because the degree to which jobs are comprised of a few tasks is the definition of work simplification. Option (C) addresses the location of authority, which refers to centralization, not modifying the job content and is therefore incorrect. The number of employees who report to a supervisor (D) is not correct because this phrase is a definition of span of control, or management.

27. **(E)** The correct response is (E), uncertainty. This situation has the least amount of information for making decisions and therefore more errors

may occur here. Risk (A) is a decision situation where options are known with some probability. Since probabilities are not known here, (A) cannot be correct. Politics (B) is not correct. The political approach was one of the approaches to decision-making but does not apply to decision situations. Option (C) is not correct as vagueness was not a term discussed in the decision-making chapter. Option (D) is not correct because certainty is a situation with full information about options and outcomes.

28. **(E)** The correct response is (E), strategy to achieve growth through a joint venture. Strategies and projects are both single-use plans. Option (A) relates to policies and option (B) relates to procedures. Both are standing plans, used repeatedly, and therefore are not correct. Both option (C) and option (D) are goals. Goals are end results but plans are the means for reaching those ends. Therefore (C) and (D) are incorrect.

29. **(C)** The correct response is (C), felt. Antonio is angry after perceiving that Otto has frustrated his goal of the promotion. Emotions are at play. Since he is angry, the conflict cannot be latent (A) or perceived (B). These choices are incorrect. The conflict is not yet manifest, as he has not taken any action, so option (D) is incorrect. Similarly there is no aftermath without the manifest stage, so (E) is incorrect also.

30. **(D)** The correct response is (D), the processes for acquiring raw materials, producing products, and delivering them to customers is supply chain management (SCM). No longer isolated activities, these elements of the chain must be coordinated for a successful business. Option (A) is not correct because physical chains have nothing to do with SCM. Option (B) is not correct because SCM is more than managing links among suppliers. It also involves inventory, manufacture, and the logistics of distribution. Determining the best way to deliver products to customers is part of logistics, only one component of SCM, making (C) not correct. Improving the layout of tasks by reducing unnecessary steps (E) is re-engineering, not SCM.

31. **(D)** The correct response is (D), socio-cultural. Consumers have attitudes that run counter to the methods used to market infant formula. Nestlé is either ignoring this attitude or is not aware of it. The general state of the economy is not influencing this church group, so option (A), economy, is not correct. There is no technological issue here, so option (B) is not correct. Option (C) is not correct. Although some may argue that the church group is being political, they are not involved with the government or regulation. They are consumers trying to influence the company. Option (E), human

capital, is not correct because there is no evidence of a competency or skill shortage.

32. **(C)** The correct response is (C), Malcolm Baldridge. He is the former secretary of commerce for whom the Malcolm Baldridge National Quality Award is named. Option (A), Edward Deming, was the most philosophical with principles of constancy of purpose and ending mass inspection and is not correct. Option (B) is not correct because Philip Crosby was most associated with zero defects and lowering costs. James Fairfield-Sonn wrote about quality and culture. Option (D) is incorrect. Joseph Juran defined quality as fitness for use, not constancy of purpose and so (E) is not correct.

33. **(B)** The correct response is (B). Clean air is part of a healthy workplace and is monitored by the Occupational Safety and Health Act of 1970. The Civil Rights Act of 1964 (A) prohibits discrimination and has nothing do with workplace health directly. Option (C) is also incorrect as the Age Discrimination Act does not relate to clean air. Option (D) is not correct because the Americans with Disabilites Act relates to helping those with disabilities and not clean air. Finally option (E) is not correct because the Family and Medical Leave Act grants unpaid leave to workers and does not impact air.

34. **(E)** The correct response is (E), task force. In contrast to a committee (D), which is permanent, the task force is temporary or ad hoc (i.e., for a specific purpose). Option (D) is incorrect. Both vertical groups (A) and functional groups (C) are groups where work is done in teams. They are not coordinating bodies. These options are incorrect. Option (B), virtual team, is not correct because the group would be geographically distributed and not meet face-to-face.

35. **(E)** The correct option is (E), job enrichment. Job enlargement (A) is not correct because enlargement adds a few more of the same tasks. Enrichment, or vertical enlargement, adds greater skill requirements to motivate workers. Option (B), staff authority, is not correct. Although it is an aspect of division of labor, it does not relate to enlargement, enrichment, or job rotation. Option (C) is not correct because rotation merely moves workers from job-to-job. Job simplification (D) is the opposite of job enrichment and is not correct.

36. **(C)** The correct response is option (C), technology planning. This choice is not part of the balanced scorecard. The four categories of Kaplan

and Norton's Balanced Scorecard in order are learning and growth (D), internal business processes (B), customer (E), and financial (A). Options (A), (B), (D), and (E) are therefore not correct.

37. **(D)** The correct response is (D), compromising. Conflicts between labor and management are often competitive, wherein each tries to satisfy their own concerns without regard for the other. When two competitors have equal power, a compromise of partial concessions by each is the only type of agreement possible. Option (A) is not correct because accommodating satisfies only one party's concerns. Avoiding (B) does not satisfy your concerns or those of another, so it would not be useful in labor-management negotiations. In the situation described, both sides are competing, but (E) is not the correct answer because they have equal power. As the power is balanced, the two competitors will each have to compromise to reach agreement. Collaboration (C) is not correct because the parties have no concern for each other's interest. Collaboration involves concern for both self and others.

38. **(B)** The correct option is (B), military organizations dating from ancient times. Military thinking and language has impacted business. Option (A) is not correct because contingency is based on situational effectiveness, which was not articulated until the 1960s. Option (C) is not correct either. Humanist approaches were derived from the Hawthorne studies, which did not give us this colorful language. Like contingency theory, systems theory (D) developed in the twentieth century and focused managers' attention on issues outside of the organization. Barnard (E) wrote about worker cooperation and acceptance of authority in the 1930s, but did not develop these terms.

39. **(D)** The correct response is (D), certainty. This option represents the classic definition of full information. Risk (A) is a decision situation where options are known with some probability. Since both options and outcomes are certain, (A) cannot be correct. Politics (B) is not correct. The political approach was one of the approaches to decision-making but does not apply to decision situations. Option (C) is not correct, as vagueness is not a term relevant to a discussion on decision-making. Uncertainty (E) involves incomplete knowledge of options. Here the options are known, making (E) incorrect.

40. **(E)** The correct response is (E), House's path-goal theory. House asserted that leaders identify paths to goals and assure rewards are delivered for performance. These actions motivate and sustain performance and are

closely linked to the expectancy theory of motivation. The remaining options are not linked to expectancy and are incorrect. Fiedler's contingency theory (A), the Ohio State University's studies (B), and the University of Michigan's studies (C) have no links to expectancy theory, nor does Hersey-Blanchard's approach (D).

41. **(C)** The correct response is (C), utilitarian. The ethical perspective suggests that choices that do the greatest good for the greatest number are best. Laying off some workers preserves jobs for a larger number of those remaining. The justice perspective treats all employees fairly and impartially, so (A) is not correct, as some are hurt by this action. Moral rights (B) involves decisions made freely with full information. This is not correct, as the laid off employees did not choose. Universalism (D) involves the golden rule, treating all with dignity and respect. Laying off workers does not follow this perspective, making (D) incorrect. Moralism (E) was not a perspective covered in the text and is therefore incorrect.

42. **(B)** The correct response is (B), Alderfer's ERG theory. He added the principle of frustration-regression to account for situations where workers cease to care about growth related factors in the job. Maslow (D) only has the satisfaction-progression element, not the frustration-regression, making it incorrect. Herzberg's (A) two categories were separate and distinct, without progression or regression components. Locke's goal-setting theory (C) is not a need-based theory and is therefore incorrect. Finally (E) is not correct, as McClelland's acquired needs were not connected to any progression or regression component.

43. **(A)** The correct option is (A), technical skills. Technical skills are used in identifying and fixing problems in the immediate work environment. The skills are acquired through experience, another feature of technical skills. Option (B) is not correct because the question does not relate to communicating or dealing with others. Conceptual skills (C) are abstract models for understanding the broader organization beyond the immediate work environment. Option (D) is not correct because functional was not a skill category mentioned in this chapter. Emotional intelligence (E) is related to human skills and is therefore not correct either.

44. **(D)** The correct response is (D). Replacement charts are part of the supply analysis in HR macro planning to see if enough supply is available to meet demand. Selection (A) involves selecting the best applicant to perform the job and is not correct. Recruitment (B) steps try to attract applicants and

do not involve replacement charts. Job analysis (C) is micro planning during which the job is studied, while macro planning involves replacement charts. Labor relations (E) is not correct because labor implies unions and replacement charts are for higher-level positions.

45. **(E)** The correct response is (E), establishing the boundaries is part of defining the problem. Knowing the scope or situation in which the problem occurred helps in focusing the information gathered in the next stage. Option (A) is incorrect because speed in problem identification can lead to the wrong problem being pursued. It is better to take more time and be deliberate. Option (B) is not correct because there are many times when decision makers need to consult experts or those with more information to define the problem and explore alternatives. Making decisions is important (C), but so is implementation. It is not automatic, making (C) incorrect. Option (D) is not correct because a manager needs to prioritize decisions. Some require little attention, and others more. Prioritizing is part of defining the problem.

46. **(E)** The correct response is (E), McClelland's acquired need theory. Of all the need perspectives, McClelland's was the only one to use power as a specific need category. He incorporated both personal and institutional into his approach. Option (A) is not correct as Herzberg did not use power, nor did Alderfer (B), nor Maslow (D). Therefore (A), (B), and (D) are not correct. Equity theory (C) is not a need-based theory and is therefore incorrect.

47. **(A)** The correct response is (A), Fielder's contingency theory. His approach began by asking individuals to describe their least preferred co-worker (LPC). This is a type of trait although he subsequently labeled his approach to be task-motivated and people-motivated. Option (B) is not correct because Ohio State University's studies were behavioral, as were the University of Michigan's studies (C), making this option incorrect too. Option (D), Hersey-Blanchard's life cycle, is not correct because they did not use least preferred co-worker. Similarly House's path-goal (E) used four types of leader behavior, not LPC or any other trait.

48. **(B)** The correct response is (B), staff. Human resources is commonly regarded as a staff department that provides service and assistance to line managers, as she is doing in this question. Functional authority (A) would give Marsha authority to direct line managers. She does not have that here so option (A) is incorrect. There is no evidence that her job is simplified. She

has ample responsibilities so option (C) is wrong. Option (D) is not correct because she is assisting line managers, making her position staff. There is no evidence that her position is centralized (E). It seems as though operations are somewhat de-centralized since she is working closely with supervisors. Option (E) is incorrect.

49. **(B)** The correct response is (B), competitors. Jenny closely monitors businesses similar to hers and tries to keep her prices below theirs, providing her with some competitive advantage although at a loss of profits. Option (A), suppliers, is not correct. There is no evidence of any supplies firms impacting Jenny's business; the only other company mentioned is a direct competitor. Community issues are not evident either and therefore option (C) is not correct. Although Jenny is winning more customers with her lower prices, this is not primarily a customer issue. Option (D) is not correct. Human capital issues are not evident either. There is no mention of Jenny having trouble hiring staff, therefore option (E) is incorrect.

50. **(D)** The correct response is (D), task interdependencies. Work done by one department is needed by another. This conflict emerges because the tasks are closely linked. Option (A) is not correct because there is no evidence of competing goals. The departments are working toward the same goals, but one hasn't completed the work needed by the other. Role ambiguities (B) involve unclear assignments and boundaries. They know their roles but need the work. Option (C) is incorrect because there is also no evidence of scarce resources. Incompatible reward systems (E) are not present either, making this option incorrect.

51. **(A)** The correct option is (A). Contingency means contingent on the situation. Success is not universal but is linked to circumstances in the context. Option (B) is not correct as ancient military did not articulate contingencies. They adjusted strategies for unexpected circumstances but were not explicit about situational effectiveness. The humanist perspective (C) explained worker and group reactions, not contingencies. Although from the same time period, systems theory (D) addressed open systems and adaptation to the environment. Chester Barnard (E) addressed worker cooperation, not contingencies. Options (C), (D), and (E) are all incorrect.

52. **(B)** The correct response is (B), reviewing processes to radically eliminate unnecessary steps and simplify the process. The key word is "radically." Business process re-engineering (BPR) strives to do more than quality improvements. It questions assumptions and seeks dramatic improvements.

Option (A), using robotics, is involved in introducing new technology but is not BPR. Option (C) is not correct because decision support systems do not eliminate steps but instead seek to develop information systems that support decision-making. Contacting suppliers (D) may yield some improvements, but not the radical ones embodied in BPR. Administering surveys to employees (E) is not a common procedure for BPR. Employees may be interviewed but surveys are not able to capture enough information to identify the steps to be eliminated. Both (D) and (E) are incorrect.

53. **(A)** The correct response is (A), justice. Consistent, fair, and impartial treatment is the foundation of human resource management. Moral rights (B) involves decisions made freely with full information and the rights of due process. Sometimes HR cannot apply all of the moral rights, such as firing in an employment-at-will company. Option (A) is more correct than option (B). Option (C), utilitarian, is not as good as option (A) either. Utilitarianism argues for the greatest benefit for the greatest number, again sometimes inconsistent with HR practice. Universalism (D) treats all employees as means and not ends, that is, with dignity and respect. HR follows these principles on many occasions, but not all. Terminating someone may be just but not in accordance with universalism. Therefore, (A) is a better choice than (D). Moralism (E) was not a perspective covered in the text and is therefore incorrect.

54. **(B)** The correct response is (B), power of buyers. The Internet provides accessible information that buyers can use to leverage businesses. Rivalry among competitors (A) is not operating here. There is no evidence of an intense rivalry with another business. Information is providing the competition. Option (C) could not be correct either because there are no suppliers operating. The pressure for products and price is not due to available substitutes (D) but from pressure from buyers. Finally new entrants (E) are not present, making (E) incorrect. Another business down the street would be a new entrant.

55. **(D)** The correct response is (D), innovation, agility, and citizenship are core values embodied in the award. Option (A) is not correct because awards are given in the areas of small business, education, and healthcare, in addition to manufacturing. Option (B) is not correct because the Baldridge criteria are much broader than just statistical precision and include social responsibility, a systems perspective, and personal learning. President Reagan instituted the award, not President Clinton, so (C) is not correct. Option (E)

is not correct because many more individuals besides workers are involved in the award. All phases of the organization should be involved.

56. **(D)**   The correct response is follower (D). Followers are important in groups, especially those with strong, task-oriented members. Some need to support ideas made by others for the group to function well, making the follower a maintenance or socio-emotional role. Avoider (A) and blocker (B) are self-oriented roles and not correct. Both initiator (C) and summarizer (E) are task-oriented roles, not socio-emotional. These options are incorrect.

57. **(C)**   The correct response is (C), matrix. With both a functional manager and a product manager, a worker in a matrix design has two supervisors, which violates Fayol's unity of command principle. Divisional structure (A) is not correct because each worker has only one manager in this form of organizing. Similarly, the functional structure (B) also has one supervisor. Options (D) and (E) are forms of divisional structure and also are not correct as they have only one supervisor.

58. **(A)**   The correct response is (A), technological forces in the general environment. Hiring the consultant is an action to learn about new technological developments in the general environment. Option (B) is not correct because this is not a ceremonial aspect of the culture; it is focused outside of the organization. Lobbying (C) is not being practiced as there is not an attempt to influence the environment, only to learn about trends. Option (D) is not correct because boundary spanning is not an influence activity but is an adaptive strategy, moving in the reverse direct from the outward-oriented influencing. Option (E), community forces, is not correct because there is no effort to help or support community stakeholders.

59. **(B)**   The correct response is option (B), telling. In the life-cycle theory, the level of readiness determines the right style. When a subordinate is unable and unwilling, they are at the first level of readiness. When the subordinate is at R1, the appropriate leadership style is S1 or telling. Option (A) is not correct because for delegating to be correct the subordinate would have to be both willing and able or R4. Option (C) is not correct because participating is associated with a readiness level where the subordinate is able but not willing to accept responsibility. Abdicating (D) is not correct because abdicating was not a style in this model. Finally, option (E), selling, is not correct because this style would be paired with a level two readiness where the subordinate was somewhat willing but not fully able.

60. **(E)**   The correct response is (E), profit center. Both revenue and expenses are included in profit centers. Option (A) is not correct because investment centers also include capital budgets. Expense centers only include expense budgets, not revenue or capital budgets, so (B) is not correct. Revenue centers only include revenue, so (C) is not correct as it does not involve expenses. Option (D) is not correct because building center is a fabricated term.

61. **(E)**   The correct response is option (E), Chester Barnard of the administrative school. His idea of zone of acceptance illustrates the informal organization that is part of worker cooperation. Contingency approaches (A) is a general principle about situational effectiveness, not specifically about the informal organization. Ancient military organizations (B) were not concerned about the informal organization, although they had concerns about the acceptance of orders. Humanist perspective (C) began the thinking about the informal organization, but was not concerned about authority and therefore is not correct. Systems theory (D) addressed open systems and adaptation to the environment, not authority.

62. **(C)**   The correct response is (C), performance management. 360 feedback solicits performance feedback from superiors, peers, and subordinates to form a more complete and accurate picture of managerial performance. Compensation (A) is not correct although the results of 360 feedback may influence merit pay. Recruitment (B) attracts applicants while 360 evaluates current employees. Like compensation, the results of 360 feedback may lead to training (D) but as part of performance management. Option (E) is also incorrect because selection evaluates applicants' suitability to perform the job before hiring. Feedback occurs after hiring.

63. **(B)**   The correct response is (B), intuition-feeling. The big picture is characteristic of an intuitive style and the people focus is found among feeling types. NF's can be found in public relations, where this style would fit well. Option (A) is incorrect because a sensing type would be detail and present oriented. The question clearly focuses on an intuitive style. Option (C) is not correct because analytic is not a Myers-Briggs category. This question describes someone who is the opposite of an ST, who would focus on details and analytic reasoning, making (D) incorrect. Although the question has intuitive elements, there is no evidence of thinking, so (E) is incorrect.

64. **(E)**   The correct response is forming (E). In the initial stage of development members are cautious and hesitate to disagree with others. Op-

tion (A), performing, is not correct, as this stage yields high levels of performance and sharing of roles. Members are open and willing to provide critical comments. Storming (B) is the second stage and is characterized by differences among members, not cautiousness. It is not correct for this question. Option (C) is not correct because norming is the third stage, following storming, where differences are resolved and norms are clarified. Option (D) is not correct because adjourning is the final stage, related to closure when the group's tasks are finished.

65. **(B)**   The correct response is (B). The acronym *SWOT* stands for strengths, weaknesses, opportunities, and threats. The remaining options are incorrect collections of words. "Strategy wins over tactics" (A) may be a nice slogan but it is not correct. Although strategic planning seeks to separate your company from others, the wedge in option (C) does not apply to SWOT analysis. Option (D) pertains more to human resource management with talent and workplace. It does not apply to SWOT in strategic analysis. The final option (E) focuses on the military metaphor which is common in strategic planning, but does not apply to the strategic planning model directly.

66. **(C)**   The correct response is (C), economic. Closing an unprofitable plant supports the economic responsibilities of the organization to use financial resources wisely and make decisions to protect shareholder interests. Option (A) is not correct because there are no legal requirements to close plants that are not profitable, only to inform employees sixty days before a plant closing. Option (B) is not correct because caring is not a category of corporate social responsibility. Discretionary (D) is not correct because this action is minimal and the discretionary acts of social responsibility go well beyond typical expectations. Similarly, ethical (E) goes somewhat beyond minimal requirements.

67. **(B)**   The correct option is (B), human. The manager is aware of an emotional problem with the employee and asks a question to find out more about it, demonstrating interpersonal, or human, skills. Option (A) is not correct because technical skills involve analyzing things, not people issues. Option (C) is not correct because a conversation about subordinate problems is primarily interpersonal, not conceptual. Option (D) is not correct because functional was not a skill category mentioned in this chapter. Analytical skills (E) are part of technical skills, not human.

68. **(E)** The correct response is (E), project. Projects have a specific purpose that is only performed once. Specific timetables are established for the beginning and end of each project. Option (A), decision support systems (DSS), is not correct because DSS's take more limited pieces of information and combines them into an information system for a specific decision purpose. The development of a DSS may use project management methodology, but it is not the same as a project. Expert systems (B) is also not correct, as they capture human knowledge, again for a decision task. Expert systems are used over and over. Option (C), enterprise resource planning, is not correct because it too is a recurring process which integrates all business data for a firm. Management of technology (D) is not correct either. It is a general term for enhancing performance and repeatedly creating innovation, not a one-time task.

69. **(A)** The correct response is (A), unfreezing. Before any planned change project can begin, the ties to the former must be loosened. Unfreezing does this. Having sufficient technical support (B) helps in making the change but is not the starting point. Designing training programs is part of re-freezing, not unfreezing, making (C) wrong. Option (D), reward systems for sustaining new changes, is also part of re-freezing and therefore wrong. Clear communication about the changes (E) is an important part of moving the change, but not the first step. Option (E) is incorrect.

70. **(C)** The correct response is (C), expectancy or E → P. Jermaine is uncertain about the new procedures. He can try hard but due to the uncertainty about procedures he is not likely to do the right thing. He will simply not make much of an effort. He values the incentives, so option (A), valence of outcomes, is not correct. He also knows that if he performs at the right level, he will receive these outcomes; therefore his instrumentality is high and (D) is not correct. Option (B) is not correct because the ratio of outputs to inputs is part of equity theory, not expectancy. Similarly, option (E) is not correct because positive reinforcement is not part of expectancy.

71. **(D)** The correct option is (D), systems theory. In addition to adaptation to the external environment, the systems theory principle of negative entropy asserts that with additional resources it can overcome the natural tendency of systems to break down (i.e., entropy). Organizational development is a field that applies the negative entropy principle. Contingency approaches (A) is a general principle about situational effectiveness, not about overcoming the tendency to wear down over time. Option (B) is not correct, as ancient military did not articulate open systems principles. Option (C),

humanist perspective, is not correct because it explained worker and group reactions, not systems wearing down. Chester Barnard (E) dealt with worker cooperation, not the larger system and overcoming its decline.

72. **(B)**   The correct response is (B), information is data that has value or meaning. Data can easily overwhelm or overload employees. It must have meaning to be useful to managers. Rockhart recommends only seven key indicators as the limit of information that managers can use. Option (A) is not correct because both data and information are stored in computers. Accessing the data does not convert it to information. Without meaning or value, it remains data. Option (C) is not correct. The distinction between customer and company characteristics is not relevant here. Either can be data or information. Similarly option (D) is not correct because the distinction between product and employee qualities is also meaningless. Finally option (E) is not correct because data and information are quite different from a manager's perspective. The latter are meaningful and used in making decisions.

73. **(D)**   The correct response is (D), hierarchy. Questions are routinely referred up the chain of command, or hierarchy, to share information and make decisions. There are two additional basic integrating mechanisms: planning and rules and procedures. Matrix design (A) is a structure that integrates but is used in highly specialized conditions and is not common. Option (B), liaison role, is another integrating mechanism, but not a common one. It is not correct either. Similarly the liaison department (C) is not correct as it is used only where high levels of integration are needed. Option (E) is not correct because functional departments are not very good at integrating across departmental boundaries.

74. **(E)**   The correct response is (E), clan control. This informal system uses internal controls of values and group influence to get employees to conform to rules and policies, in contrast to the external approach of bureaucratic control. Quality control (A) is not correct because this system is more formal and addresses improvements in product and service quality, not employee behavior. Option (B) is not correct because progressive discipline is a formal system administered by supervisors. Market control (C) is an informal system that influences prices, not employees. Incremental discipline (D) is a fabricated term that describes progressive discipline, but is not an official term. It is incorrect.

75. **(D)**   The correct response is option (D), increasing awareness of the environment outside the company. Marketing research gathers data about

customer preferences to help the company adapt. Coping with technological forces (A) is not correct because the focus is on customers in the immediate environment, not technology in the general environment. Although marketing research is identifying an immediate environment issue, competitors (B) are not being studied. Researchers are gauging opinions of company prototypes, not comparing company products with competitors. Option (B) is not correct. The internal culture (C) is not being addressed with marketing research and is not correct. Option (E) is not correct because researchers are not influencing but instead are adapting to the environment. An advertising campaign attempts to influence customers.

76. **(A)** The correct response is (A), variable ratio schedule. Praise is best administered on this variable schedule because it is the hardest to extinguish. If a manager issues praise too much, its effects will be watered down. Variable ratio schedules work best in these situations. A fixed interval schedule (B) would not work as it would lead to long lapses in behavior between fixed time points. Variable schedules are better. Option (C), continuous schedule, is not correct, as managers cannot administer any type of reward for every behavior; it is not practical. A spontaneous schedule (D) is not a schedule in reinforcement theory and is therefore incorrect. Option (E), fixed ratio schedule, is not correct for similar reasons as option (B)—fixed schedules do not work well with praise.

77. **(B)** The correct response is (A), participation and involvement. Lewin found that participating was effective in overcoming resistance to change. Lewin never advocated coercion (B) or manipulation (D); contemporary views suggest that these tactics are last resorts. Options (B) and (D) are incorrect. Negotiated agreement (C) is a more contemporary perspective than Lewin, so it is not correct here. Education and communication (E) represents effective change strategies but is not as closely tied to Lewin.

78. **(B)** The correct response is (B). Social loafing is a disadvantage, not an advantage. Social loafing hurts the group, as those members are nonproductive and don't share information. Option (A) is not correct because greater acceptance of decisions is a benefit. Having members participate (C) is a benefit and therefore incorrect. Similarly option (D) is not correct, as synergy is a benefit of group decision-making. Another benefit of groups is greater understanding of the issues, making (E) incorrect.

79. **(C)** The correct response is (C), contingency plan. A disaster plan prepares for unexpected events or contingencies. Option (A) refers to strat-

egy formulation, which is developed to achieve planned outcomes. It is incorrect here. A policy is a recurring plan designed to provide guidance for activities that occur repeatedly, not rare disasters, making option (B) incorrect. Benchmarking (D) is a planning process that compares the way other companies perform a process to identify better ways of accomplishing the task. Option (D) does not relate to unexpected events and is wrong. A project is a single-time event, like a contingency plan, but it is not for unexpected events, so (E) is incorrect.

80. **(C)**   The correct option is (C), conceptual skills. Figure 1.2 illustrated that conceptual skills represent the largest proportion for senior managers. Conceptual skills are essential for plotting future directions and developing strategy. Option (A) is not correct because technical skills are most important for first- or lower-level, not top management. Option (B) is not correct because human skills are equally important at all levels. Option (D) is not correct because functional was not a skill category mentioned in this chapter. Expressive skills (E) are more closely related to human skills, which was not as important as conceptual skills at this level.

81. **(D)**   The correct response is (D), weak financial skills. This option is the only one not identified in the research at the Center for Creative Leadership. Not meeting business objectives (A), poor interpersonal relationships (B), inability to change (D), and failure to build a team (E) were all identified, making them incorrect options.

82. **(D)**   The correct response is (D), accommodation. Giving employees one hour of paid time to work with urban grammar students is progressive, going beyond the minimum. As they do not share profits or engage in other actions, it would not be considered proaction (A). Consequently option (A) is not correct. Reaction (B) is not correct as the company is not fighting social expectations but meeting them willingly. Option (C), activation, is not correct as this is not a category of social responsiveness described in the chapter. Defense (E) is not correct either. Clearly the company is going beyond what is required.

83. **(D)**   The correct response is (D), external equity. Wage surveys provide information about what comparable firms in the area are paying for certain jobs. Internal equity (A) is not correct as it is based on job evaluation comparing internal jobs not external surveys. Wage surveys are not part of valid selection and so option (B) is not correct. Affirmative action (C) is

part of recruitment and therefore is not correct. Labor relations (E) involves working with unionized employees and is not correct.

84. **(D)** The correct response is (D), face-to-face. Of all the media presented, face-to-face is the richest and is able to transmit the greatest amount of information. Formal written communication (A) is the least rich and is incorrect. Face-to-face contains words, intonation, and facial expressions. As a medium, the telephone is moderately rich. It contains voice inflections and words, but not nonverbal or facial expressions. Option (B) is not correct because face-to-face is richer. E-mail (C) is lower in richness than telephone, making (C) incorrect. Video conferencing (E) is nearly as rich as face-to-face, but not as rich, so option (E) is wrong.

85. **(A)** The correct answer is (A), planning. The setting of objectives defines future performance and provides direction for the secretary as part of planning. This activity is not part of organizing (B) because it does not involve relationships or arrangements among workers. It focuses solely on the secretary's work. Option (C) is not correct because coordinating is not one of the contemporary functions of management. In trying to improve the secretary's performance, Brenda may use the leading (D) function, but setting objectives is more clearly part of planning. Brenda may have assessed performance earlier as part of controlling (E), but planning is more correct for setting future objectives.

86. **(E)** The correct response is (E), strategic choice influences structure. The General Motors structure developed by Alfred Sloan made the case that the choice of strategy then influences the best structural design. Option (A) is incorrect because this states that structure influences strategy, the reverse of the correct order. Option (B) is not correct because Woodward's research demonstrated that technology influences which structure works best. Although General Motors has become very large, and size influences structure, a study at General Motors did not contribute to these conclusions; thus option (C) is not correct. Environment (D) is an influence on structure and therefore this option is not correct.

87. **(B)** The correct response is (B), group norms play a role in determining the impact of cohesiveness on performance. Cohesiveness leads to greater uniformity pressures but the norms determine the level, either high or low. Option (A) reflects a common misconception that cohesiveness leads to better performance. Cohesiveness tends to lead to more uniform performance, not high levels. Option (C) is not correct because cohesiveness creates more

pressure to perform, which could reduce individual freedom. Option (D) is not correct because cohesiveness does influence performance in that it creates pressure for all to perform at the same level. Whether the level is high or low depends on the norms or performance goals. Option (E) is not correct because cohesiveness does not always hurt performance; it can lead to high performance if group norms are high.

88. **(A)** The correct response is (A), failing to adequately review an applicant's prior work record. Suits are filed against employers who do not perform due diligence in investigating the past. It is wrong to hire applicants with prior records of abuse or committing crimes against people. If they are placed in positions where they can harm people, such as a daycare center, then the company is negligent. Negligent hiring is not just about hiring someone who cannot do the job, as in option (B), but about hiring employees who harm others. Not accepting an offer (C) is not the basis for negligent hiring and is not correct. Similarly not having money in the budget (D) does not constitute negligent hiring. Having a bad first day (E) can be unpleasant but is not negligent hiring. The employee with a prior record has to harm others on the job.

89. **(A)** The correct response is (A), start easy and work up. Goal setting advocates setting challenging goals (B) from the start with high commitment to them (C). Therefore, options (B) and (C) are incorrect. There is no principle related to starting easy. High self-efficacy persons do set more difficult goals, making (D) incorrect. Finally rewarding goal attainment is important in goal setting, making (E) incorrect.

90. **(C)** The correct response is (C), policies. Policies are formal and official while culture is informal. Option (A) is not correct because ceremonies are manifestations of culture. Slogans (B) are a component of language, which is a part of culture and is not correct. Rituals (D) is not correct because they are also a practice that constitutes the culture. Option (E) is not correct because jargon is part of the language which represents the culture of an organization.

91. **(C)** The correct response is (C), equity. Fairness by comparing output/input ratios with relevant coworkers is the heart of equity theory. Goal setting (A) does not deal with the issue of fairness relative to others, nor does reinforcement theory (D), other process approaches. Both options (A) and (D) are incorrect. McClelland's acquired need theory (E) does not deal with any processes and is incorrect. The closest other option is option (B), ex-

pectancy, as individuals may choose between conflicting options in that approach. Option (B) is incorrect, however, because it does not deal with fairness in comparison to others.

92. **(D)** The correct response is (D), punishments for failure to meet standards. A desired feature of effective systems is the opposite—rewarding conformance and high performance. *Focused on results* is a characteristic of effective control systems, making (A) incorrect. Employees need to have the ultimate goal in mind and not become overly concerned with the means or process. Option (B), an internal orientation of self-control, is not correct. Self-control is very important in control systems. External checking does not work as the sole approach. Similarly, measure strategically (C) is another key component of effective control systems, making it incorrect for this question. Option (E), flexibility, is also important. Provisions for breaking the rule should be allowed. Flexibility for measured risks can lead to greater gains.

93. **(A)** The correct response is (A). Use the meeting for the right purposes. Meetings bring people together. The group should evaluate information and make decisions, not listen to announcements. Option (B) is not correct because sharing your opinion in important matters could lead to groupthink and bias the decision. Not interfering with discussion (C) is also not a good idea. Some members may dominate, causing others to withhold ideas. Waiting until all have arrived (D) essentially states to the group that being late is acceptable. Start on time and send a clear message about punctuality. Option (E) is also wrong because members should be informed of the agenda prior to the meeting. You want attendees to be prepared. Don't spring business items on them.

94. **(C)** The correct response is (C), entrepreneur. The decisional role of entrepreneur involves planned change. Marqus has carefully deliberated over these changes. They are designed to improve performance, clearly part of the entrepreneur role. Option (A) is not correct because the monitor role involves gathering information. Marqus is making decisions here, doing more than gathering information. Option (B) is not correct because the liaison role involves establishing contacts as part of an interpersonal role. Marqus already has relationships with his team. This activity is not disturbance handling (D) because it is not unexpected, it is planned. Option (E) is not correct because Marqus is not deciding how to distribute resources among subordinates.

95. **(B)**   The correct response is (B), healthcare. For the past few years HR professionals have rated healthcare costs as their number one problem.[1] Managers are reluctant to hire full-time employees because of the high cost of healthcare benefits, which have risen at the rate of 10–20 percent over the past few years[1]. Employees also want adequate healthcare coverage, so option (A) is not correct. Labor unions are striking over the loss of benefits or over having to pay a greater percentage of cost. Option (C) is not correct because some employees seek jobs in specific organizations because of the benefits, so it is a source of attraction. Benefits are not a source of motivation, as employees tend to receive the same benefits regardless of performance. Turnover (D) is related to pay and supervision, but also to benefits. As suggested in option (C), employees leave for better benefits, so option (D) is wrong. Option (E) is not correct because new benefits are being developed to find cost effective and innovative ways to support employees.

96. **(D)**   The correct response is (D), immediately fire the ethical offender. Such response would not be correct because being accused is not the same as being guilty. Ethical questions must be investigated to be fair to all parties. Each of the other four options represents legitimate actions for improving ethics in organizations and all are therefore incorrect. Companies should establish an ethical code of conduct (A), communicate it (E), create ethical training programs (B), and create a hotline for reporting violations (C).

97. **(C)**   The correct option is (C), only those workers with higher-order needs prefer enriched jobs. In general there are few absolutes or universal principles, so options that say "all" or imply that something always works tend not to be correct, but workers with lower order needs do, in fact, tend to prefer more routine jobs. Option (A) is not correct because some decisions are centralized. Decentralization helps spur innovation and change but employs less control. At times an organization may re-centralize some decisions for greater control. Cycles of decentralization and centralization do occur. Work specialization, when taken to the extreme, does lead to boring jobs, but some specialization is needed to foster efficiency. Therefore, option (B) is not correct. Staff positions have less power than line positions, so option (D) is incorrect. Finally the absolute statement that all organizations should have a wide span (E) is incorrect. Some technologies and organizational situations may require a narrow span. To repeat, few absolutes are correct.

98. **(B)** The correct response is (B), speaking too softly. All of the other options are typical barriers in communicating. Overload (A), language (C), selective perception (D), and noise (E) are barriers and are incorrect.

99. **(A)** The correct response is option (A). Groups need to work on both content and process. Neglecting either one will lead to lower results and performance. Following from that conclusion, option (B) is not correct because content is not the most important. Similarly, option (C) is wrong, as process is not more important than content—both are needed. Group process may not evolve over time, rendering option (D) incorrect. Explicit attention to process is needed. Finally, group process does relate to task accomplishment. With attention and proper management, process can help groups optimize performance. Therefore, option (E) is incorrect.

100. **(D)** The correct response is (D). Emotional intelligence involves self-awareness, self-regulation, and the social skills to influence others. Empathy is part of these social skills. Option (A) is not correct because delegating the right task at the right time is more of a cognitive skill. Option (B) is not correct because being funny is not the same as emotional intelligence. Many people who feel good about themselves are insensitive and unaware of others' feelings, so option (C) is not correct. Finally, rewards and praise (E) can be given indiscriminately; therefore, this option is not part of emotional intelligence.

Endnote

1. SHRM survey results found at http://www.shrm.org/press_published/CMS_006861.asp

CLEP PRINCIPLES OF MANAGEMENT
PRACTICE TEST 1

ANSWER SHEETS

1. (A) (B) (C) (D) (E)	35. (A) (B) (C) (D) (E)	69. (A) (B) (C) (D) (E)
2. (A) (B) (C) (D) (E)	36. (A) (B) (C) (D) (E)	70. (A) (B) (C) (D) (E)
3. (A) (B) (C) (D) (E)	37. (A) (B) (C) (D) (E)	71. (A) (B) (C) (D) (E)
4. (A) (B) (C) (D) (E)	38. (A) (B) (C) (D) (E)	72. (A) (B) (C) (D) (E)
5. (A) (B) (C) (D) (E)	39. (A) (B) (C) (D) (E)	73. (A) (B) (C) (D) (E)
6. (A) (B) (C) (D) (E)	40. (A) (B) (C) (D) (E)	74. (A) (B) (C) (D) (E)
7. (A) (B) (C) (D) (E)	41. (A) (B) (C) (D) (E)	75. (A) (B) (C) (D) (E)
8. (A) (B) (C) (D) (E)	42. (A) (B) (C) (D) (E)	76. (A) (B) (C) (D) (E)
9. (A) (B) (C) (D) (E)	43. (A) (B) (C) (D) (E)	77. (A) (B) (C) (D) (E)
10. (A) (B) (C) (D) (E)	44. (A) (B) (C) (D) (E)	78. (A) (B) (C) (D) (E)
11. (A) (B) (C) (D) (E)	45. (A) (B) (C) (D) (E)	79. (A) (B) (C) (D) (E)
12. (A) (B) (C) (D) (E)	46. (A) (B) (C) (D) (E)	80. (A) (B) (C) (D) (E)
13. (A) (B) (C) (D) (E)	47. (A) (B) (C) (D) (E)	81. (A) (B) (C) (D) (E)
14. (A) (B) (C) (D) (E)	48. (A) (B) (C) (D) (E)	82. (A) (B) (C) (D) (E)
15. (A) (B) (C) (D) (E)	49. (A) (B) (C) (D) (E)	83. (A) (B) (C) (D) (E)
16. (A) (B) (C) (D) (E)	50. (A) (B) (C) (D) (E)	84. (A) (B) (C) (D) (E)
17. (A) (B) (C) (D) (E)	51. (A) (B) (C) (D) (E)	85. (A) (B) (C) (D) (E)
18. (A) (B) (C) (D) (E)	52. (A) (B) (C) (D) (E)	86. (A) (B) (C) (D) (E)
19. (A) (B) (C) (D) (E)	53. (A) (B) (C) (D) (E)	87. (A) (B) (C) (D) (E)
20. (A) (B) (C) (D) (E)	54. (A) (B) (C) (D) (E)	88. (A) (B) (C) (D) (E)
21. (A) (B) (C) (D) (E)	55. (A) (B) (C) (D) (E)	89. (A) (B) (C) (D) (E)
22. (A) (B) (C) (D) (E)	56. (A) (B) (C) (D) (E)	90. (A) (B) (C) (D) (E)
23. (A) (B) (C) (D) (E)	57. (A) (B) (C) (D) (E)	91. (A) (B) (C) (D) (E)
24. (A) (B) (C) (D) (E)	58. (A) (B) (C) (D) (E)	92. (A) (B) (C) (D) (E)
25. (A) (B) (C) (D) (E)	59. (A) (B) (C) (D) (E)	93. (A) (B) (C) (D) (E)
26. (A) (B) (C) (D) (E)	60. (A) (B) (C) (D) (E)	94. (A) (B) (C) (D) (E)
27. (A) (B) (C) (D) (E)	61. (A) (B) (C) (D) (E)	95. (A) (B) (C) (D) (E)
28. (A) (B) (C) (D) (E)	62. (A) (B) (C) (D) (E)	96. (A) (B) (C) (D) (E)
29. (A) (B) (C) (D) (E)	63. (A) (B) (C) (D) (E)	97. (A) (B) (C) (D) (E)
30. (A) (B) (C) (D) (E)	64. (A) (B) (C) (D) (E)	98. (A) (B) (C) (D) (E)
31. (A) (B) (C) (D) (E)	65. (A) (B) (C) (D) (E)	99. (A) (B) (C) (D) (E)
32. (A) (B) (C) (D) (E)	66. (A) (B) (C) (D) (E)	100. (A) (B) (C) (D) (E)
33. (A) (B) (C) (D) (E)	67. (A) (B) (C) (D) (E)	
34. (A) (B) (C) (D) (E)	68. (A) (B) (C) (D) (E)	

CLEP PRINCIPLES OF MANAGEMENT
PRACTICE TEST 2

ANSWER SHEETS

1. Ⓐ Ⓑ Ⓒ Ⓓ Ⓔ	35. Ⓐ Ⓑ Ⓒ Ⓓ Ⓔ	69. Ⓐ Ⓑ Ⓒ Ⓓ Ⓔ
2. Ⓐ Ⓑ Ⓒ Ⓓ Ⓔ	36. Ⓐ Ⓑ Ⓒ Ⓓ Ⓔ	70. Ⓐ Ⓑ Ⓒ Ⓓ Ⓔ
3. Ⓐ Ⓑ Ⓒ Ⓓ Ⓔ	37. Ⓐ Ⓑ Ⓒ Ⓓ Ⓔ	71. Ⓐ Ⓑ Ⓒ Ⓓ Ⓔ
4. Ⓐ Ⓑ Ⓒ Ⓓ Ⓔ	38. Ⓐ Ⓑ Ⓒ Ⓓ Ⓔ	72. Ⓐ Ⓑ Ⓒ Ⓓ Ⓔ
5. Ⓐ Ⓑ Ⓒ Ⓓ Ⓔ	39. Ⓐ Ⓑ Ⓒ Ⓓ Ⓔ	73. Ⓐ Ⓑ Ⓒ Ⓓ Ⓔ
6. Ⓐ Ⓑ Ⓒ Ⓓ Ⓔ	40. Ⓐ Ⓑ Ⓒ Ⓓ Ⓔ	74. Ⓐ Ⓑ Ⓒ Ⓓ Ⓔ
7. Ⓐ Ⓑ Ⓒ Ⓓ Ⓔ	41. Ⓐ Ⓑ Ⓒ Ⓓ Ⓔ	75. Ⓐ Ⓑ Ⓒ Ⓓ Ⓔ
8. Ⓐ Ⓑ Ⓒ Ⓓ Ⓔ	42. Ⓐ Ⓑ Ⓒ Ⓓ Ⓔ	76. Ⓐ Ⓑ Ⓒ Ⓓ Ⓔ
9. Ⓐ Ⓑ Ⓒ Ⓓ Ⓔ	43. Ⓐ Ⓑ Ⓒ Ⓓ Ⓔ	77. Ⓐ Ⓑ Ⓒ Ⓓ Ⓔ
10. Ⓐ Ⓑ Ⓒ Ⓓ Ⓔ	44. Ⓐ Ⓑ Ⓒ Ⓓ Ⓔ	78. Ⓐ Ⓑ Ⓒ Ⓓ Ⓔ
11. Ⓐ Ⓑ Ⓒ Ⓓ Ⓔ	45. Ⓐ Ⓑ Ⓒ Ⓓ Ⓔ	79. Ⓐ Ⓑ Ⓒ Ⓓ Ⓔ
12. Ⓐ Ⓑ Ⓒ Ⓓ Ⓔ	46. Ⓐ Ⓑ Ⓒ Ⓓ Ⓔ	80. Ⓐ Ⓑ Ⓒ Ⓓ Ⓔ
13. Ⓐ Ⓑ Ⓒ Ⓓ Ⓔ	47. Ⓐ Ⓑ Ⓒ Ⓓ Ⓔ	81. Ⓐ Ⓑ Ⓒ Ⓓ Ⓔ
14. Ⓐ Ⓑ Ⓒ Ⓓ Ⓔ	48. Ⓐ Ⓑ Ⓒ Ⓓ Ⓔ	82. Ⓐ Ⓑ Ⓒ Ⓓ Ⓔ
15. Ⓐ Ⓑ Ⓒ Ⓓ Ⓔ	49. Ⓐ Ⓑ Ⓒ Ⓓ Ⓔ	83. Ⓐ Ⓑ Ⓒ Ⓓ Ⓔ
16. Ⓐ Ⓑ Ⓒ Ⓓ Ⓔ	50. Ⓐ Ⓑ Ⓒ Ⓓ Ⓔ	84. Ⓐ Ⓑ Ⓒ Ⓓ Ⓔ
17. Ⓐ Ⓑ Ⓒ Ⓓ Ⓔ	51. Ⓐ Ⓑ Ⓒ Ⓓ Ⓔ	85. Ⓐ Ⓑ Ⓒ Ⓓ Ⓔ
18. Ⓐ Ⓑ Ⓒ Ⓓ Ⓔ	52. Ⓐ Ⓑ Ⓒ Ⓓ Ⓔ	86. Ⓐ Ⓑ Ⓒ Ⓓ Ⓔ
19. Ⓐ Ⓑ Ⓒ Ⓓ Ⓔ	53. Ⓐ Ⓑ Ⓒ Ⓓ Ⓔ	87. Ⓐ Ⓑ Ⓒ Ⓓ Ⓔ
20. Ⓐ Ⓑ Ⓒ Ⓓ Ⓔ	54. Ⓐ Ⓑ Ⓒ Ⓓ Ⓔ	88. Ⓐ Ⓑ Ⓒ Ⓓ Ⓔ
21. Ⓐ Ⓑ Ⓒ Ⓓ Ⓔ	55. Ⓐ Ⓑ Ⓒ Ⓓ Ⓔ	89. Ⓐ Ⓑ Ⓒ Ⓓ Ⓔ
22. Ⓐ Ⓑ Ⓒ Ⓓ Ⓔ	56. Ⓐ Ⓑ Ⓒ Ⓓ Ⓔ	90. Ⓐ Ⓑ Ⓒ Ⓓ Ⓔ
23. Ⓐ Ⓑ Ⓒ Ⓓ Ⓔ	57. Ⓐ Ⓑ Ⓒ Ⓓ Ⓔ	91. Ⓐ Ⓑ Ⓒ Ⓓ Ⓔ
24. Ⓐ Ⓑ Ⓒ Ⓓ Ⓔ	58. Ⓐ Ⓑ Ⓒ Ⓓ Ⓔ	92. Ⓐ Ⓑ Ⓒ Ⓓ Ⓔ
25. Ⓐ Ⓑ Ⓒ Ⓓ Ⓔ	59. Ⓐ Ⓑ Ⓒ Ⓓ Ⓔ	93. Ⓐ Ⓑ Ⓒ Ⓓ Ⓔ
26. Ⓐ Ⓑ Ⓒ Ⓓ Ⓔ	60. Ⓐ Ⓑ Ⓒ Ⓓ Ⓔ	94. Ⓐ Ⓑ Ⓒ Ⓓ Ⓔ
27. Ⓐ Ⓑ Ⓒ Ⓓ Ⓔ	61. Ⓐ Ⓑ Ⓒ Ⓓ Ⓔ	95. Ⓐ Ⓑ Ⓒ Ⓓ Ⓔ
28. Ⓐ Ⓑ Ⓒ Ⓓ Ⓔ	62. Ⓐ Ⓑ Ⓒ Ⓓ Ⓔ	96. Ⓐ Ⓑ Ⓒ Ⓓ Ⓔ
29. Ⓐ Ⓑ Ⓒ Ⓓ Ⓔ	63. Ⓐ Ⓑ Ⓒ Ⓓ Ⓔ	97. Ⓐ Ⓑ Ⓒ Ⓓ Ⓔ
30. Ⓐ Ⓑ Ⓒ Ⓓ Ⓔ	64. Ⓐ Ⓑ Ⓒ Ⓓ Ⓔ	98. Ⓐ Ⓑ Ⓒ Ⓓ Ⓔ
31. Ⓐ Ⓑ Ⓒ Ⓓ Ⓔ	65. Ⓐ Ⓑ Ⓒ Ⓓ Ⓔ	99. Ⓐ Ⓑ Ⓒ Ⓓ Ⓔ
32. Ⓐ Ⓑ Ⓒ Ⓓ Ⓔ	66. Ⓐ Ⓑ Ⓒ Ⓓ Ⓔ	100. Ⓐ Ⓑ Ⓒ Ⓓ Ⓔ
33. Ⓐ Ⓑ Ⓒ Ⓓ Ⓔ	67. Ⓐ Ⓑ Ⓒ Ⓓ Ⓔ	
34. Ⓐ Ⓑ Ⓒ Ⓓ Ⓔ	68. Ⓐ Ⓑ Ⓒ Ⓓ Ⓔ	

INDEX

Index

3M, 97
360° feedback, 140
9/11 Commission, 103, 117

A

accommodation, 229–230
adaptation to environment, 43–44
adjourning, 203
administrative management, 22–24, 56
affirmative action, 130
Age Discrimination Act of 1967, 129, 130
agendas, 61–62
Alderfer, Clayton, 180
American Amicable Life Insurance Company,
   69–70, 76
Americans with Disabilities Act of 1990, 38,
   129, 130
assemble-to-order, 162
authority and responsibility, 22, 24
autonomy, 107
avoidance, 230

B

background checks, 137–138
balanced scorecard, 89, 128
Barnard, Chester, 23, 221
barriers to communication, 242–243
Bass, Bernard, 223
benchmarking, 98
benefits, 140–141
best practices, 98
Blake, Robert, 213
Blanchard, Ken, 213
BMW, 97
bottom-up communication, 241
boundary spanning roles, 43–44

bounded rationality, 56, 170
brainstorming, 63–64
budgeting, 153–155
bureaucracy, 21, 106
business ethics. See ethics
business process goals, 89–90
business process reengineering, 166–167

C

career, 21
Center for Creative Leadership, 219–220
Center for Responsible Business, 79
centralization, 22, 23, 109
ceremonies, 47
certainty, 55
chain of command, 23, 105. See also coordination
Champy, James, 166
change management, 235–238
charisma, 222–223
Chevron-Texaco, 79
ChoicePoint, 171
Civil Rights Act of 1964, 129, 130, 131
clan control, 153
closed system, 27
coaching, 140
coercive power, 222, 238
cohesiveness, 204–205
collaboration, 231
committees, 199
communication, 238–243
community, 42. See also ethics; social responsibility
compensation, 140–141. See also remuneration
competitive forces, 93–95
competitors, 41, 229–230
conceptual skills, 7
concurrent control, 148

conflict management, 227–235

consideration, 213

content theories of motivation, 179–185

    Alderfer's hierarchy of needs, 183

    Herzberg's two-factor theory, 182–183

    Maslow's hierarchy of needs, 26, 180–182

    McClelland's acquired needs, 184–185

contingency management, 29. *See also* situational theories of leadership

    organization, 118–120

    planning, 98, 134

continuous processes, 119–120

control, 10, 52, 88, 145–148, 155–156

    and budgeting, 153–155

    of human resources, 152–153

    operations management, 159–168

    project management, 171–173

    quality standards, 149–152

co-optation, 237

coordination, 112, 116–118

core technology, 119–120

corporate culture, 45–47, 153

corporate engagement and governance, 79–80

cost leadership, 97

costs, 160

Crosby, Philip, 149, 150

culture, elements of, 46–47, 153, 203

customer goals, 89–90

customers, 41, 94

customized services, 162

D

decentralization, 22, 23, 109

decisional role, 12–13

decision-making, 51

    group, 60–64

    managerial, 51–59

    theory of, 52–59

decision support system (DSS), 170

Deming, Edward, 149–150

demographic groups, 39

departmentalization, 109

derailment, 219–220

development of workers, 138

diagonal communication, 241–242

differential piece rate, 20

differentiation, 28, 29, 97

disabilities, 130–131

discrimination, 130

dissatisfiers, 182

disseminator, 12

distributive justice, 54. *See also* ethics

disturbance handler, 13

divisional organization, 112–115

division of labor, 22, 105

documentation, 240

drives. *See* content theories of motivation

Drucker, Peter, 127

duality of command, 116

DuPont, 45, 47

E

economic environment, 37

economic order quantity (EOQ), 165

effectiveness, 5, 89

    operational, 161–162

efficiency, 5, 89, 127, 160–161, 240

emergent strategy, 98

emotional intelligence, 7, 221

employee relations, 141–142

employment agencies, 135–136

enlargement of jobs, 106

enrichment of jobs, 107

Enterprise Rent-A-Car, 97

enterprise resource planning, 168. *See also* information management

entrepreneur, 13

environment, 27–28, 35–36, 40, 120

    competitive forces, 93–95

    external, 36–45, 80–81

    immediate, 39–42

    internal, 45–47

    responses to, 42–45, 80–81

    SWOT analysis, 96–96

Environmental Protection Agency (EPA), 37–38

Equal Employment Opportunity Act of 1972, 129, 130

Equal Pay Act of 1963, 129, 130

equity, 22, 23, 140–141

equity theory of motivation, 191–192

ethics, 70–76. *See also* social responsibility

European Union, 38

expectancy theory, 185–188, 218

expense center, 153–154

expertise, 222
expert system (ES), 170–171
external equity, 140–141

F

facilities, 165–166
Fairfield-Sonn, Jim, 46, 47, 151
Fair Labor Standards Act of 1938, 129, 130
Family and Medical Leave Act of 1993, 129, 131
Fayol, Henri, 9, 22, 109
    fourteen administrative principles, 22–23, 104, 105
feedback, 28, 29, 62–63, 107, 140, 148–149, 243
feedforward control, 148
Fiedler, Fred, 29, 214–215
figurehead, 12
financial process goals, 89–90
finished goods, 164
flat organizational structure, 108–109
flexibility, 160–161
flexible manufacturing, 167–168
flow approach to HRM, 132–142
focus, strategic, 97–98
Follett, Mary Parker, 24
Ford, Charles, 53, 57
Ford Motor Company, 167
forming, 202
Fort Benning (Georgia), 69–70, 76
framing, 52
Friedman, Milton, 77
frustration regression, 183
functional departmentalization, 109–111
fundamental attribution error, 178

G

Gannt chart, 21, 172–173. *See also* operations management; project management
Gannt, Henry, 21
gender differences in leadership, 223
general environment, 36–39
General Electric, 140
General Motors, 6, 119
Gilbreth, Frank and Lillian, 21
GlaxoSmithKline, 95
goal displacement, 154
goals, 87, 89–90, 154, 190–191

goal-setting theory of motivation, 190–191
Godfrey, Paul, 79
group dynamics, 25, 57. *See also* decision-making; teams
groupthink, 207–208, 228

H

Hackman, Richard, 107
Hammer, 166
Hawthorne effect, 25
Hawthorne studies, 24–26
Hersey, Paul, 216
Herzberg, Frederick, 107, 180, 182
high-performing team, 204–207
hiring. *See* human resource management
horizontal communication, 241
Hosmer, LaRue Tone, 75
hostile work environment, 131
House, Robert, 218
human capital, 42, 127
human perspectives on management, 24–27
human relations movement, 25–26
human resource approach, 27, 90
human resource information system (HRIS), 133–134
human resource management (HRM), 126–128
    control methods, 152–153
    flow approach to, 132–142
    HR triad, 126
    legal and legislative environment, 128–132
human skills, 7
human skills goals, 89–90

I

immediate environment, 39–42
incentives, 20, 23
incumbents, 133
Industrial Revolution, 18–19
influencing the environment, 44–45
informal organization, 23–24
informal strategy, 98
information management, 168–169
    characteristics of information, 169–170
    project information, 171–173
    security issues, 171
information-processing role, 11–12
initiation of structure, 213

instrumentality, 186
integration, 28, 29
internal equity, 140–141
interpersonal role, 11–12
interval reinforcement, 189–190
interviews, 137
inventory management, 164–166
investment center, 154

J

Jackson, Susan, 126
Janis, Irving, 207
job analysis, 126, 133
job incumbent, 133
job samples, 137
job specialization options, 106–108
joint ventures, 44
Juran, Joseph, 149, 150
justice, 54, 75–76. *See also* ethics
just-in-time inventory systems. *See* lean
     inventory systems

K

Kahn, Robert, 28
kanban, 165
Kaplan, Robert, 89, 128
Katz, Daniel, 28
Katzenbach, Jon, 205
Kepner-Tregoe, Inc., 54
Kotter, John, 237

L

labor relations, 141–142
large batch processes, 119–120
laws, 71–72. *See also* ethics; justice
leader, 12
leading and leadership, 10, 24, 88, 177–178,
     211–212, 219–223. *See also* motivation
   characteristics of leaders, 211–213
   change, 235–238
   charisma, 222–223
   conflict, 227–235
   derailment, 219–220
   emotional intelligence, 7, 221
   gender differences, 223
   managerial styles, 213, 215
   power, bases of, 221–222
   situational approaches, 214–219
lean inventory systems, 165
least-preferred coworker, 214
legal-political environment, 37–38, 128–132
Lewin, Kurt, 212, 235
liaison, 12, 116–117
life-cycle (Hersey-Blanchard) model, 216–218
line employees, 108
loafing, 61
lobbyists, 44
logistics, 166

M

make-to-order strategy, 163
make-to-stock strategy, 163
Malcom Baldridge National Quality Award
     (MBNQA), 150–151
management. *See also* communication;
     decision-making
   administrative, 22–24, 56
   bureaucracy, 21
   change, 235–238
   conflict, 227–235
   contingency approach to, 29
   corporate culture, 45–47
   functional view of, 9–10
   history of, 3, 17–19, 30–31
   human issues in, 24–27
   human resource (*see* human resource
     management)
   information (*see* information management)
   levels of, 6–9
   operations (*see* operations management)
   organizational structures, 108–116
   project, 171–173
   roles, 12–13
   scientific, 11–13, 19–21, 56
   skills, 6–8
   systems theory approach to, 27–29
managerial styles, 213
manager-subordinate relationship, 4
manufacturing strategies, 162–163, 167–168
Maslow, Abraham, 26, 180
matrix organization, 115–116, 117
Mazda, 167
McClelland, 180
McGregor, Douglas, 26

meetings, 61–63
Merck, 170
merit pay, 141
Meyers-Briggs Type Indicator, 58–59
military heritage of management, 18
Mintzberg, Henry, 11, 98
mission statement, 95
monitor, 12
moral rights, 75
morals, 70–71. *See also* ethics
Moran, Linda, 117
motivation, 107, 177–178
    content theories, 179–185
    process theories, 185–192
Mouton, Jane, 213
moving, 235
multitasking, 11

N

narratives, 47
National Labor Relations Act of 1935, 129, 130
needs. *See* content theories of motivation
negative entropy, 28, 29
negligent hiring, 137–138
negotiation. *See* conflict management
negotiator, 13
networked teams, 118
niche, 97–98
nominal group technique, 63–64
norming, 202, 203
norms, 203–205
Norton, David, 89, 128

O

objectives, 87, 91–92
open system, 27. *See also* environment
Occupational Safety and Health Act of 1970, 129, 131
operational effectiveness, 161–162
operations management, 159–161
    component activities, 163–166
    improvement, 166–168
    information and decision making, 168–173
organizing, 10, 24, 44, 88, 103–105
    contingency approach toward, 118–120
    coordination, 112, 116–118
    and job specialization, 106–108

organizational chart, 104–105, 109, 110, 111
organizational structures, 108–116
orientation of workers, 138
Osburn, Jack, 117
Ouchi, William, 153

P

PalmOne, 35, 41, 87, 94, 96–97
partnerships. *See* joint ventures
path-goal theory of leadership, 218–219
performance. *See also* motivation
    and compensation, 140–141
    and corporate culture, impact of, 46
    criteria of success, 5–6
    determiners of, 178–179
    evaluation of, 89–92, 98, 126–127, 139–140, 160–161, 170
    scientific measurement of, 20
performing, 202, 203
personnel. *See* human resource management
Pfeffer, Jeff, 46
planning, 10, 24, 87–89. *See also* control
    plans and strategies, 92–98
    projects, 171–173
Plant Closing Act of 1988, 75
political model of decision-making, 57
policies, 92, 152
Porter, Michael, 93, 161
    five competitive forces of, 93–95
power, bases of, 221–222
practices, cultural, 47
Pregnancy Discrimination Act of 1978, 129, 131
problem-solving. *See* decision-making
procedural justice, 54, 60. *See also* ethics
procedures, 92, 152
process conflict, 232
process loss, 61, 63, 199
process observer, 63, 200–201
process technologies, 119–120
process theories of motivation
    equity theory, 191–192
    expectancy theory, 185–188
    goal-setting theory, 190–191
    reinforcement theory, 188–190
profit center, 153–154
progressive discipline, 152, 189
project management, 171–173
Prussian army, 18

pseudo-team, 204–207
public relations, 44–45
punishment, 188
purchasing, 164

Q

quality control, 149–152, 160

R

raw materials, 164
real-time systems, 169
reasonable accommodations, 130–131
recruitment, 134–136
redundancy, 243
reengineering. *See* business process reengineering
referent power, 222
referral, 134–135
refreezing, 235
reinforcement theory, 188–190
relationship conflict, 232
remuneration, 22, 23. *See also* compensation
replacement chart, 134
resource allocator, 13
responsibility, 77–79. *See also* authority and
    responsibility; social responsibility
responsibility centers, 153–154
responsiveness, 80–81
revenue center, 153–154
richness of communication media, 239–240
risk, 55, 57, 61
rites, 47
rituals, 47
Rockhart, John, 52, 170
rotation of jobs, 106

S

Sarbanes-Oxley Act, 38, 72
satisfaction progression, 182, 183
satisficing, 56
satisfiers, 182
Schein, Edgar, 46
Schlesinger, Leonard, 237
scientific management concepts
    of Frederick W. Taylor, 19
    of Henry Mintzberg, 11–13
Sears, 109, 128

selection of workers, 136–137
self-directed teams, 117
self-oriented roles, 201
service strategies, 162–163
sexual harrassment, 131
shareholders, 77
Shuler, Randall, 126
Simon, Herbert, 56
single-use plans, 92, 93
situational theories of leadership
    Fiedler's contingency theory, 214–215
    Hersey-Blanchard life-cycle theory, 216–218
    House's path-goal theory, 218–219
Six Sigma, 151
skill pay, 141
skill variety, 107
Sloan, Alfred, 119
slogans, 47
small batch processes, 119–120
SMART objectives, 91–92
Smith, Adam, 105
Smith, Douglas, 205
social enterprise, 79–80
social performance metrics, 79
social responsibility, 77–82. *See also* ethics
socio-cultural environment, 38–39
socio-emotional roles, 200–201
Southwest Airlines, 162
span of management, 109
specialization, 105, 106–108
spokesperson, 12
staff employees, 108
stakeholders, 6, 39–42, 77
standardized services, 162
standard operating procedures (SOPs), 92
standing plans, 92
storming, 202
strategic business units (SBUs), 90
strategy, 93–98, 119
subordinates. *See also* human capital; motivation
    attitudes of, 24
    and group dynamics, 25–26
    relationship to managers, 4
    zone of indifference, 24
success, managerial, 5–6
suppliers, 41–42, 94, 164
supply chain management, 164. *See also* opera-
    tions management

SWOT analysis, 95–96
symbols, cultural, 46
synergy, 60, 199
systems theory, 27–29

T

tall organizational structure, 108
task conflict, 232
task forces, 117, 199
task identity and significance, 107
task-oriented roles, 200
Taylor, Frederick W., 19, 106
teams, 117–118, 197–199, 205–208
  stages of development, 202–203
  types of and roles within, 199–201
team spirit, 22, 23
technical skills, 6–7
technological environment, 37
technology
  core, 119–120
  management of, 167
Terrorist Threat Integration Center, 117
Theory X, 26–27, 177
Theory Y, 26, 183
time and motion studies, 20, 106
time frame, 9
top-down communication, 241
training of workers, 138–139
transformational leadership, 222–223
TRW Systems, 115

U

uncertainty, 55–56
unfreezing, 235
unions, 142
unity of direction, 22, 23
universalism, 74–75
University of Phoenix, 96
utilitarianism, 73–74, 77

V

valence, 186
Vaughn, Clyde, 138
virtual organization. *See* networked teams
vocation, 21

W

Wal-Mart, 97
Weber, Max, 21, 106, 109
W.L. Gore and Associates, 242
Woodward, Joan, 29, 119
workers. *See* human capital; human resource
    management; motivation; subordinates
work-in-progress, 164
workplace safety, 131

Z

zone of indifference, 24